Praise for *The Murderer Next Door*

"A persuasive explanation for murder—and a provocative one at that.... Highly recommended."
—*Library Journal*

"Intriguing ... Examples offer powerful support for the author's evolutionary theory and give the reader a startling, and at times unsettlingly familiar, glimpse into the mind of a killer."
—*Science News*

"What marks the book more than any other element is [Buss's] support for his central claim. In his design, implementation, and presentation of this research, Buss is at his most persuasive."
—*PsycCritiques: APA Review of Books*

"Buss is adept at keeping the reader interested.... The book makes a great deal of sense. —*Minneapolis/St. Paul City Pages*

"Provocative ... Ominous but enormously intriguing."
—*San Antonio Express-News*

"Provocative"   —*Austin American-Statesman*

"Provocative ... unnerving." —*The Indianapolis Star*

ABOUT THE AUTHOR

David M. Buss is a professor of psychology at the University of Texas at Austin. His path-breaking research has received extensive media coverage, including features in *Newsweek, U.S. News & World Report, The New York Times,* and *The Washington Post,* and he has appeared on *Dateline, 20/20,* the *Today* show, and *CBS This Morning.* His books include *The Evolution of Desire* and *The Dangerous Passion.*

THE MURDERER NEXT DOOR

Why the Mind Is Designed to Kill

- -

DAVID M. BUSS

PENGUIN BOOKS

PENGUIN BOOKS
Published by the Penguin Group
Penguin Group (USA) Inc., 375 Hudson Street, New York, New York 10014, U.S.A.
Penguin Group (Canada), 90 Eglinton Avenue East, Suite 700, Toronto,
Ontario, Canada M4P 2Y3 (a division of Pearson Penguin Canada Inc.)
Penguin Books Ltd, 80 Strand, London WC2R 0RL, England
Penguin Ireland, 25 St Stephen's Green, Dublin 2, Ireland (a division of Penguin Books Ltd)
Penguin Group (Australia), 250 Camberwell Road, Camberwell,
Victoria 3124, Australia (a division of Pearson Australia Group Pty Ltd)
Penguin Books India Pvt Ltd, 11 Community Centre,
Panchsheel Park, New Delhi – 110 017, India
Penguin Group (NZ), cnr Airborne and Rosedale Roads, Albany,
Auckland 1310, New Zealand (a division of Pearson New Zealand Ltd)
Penguin Books (South Africa) (Pty) Ltd, 24 Sturdee Avenue,
Rosebank, Johannesburg 2196, South Africa

Penguin Books Ltd, Registered Offices:
80 Strand, London WC2R 0RL, England

First published in the United States of America by The Penguin Press,
a member of Penguin Group (USA) Inc. 2005
Published in Penguin Books 2006

3   5   7   9   10   8   6   4

THE LIBRARY OF CONGRESS HAS CATALOGED THE HARDCOVER EDITION AS FOLLOWS:
Buss, David M.
The murderer next door : why the mind is designed to kill / David M. Buss.
p.   cm.
Includes bibliographical references and index.
ISBN 1-59420-043-2 (hc.)
ISBN 0 14 30.3705 6 (pbk.)
1. Murder—Psychological aspects.   2. Murderers—Psychology.   I. Title.
HV6515.B88 2005   2005043105

Printed in the United States of America
DESIGNED BY AMANDA DEWEY

for Cindy

CONTENTS

One

THE MURDERING MIND

— —

"There is no single crime that fascinates us more than murder. . . .
We have been fascinated with murder since Cain killed Abel."

—EDWARD L. GREENSPAN, Introduction, *Crimes of Passion*.[1]

"For murder, though it have no tongue, will speak with almost
miraculous organ." —WILLIAM SHAKESPEARE, *Hamlet*

M Y INTEREST in studying murder was sparked when I witnessed a
close friend fly into a murderous rage one night at a cocktail party. I
had known him for years and spent many pleasant nights socializing with
him and his wife. They had always seemed a happy couple with a strong
bond, though, as we all know, much goes on between couples about which
others aren't aware. As I was to learn, their marriage was rife with tensions.

The party was already in full swing when I arrived, but my friend was
nowhere to be found. When I asked his wife where he was, she told me with
disgust that he was in another room. Though he greeted me warmly when I
found him, I could tell he was out of sorts.

We passed his wife a short time later, and she was chatting with one of
the other men at the party, radiating beauty and charm as she talked flirta-
tiously with him. She was a striking woman, and men were generally
enchanted by her. As we went by, she looked at her husband derisively and

made a derogatory remark about the way he looked, then turned right back to her flirtatious conversation. He immediately became enraged, in a way I'd never seen him before. Grabbing my arm, he said, "Let's get out of here," and stormed out of the house, with me following close behind. The second we hit the street, he started fuming. Her public flirtation incensed him, he said. Her flagrant "dissing" of him in front of others enraged him. Then he said he wanted to kill her. Tonight, right now, at this moment. I was stunned. And I had no doubt that he would do it.

Then a strange feeling came over me—I became frightened for my *own* life. As I look back on that night, that instinctive fear reaction still amazes me. He wasn't angry at me, but he was so wild with rage, such a transformed man, that he seemed capable of killing any living thing within arm's reach. I'd never seen anyone in such an unbridled murderous state, and it was terrifying.

I spent the next half-hour talking him out of his rage, trying every tactic I could think of. I appealed to his self-interest, telling him that he'd be throwing away his career if he so much as touched her. I told him he'd spend the rest of his life in prison. I stammered out everything that rushed into my mind. Finally he calmed down, and then we returned to the party. After a while, I left for my hotel, still shaken and more than a little worried. And I should have been. The drama wasn't over. At two in the morning, he called and asked if he could come over and sleep on my couch. After the party, he said, he immediately started a horrible fight with his wife, and had threatened to kill her, slamming his fist into the bathroom mirror and shattering it. Then, fortunately, he had left the house. He told me he had realized that if he didn't leave right then he would kill her.

Perhaps the most remarkable part of the story is that his wife moved out of their house that night and went into hiding. Eventually she divorced him, and they have never seen each other again since the night of that party. I was shocked that a marriage that I knew to be founded on genuine love, between two exceptionally intelligent, thoughtful, and successful people, had ended that way, and that a close friend of mine might well have become a murderer.

One thing my subsequent study of murder has taught me is that his wife recognized something that all too many of us don't quite fully appreciate—that we must be alert to the deeply ingrained capacity for murder that lurks inside us all, even those whom we love and who love us. When her husband went into a murderous rage, she understood with exquisite awareness that she was in mortal danger.

If her reaction seems overdone, and her flight out of town and filing for divorce without ever seeing her husband again seem extreme, then consider the story of Sheila Bellush, the ex-wife of Texas multimillionaire Allen Blackthorne. Blackthorne was, as news accounts said, a man who had everything. He'd made a fortune in the medical-equipment business; he was handsome, and he had married again after he and Sheila Bellush divorced—his fourth marriage—to a beautiful woman with whom he had two children. Sheila had also remarried, to Jamie Bellush, but she was haunted by an intense fear that Blackthorne might try to kill her. Their divorce had been nasty, and she had won custody of their two daughters in a horrible battle. For years he had continued to harass her, even after his remarriage. She even told her sister: "If anything ever happens to me, promise me that you will see that there's an investigation. . . . And find Ann Rule and ask her to write my story."[2] So afraid did she become that one night she gathered up her family—her two daughters by Blackthorne, and quadruplets she had by her new husband—and fled from her home in San Antonio. They moved to Sarasota, Florida, and Sheila was so afraid that she didn't even give her own sister her new address.

With all that distance between her and Allen Blackthorne, Sheila finally began to feel safe. It was a fatal mistake. Within months, she was murdered at her home in the middle of the day, and her quadruplet babies were found crying and covered with their mother's blood. Sheila's thirteen-year-old daughter discovered her mother dead in the kitchen, her face shot and her throat slit. When the daughter was asked by the police, "Do you know who might have done this?" she replied, "Yes, I know who did it, but he didn't do it himself. He probably hired someone to do it." "Who?" "My father did it. My father—Allen Blackthorne."[3]

Allen Blackthorne now makes his home in the state prison in Huntsville, Texas. He was convicted of hiring a young thug to drive the fourteen hundred miles from Austin to Sarasota to murder his ex-wife. According to the *Star-Telegram*, on May 3, 2002, a federal appeals court upheld Blackthorne's conviction for his role in arranging the killing. Ann Rule actually did write a book about the murder, titled *Every Breath You Take*.

When people sense that they are in mortal danger, their intuitions are probably quite good. But those we might least expect to become murderers may well be capable of killing under certain circumstances. Allen Blackthorne had a history of abuse and had been harassing his ex-wife, factors that weighed heavily on the jury's decision to convict him. Some husbands who kill their wives, however, do not exhibit any prior indications that they will murder. My friend's rage that night at the party made a profound impression on me, and my puzzlement about why he would have become so intent on murdering his wife set me on the road to investigating the deep psychology of murder. Until I sensed so palpably that someone I knew well and respected—someone whose judgment, good sense, and thoughtfulness I had come to rely on—was perfectly capable of committing a violent murder, I had thought of murderers as a special type: people given to violence in general, people conditioned to violence because of their upbringing, or hardened criminals, and at the extreme, psychopaths.

Only crazy or desperate people think about committing murder, I had thought, or people brought up in subcultures of violence that have desensitized them to violent acts. Certainly, normal, educated, successful people, like my friend, don't seriously consider becoming killers. So I was left wondering what could have produced the homicidal rage I had seen in my friend. The anger I could understand perfectly well, but the murderous intent seemed to indicate deeper psychological processes at work. I also wondered why, even though I had never witnessed murderous fury before in my life, I had felt so keenly that I myself might have been in danger that night.

The cases of cold-blooded contract killers, or those who murder in the midst of committing a crime, aren't so puzzling. These people kill for money or to eliminate a witness to a crime. So many other kinds of murder, however, seem baffling. We struggle to comprehend how a young pregnant woman can go to her high-school prom, give birth in the bathroom, stuff the newborn into the trash, and return to her date at the dance. We are horrified when a spurned man refuses to accept that his lover is leaving him, slashes the tires on her car, and leaves her body in a bloody pool. We are stunned when, en masse, Serbs rape and slaughter Albanians, and as soon as the tables are turned, Albanians rape and kill Serbs in revenge. And we are mystified by what must surely be the seething evil that motivates terrorists to sacrifice their lives so readily in order to kill for the glory of God.

People are mesmerized by murder. It commands our attention like no other human phenomenon. After studying murder extensively, I believe the reason for the fascination we feel is that we are imbued with a deep intuition born of a long history. No matter how alien, unbelievable, and extreme the cases of murder we hear about may seem, the impulse to murder is a part of us. The inclination to murder emanates from our deep, unconscious psychological mechanisms. Our fascination with it makes perfect sense—it's a good survival strategy. We must pay close attention to the parts of human nature that may one day threaten our own lives.

Some experts who have studied violent behavior, especially those concerned with violence by children, have put forth the argument that the rampant violence portrayed in movies and on TV has made us more violent, and pushes some people over the edge into murder. They caution that children's repeated exposure to Arnold Schwarzenegger in *The Terminator,* or Bruce Willis in *Die Hard,* warps them. Some are convinced that the consumption of sadistic pornography compels the Night Stalkers and Hillside Stranglers of the world. Others stress the roles of poverty, drugs, and subcultures of violence. I am convinced that none of these arguments is adequate, or gets at the real underlying motivations behind the vast majority of murders.

My investigations demonstrate that every one of these widely held beliefs is wrong—dead wrong. To understand why, we must journey into the depths of the murdering mind, and we'll discover that there is a fundamental logic to murder—ruthless but rational—and that it resides not only in the minds of people who actually become murderers, but in the minds of all of us.

Seven years ago, I taught a seminar on human nature that included a session on murder. As an exercise to get the class engaged, I had the students complete a questionnaire asking, "Have you ever thought about killing someone?" If the answer turned out to be "yes," they were instructed to describe the specific circumstances that had triggered their homicidal thought, their relationship to the victim, and the method of killing that they had fantasized about. My research into murder began in earnest after this astonishing experience.

As I read through their responses in my office, I was stunned. Nothing had prepared me for the outpouring of murderous thoughts my students reported. These were intelligent, well-scrubbed, mostly middle-class kids, not the gang members or troubled runaways one might expect to express violent rage. Yet most of them had experienced at least one intense episode in which they had fantasized about killing someone. As I sat in my office reading through these homicidal fantasies, I began to suspect that actual homicides were just the tip of the deep psychological iceberg of murder. Could actual murder be only the most flagrant outcome of a fundamental human drive to kill? Do our minds really course with homicidal thoughts? Is there a purpose to our killing fantasies?

Pursuing this line of research, my lab went on to conduct the largest scientific study ever carried out on people's homicidal fantasies, looking into why they have them and the specific circumstances in which they contemplate killing. This groundbreaking international study involved more than five thousand individuals from San Antonio to Singapore, who were interviewed intensively. Here are a few excerpts from those remarkable interviews.

CASE #5537, *female, age 20.* [Who did you think about killing?] *My ex-boyfriend. We lived together for a couple of months. He was very aggressive. He started calling me a whore, and told me that he didn't love me anymore. So I broke up with him. Then a few months later he started calling me trying to get back together, but I didn't want to. He said that if I ever had a relationship with another man, he was going to send videos, where we appear having sex, to all the people in my university. The thing is that I do have a new boyfriend, but my ex-boyfriend doesn't know it yet, and I'm terrified that he'll do what he says. Then suddenly the thought occurred to me that my life would be so much happier without him in existence.* [Please describe step by step how you thought about killing this person.] *I actually did this. I invited him over for dinner. And as he was in the kitchen, looking stupid peeling the carrots to make a salad, I came up to him laughing, gently, so that he wouldn't suspect anything. I thought about grabbing a knife quickly and stabbing him in the chest repeatedly until he was dead. I actually did the first thing, but he saw my intentions and ran away.* [When asked how close she came to killing him, she estimated 60%.]

CASE #967, *male, age 28.* [Who did you think about killing?] *He was a very good friend whom I defended on a number of occasions. On my 20th birthday, he told my paranoid fiancée that I had been unfaithful. This was a pack of lies. Then he made a move on her. It has been a huge problem in my relationship, one that will probably never be resolved. He was like my little brother and he stabbed me in the back, in the worst possible place, on my birthday nonetheless. . . .* [What method did you envision using to kill him?] *First, I would break every bone in his body, starting with his fingers and toes, slowly making my way to larger ones. Then I would puncture his lung and maybe a few other organs. Basically give him as much pain as possible before killing him.* [When asked how close he actually came to killing, he estimated 80%.]

CASE #108, *male.* [Who did you think about killing?] *I was in a parking lot, and he was going about 30 miles per hour. He almost hit me (even though I had the right of way). He jumped out of his car, threw his cigarette at me, then started kicking my car and trying to break my window. I grabbed my bat and got out of the car, and hadn't even had a chance to swing it at him when he ran away like a little pansy. I calmed down a little bit after he bolted, but when he started to try to get at me and my girlfriend, to cause harm to us, that's when I felt the desire to take his life. . . . I would have beaten him to death with my baseball bat.* [What did you actually do?] *I thought about what I would have done if he wouldn't have taken off, which is probably beat him to a bloody pulp with my bat. I don't know if I would have killed him, but it definitely crossed my mind.* [What could have pushed you over the edge to actually kill him?] *If he would have touched my girlfriend, I would have beat him to death. No questions asked.*

According to our findings, 91 percent of men and 84 percent of women have had at least one such vivid fantasy about killing someone. As I contemplated these surprising findings, and considered that the human mind has been exquisitely fine-tuned by evolution, I began to suspect that these fantasies were the expressions of deep psychological underpinnings that motivate us to kill for quite specific, calculated reasons. Seven years of near-obsessive subsequent research into murder has led me to the conclusion that, yes, the human mind has developed adaptations for killing—deeply ingrained patterns of thought, often accompanied by internal dialogue, anchored in powerful emotions—that motivate us to murder.

The simple explanations that are so frequently proffered to explain murder—poverty, pathology, parents, media violence—fail crashingly at getting to the heart of the darkness, the underlying architecture of the murdering mind. They fall short for many reasons, but the most obvious is that murder does not flow from any singular motivation. Consider the panoply of emotions that roil our blood and drive us to kill. Sometimes *hate* motivates murder; sometimes *envy*; sometimes *greed*; sometimes *fear*; sometimes *jealousy*; sometimes *spite*. And sometimes, a complex combination of emotions motivates murder.

Moreover, a single emotion can cause quite different kinds of murder. Jealousy compels one man to gun down a rival. But that same rage causes a second to strangle his wife, and a third to put the gun in his own mouth. Some people kill in order to secure a mate they think might stray into the arms of another; others kill to get rid of a mate. Some kill for love, others for hate. Some murders are strangely devoid of emotion, such as when a Mafia hit man kills. Others seem to cut against the grain of fundamental human nature, as when a single mother abandons a newborn. From malice to mercy, the range of psychological states that propel people to kill is staggering and begs for deeper understanding. Ted Bundy, Susan Smith, Jack Kevorkian, and Osama bin Laden are miles apart in motive.

Behind the apparent diversity of motives, and across the variability of circumstances that lead up to murder, lies a hidden web containing a collage of motives, a variety of means, and an assortment of opportunities. The powerful threads of this web stretch back millions of years, into the ancient mists of human evolutionary history.

According to the theory I've developed, nearly all the many kinds of murder—from crimes of passion to the methodically planned contract kill—can be explained by the twists and turns of a harsh evolutionary logic. Killing is surely ruthless, but it is also most often not the result of either psychosis or cultural conditioning. Murder is a product of the evolutionary pressures our species confronted and adapted to.

Recent findings about the murderous impulses of our ancestors strongly suggest that we became murderers very early in the course of our evolution. The "Iceman," a frozen corpse discovered in the Italian Alps, lived fifty-three hundred years ago. In 1991, two German hikers found him, the best-preserved human specimen yet discovered. With bread and meat in his intestines, and a bow and quiver of fourteen arrows by his side, he lay face-down in the snow. Scientists advanced several theories about his demise. One claimed that he froze to death in his sleep when he lay down to rest after an exhausting climb. Another suggested that he died because he had fallen and broken his ribs. A third suggested that an avalanche buried him under the snow.

All were proved wrong when scientists discovered the real reason. He died from an arrow that ripped into his back, tore through his insides, shattered his scapula, and lodged itself into his left shoulder. He suffered internal bleeding, and lived no longer than a few hours after being shot. Those who had examined his remains had initially missed the signs of this wound. The inch-long arrowhead was finally discovered through a multidimensional imaging procedure known as computerized tomography. We do not know whether he died trying to flee his attacker, whether he was caught by surprise and felled unawares, or whether a single enemy or a gang attacked him. What we now know with the certainty of forensic science, however, is that he was murdered. The "Iceman" was found clutching a dagger in his right hand. His forearms and hands revealed defensive wounds. And his body was covered with the blood of at least two other individuals.

Additional archeological evidence of our murderous nature is leading a reassessment of just how long ago murder entered our lives. Fifty-nine human skeletons were recently found in a cemetery at Gebel Sahaba in Egyptian Nubia, dating from the Late Paleolithic, some twelve to fourteen thousand years ago. More than 40 percent contained embedded stone projectiles. Many had multiple wounds. The majority of injuries appear on male skeletons. Most wounds pierced the left sides of the crania and rib cages, suggesting right-handed killers who attacked while their victims faced them. Other fresh evidence among the Anasazi Indians of the American Southwest suggests the sinister practice of cannibalism. It turns out that the scalping of skulls leaves characteristic cut-marks on the cranial bones. Did ancestral humans feast on other humans? Analyses of ancient fossilized human feces from the Anasazi recently revealed the presence of human myoglobin, which could only get there through the consumption of human muscle or heart.

Another study of human skeletons from California from more than a thousand years ago revealed that 5 percent contained arrowheads embedded within them, a finding that constitutes only the most direct evidence of warfare death.[4] A study of prehistoric sites dating to around 1325 A.D. in South and North Dakota also reveals dramatic evidence of war between tribal groups. Analysis of roughly five hundred skeletons buried in one pit provides evidence that they were all massacred during a single raid.[5] Almost all had *unhealed* cut-marks and cranial trauma indicative of scalping with sharp stones or knives, suggesting that they did not survive their attackers. Roughly 40 percent had depressed cranial fractures in addition to scalping. Interestingly, among the five hundred skeletons there was a striking absence of young women, providing a telltale clue about the purpose of the slaughter.

A study of skeletons from the Oneota culture residing along the Illinois

River floodplain, from roughly 1300 A.D., revealed that 16 percent experienced violent death. These murder victims tell their stories with unhealed trauma to the body, upper limbs, and cranium from projectiles, depressed fractures on the top and back of their skulls indicating clubbing, and holes in skulls that match the dimensions of stone weapons found at the same location. Some of the skeletons also revealed healed wounds, including punctures and cranial depressions, suggesting that they had survived at least one previous attack. Another study of the American Great Plains revealed that 19 percent had died from large projectile wounds that had penetrated pelvic bones, spinal columns, and limbs. Similar victims of mass slaughter among Native Americans have been found along the Pacific coast of southern California, dating back more than a millennium. Two-thirds of the injuries to the skeletons were inflicted on the left side of the front of the skull, indicating face-to-face combat with mostly right-handed attackers.

These and other new findings, such as discoveries of ancient weapons like maces, lances, tomahawks, daggers, and swords, leave no doubt that homicide has been prevalent over a vast expanse of human evolutionary history. Although obviously fragmentary and incomplete, this new paleontological and bioarcheological evidence has provided fascinating insights into the long history of murder, and has informed the theory of murder I've developed.

As I delved into the mystery of why we had become so violent so early on as a species, I realized that, according to the cold calculus of evolution, killing—especially the kinds of killing that are most prevalent—offered an abundance of advantages to our early ancestors in the competition for survival and reproduction, and I will explain those advantages through the course of the book. It may seem bizarre to talk about killing as adaptive, or murder as advantageous, but in fact the benefits of killing, in an evolutionary sense, are so substantial that the real mystery is not why killing has been so prevalent over our evolutionary history, but why killing has not been *more* prevalent.

The evolution of the psychology of murder has been like an arms race: in response to the threat of murder, we've developed a well-honed set of defenses against it, and they have acted as powerful deterrents.

Through the course of our evolution from primate proto-humans into *Homo sapiens*, we've had to struggle for survival against three primary dangers. The first is against the physical environment—falls from heights, starvation from food deprivation, death from drowning. The second is against other species—parasites from within and predators from without. Our natural revulsion toward people who appear diseased, our fear of spiders and snakes, and our acute sensitivity to when we are followed are all evolved defenses against these dangers. The third struggle is against members of our own species. Indeed, we are now at a stage of development where humans have become our most savage "hostile force of nature."

This long history of mortal danger from our own species is the reason that we have also developed a set of exquisitely tuned defenses to prevent being murdered. According to the workings of natural selection, the more costly it is to get killed—and of course nothing in our lives is more costly—the more rapidly will selection design weapons of defense against being killed. And, sure enough, just as humans have evolved fears of spiders and heights, we've evolved an impressive set of capabilities to ward off murder.

In an amazing scientific discovery, we have now come to know that these defenses start early in life—even before we are born, when we still inhabit the presumably cozy environment of our mother's womb. As Harvard biologist David Haig has discovered, even the womb presents its own dangers; a chief one of those is what is known as spontaneous abortions, many of which happen before a woman even knows she is pregnant. Indeed, we now know that many women who experience late periods and worry that they are pregnant, only to be relieved later when their periods begin again, have actually experienced spontaneous abortion of the growing fetus. According to Haig's findings, these often undetected miscarriages occur when the mother's body has sensed that the fetus is in poor health or possesses genetic abnormalities.

Remarkably, Haig also discovered that a defense mechanism has evolved to outwit the mother's body and protect the fetus. This is the fetal production of human chorionic gonadotropin (hCG), which is a hormone the fetus secretes into the mother's bloodstream. The female body appears to "interpret" high levels of hCG as a sign that a fetus is healthy and viable, and so does not spontaneously abort. Even the womb is a hostile environment where one's own interests must be protected at the cost of another's. Even in that most sacred place we are potential murder victims.

After birth, the next antihomicide mechanism that occurs is crying—a distress signal that alerts parents to a baby's hunger or any experience of pain. By six months of age, just when infants become more mobile, a specialized fear emerges—the fear of strangers. And this fear is not indiscriminate: infants' stranger-anxiety centers primarily on strange *men*, corresponding precisely to the sex of strangers who have posed the greatest threat to infants throughout human evolutionary history.

The antihomicidal defenses we've developed include our wariness when walking alone at night down a dark street, as well as the hypervigilance and acute anxiety that so many Americans experienced in the aftermath of the September 11 terrorist attacks. We have also evolved an amazing ability to read the minds of those with homicidal intent.

That is why Sheila Bellush sensed the danger that Allen Blackthorne might kill her. Think also of the O. J. Simpson case. Nicole Brown Simpson suspected that her life was in danger. She said on several occasions, "He's going to kill me and get away with it, because he's O. J. Simpson." Though we don't know for sure that O. J. Simpson was in fact her murderer, and he was of course acquitted of that crime, we do know that Nicole Brown Simpson's antihomicide defenses had been triggered. Unfortunately, they ultimately failed her; her killer was extraordinarily determined. The irony is that, even as natural selection fashioned our defenses against being murdered, it simultaneously created more finely developed killing strategies to evade and circumvent these defenses. As we evolved means of detecting danger from others, we also evolved the ability to deceive and surprise our victims. In effect, we evolved to disguise our own homicidal designs, concealing them from our victims. Even so, thousands of us owe our lives today to an uncanny and powerful urge to protect ourselves from the stealth tactics of the killers among us.

Our fascination with blood, our astonishing ability to pick out the angry face in a crowd of hundreds, and our thirst for the details of murders are all features of these defensive armaments. These mechanisms are designed not only to help us avoid situations in which our lives may be in peril, but also to strike back when we are in danger. As many potential murderers have discovered, it can be very dangerous to try to kill someone. Through the course of our evolution, our arsenal of self-defense strategies created monumental deterrents to those who might otherwise be tempted to kill. Potential killers are keenly aware of these defenses and deterrents, and that awareness prevents many potential murders. It's a tribute to our evolved antihomicide defenses, and to the mental calculations made by potential murderers of the risks of killing—both consciously and subconsciously—that murder is not more common.

Does this mean, then, that most murders happen because someone has lost his mind, lost his ability to understand or care about either the danger presented by self-defense mechanisms or the danger of punishment? Not at all.

Many people may believe that, whatever remaining residue of base instincts humans possess that might drive a man—or woman—to murder, they are held in check by the powerful brake we call rationality. According to this line of thinking, it simply isn't rational to kill. In their influential book *Crime of Passion,* psychologists David and Gene Lester express this traditional view of the occasional moments when the brakes fail: "Most murders occur on sudden impulse and in the heat of passion, in situations where the killer's emotions overcome his ability to reason."[6] Most experts argue that homicides typically occur when rage supplants reason; when judgment is set aside; when deeply rooted ancient emotions take over; when logic is overwhelmed by passion.

These assumptions, rooted in an artificial contrast between emotion and rationality, are wrong for two fundamental reasons.

First, many murders are premeditated. In one of the largest studies of female homicides, for example, 56 percent were judged to fulfill the criteria of premeditated (first-degree) murder, and the planning, reflection, and deliberation often extended over days, weeks, months, and occasionally years.[7] Killers often prepare elaborate scenarios—acquiring a weapon, selecting a time when the victim is vulnerable, and staging an alibi. Such deliberate planning is hardly the mark of irrationality, and though some of those who so intricately calculate their murders are discovered to be psychopaths, the vast majority are not.

Second, although it is clearly true that some killings are motivated by intense emotions, such as rage, jealousy, and envy, it does not follow that emotions defy reason. Indeed, a core argument that I will make in this book is that passions are rational. They function as well-designed components of human psychological machinery, facilitating effective solutions to specific adaptive problems. They succeed at precisely those critical junctures in life when dispassionate cold calculation would fail. Emotions, far from opposing reason, are extraordinarily effective means for implementing goals. Passions possess a functional, subconscious logic. In the case of homicide, passions provide the motivational fuel to enact a murder—but the murder is most often a solution arrived at through careful and complex, although sometimes speedy, calculation. The saying "Don't get mad, get even," misses this basic point: getting mad exists, in part, precisely for the purpose of "getting even."[8]

Case records do show that often people who kill do so while seized by a blinding rage, and they often seem oblivious to the consequences of their actions. We tend to think, then, that killers must be crazy. But they aren't. Or at least the majority are not. In the state of Michigan, as in most of the United States, nearly all people accused of the crime of killing end up being evaluated by trained psychologists and psychiatrists. They must be assessed as sane or insane, competent or incompetent to stand trial, psychotic or not psychotic. Surprisingly, in our study of 375 Michigan murders, we found that 96 percent were judged to be legally sane, competent, and nonpsychotic. They fully understood that their actions were wrong and illegal.

Most killers, in a nutshell, are not crazy. They kill for specific reasons, such as lust, greed, envy, fear, revenge, status, and reputation, or to get rid of someone who they perceive is inflicting costs on them. They are like you. They are like me. As forensic psychologist Dr. Carol Holden observed, after more than eighteen years of interviewing murderers, "The line between us and them is virtually non-existent."[9] But, perhaps unlike you and me, their cost-benefit calculators have arrived at a deadly solution to their problems.

This observation raises questions about why and when people kill. Precisely how do killers arrive at their lethal solutions? How many alternative solutions do they tend to entertain before deciding on murder? How do they determine that the benefits they would obtain from killing, the plums they would pluck, are worth the risks? How do they arrive at the means and the motive? And how do they choose the opportunity? In my investigations, I've discovered fascinating answers to these questions.

The logic of the evolutionary theory of murder that I've arrived at may well be disturbing, and I have not reached my conclusions lightly. In the course of developing this theory, I and my research colleagues, most notably Joshua Duntley, have conducted extensive studies and pored through vast numbers of case studies, honing and testing the theory. In addition to our massive study of homicidal fantasies, our work includes:

- **Homicide Defense Adaptations.** My lab has explored the specialized circumstances in which people feel that their lives are in mortal danger. Studying a sample of nearly a thousand participants from five cultures, we started by asking people: "Have you ever thought that another person might want to kill you?" An astonishing 91 percent of the men and 83 percent of the women from our age-diverse community sample answered in the affirmative. Then we probed deeper to find out *who* they feared might want to kill them, *what happened* to trigger the fear, *physical and behavioral changes* in the potential killer, the *method of murder* they envisioned the potential killer using, and most important, *what they did to avoid being killed*. In conjunction with the other studies, this study provides us with a roadmap of the precise circumstances in which our lives are most in danger and what murder-prevention strategies are most effective.

- **FBI Homicide Databases.** We have secured access to new and previously unstudied FBI databases, involving a total of 429,729 homicides. The sample contains 13,670 cases in which husbands kill their wives. A startling finding is that key contexts in which women's lives are at risk are "lovers' triangles" in which the woman is substantially younger than her husband. Women in "May–December" marriages, in which the man is substantially older than the woman, show a sharply elevated risk of murder.

- **Michigan Murders.** More than 50 percent of all people accused of murder in the state of Michigan go through the Center for Forensic Psychiatry, located in Ann Arbor, Michigan. In collaboration with Dr. Carol Holden, director of Evaluation Services at the Forensic Center, and Joshua Duntley, I have studied case files of 375 murders committed over the past fifteen years. These previously untapped files include rich and informative interviews with the killers, statements from eyewitnesses to the murder, police reports, psychiatric assessments, and autopsy reports.

- **What Would Push You Over the Edge to Kill?** My lab has conducted the first systematic research on what would tip people over the edge and cause them to kill. We presented participants with more than a hundred different scenarios, in which they recorded the probability that they would kill using percent likelihood. Nearly all people express a willingness to kill in some circumstances—to prevent being killed or to defend their children from killers. Our studies reveal the specific circumstances in which normal people state that they would kill, with some surprising findings. For example, men indicate an increased willingness to kill as their mating prospects become dire; women do not. Jim Morrison of the Doors noted, "Women seem wicked when you're unwanted," and this disturbing sentiment is reflected in our research on the circumstances in which men express a willingness to kill. These new findings simultaneously reveal when our lives are most in danger—a theme explored throughout the book.

- **Expressed Motives for Murder.** In another line of research, we have assembled the most comprehensive master-list of motives for murder. This research is based on a combined strategy of first extracting (1) all stated motives for murder depicted in criminology and forensic sciences literature, supplemented by (2) motives obtained from a review of our own sample of 375 Michigan murders, and (3) individual nominations of motives for murder by a community sample of everyday people. This is the first comprehensive scientific taxonomy of motives for murder. My research lab has used this taxonomy in our research to obtain a hierarchy of motives for murder, and to test specific facets of our new theory.

- **Interviews with Homicide Detectives and Forensic Psychiatrists.** One unusual source of evidence for the new theory of homicide comes from my personal interviews with homicide detectives and forensic psychiatrists. Those who devote their professional careers to investigating and solving murders have special insight into why people kill. I have also worked closely with forensic psychologists and psychiatrists who interview killers for a living. The insights provided by these professionals complement the other sources of empirical data.

To test our growing realization that murder is deeply ingrained in the human mind, and has been since the human mind evolved, we also investigated a series of new bioarcheological discoveries, such as those I mentioned earlier. No single source of scientific evidence can definitively prove the truth of any new theory. But my research lab over the past seven years has secured an unprecedented variety of different sources of evidence that have never been obtained and never assembled together pertaining to the underlying psychology of homicide. This unique research has enabled the development of the most penetrating, comprehensive, and scientifically sound theory of murder ever proposed, and I will walk you through it step by step in the chapters that follow.

Two

THE EVOLUTION OF KILLING

—**⦁—**

"We, the lineal representatives of the successful enactors of one scene of slaughter after another, must, whatever more pacific virtues we may also possess, still carry about with us ready at any moment to burst into flame, the smoldering and sinister traits of character by means of which they lived through so many massacres, harming others, but themselves unharmed."

—WILLIAM JAMES (1890), *The Principles of Psychology*

"To deprive others of their life is one of the most effective means of increasing one's fitness."

—JOSEPH LOPREATO, *Human Nature and Biocultural Evolution*[1]

MURDER HAS been studied a great deal and for good reason. It's the most fascinating, mysterious, and momentous act a human being can perform. So it's not remarkable that thousands of studies of homicide fill the scientific journals, and hundreds of books about murder line the shelves of libraries. We have reasonably good evidence on homicide rates, sex of perpetrator and victim, the age distributions of killers and their victims, solve rates, and many other important details. Study of the literature and statistics about murder, however, reveals that we have many mistaken beliefs, and also that surprisingly little serious scientific attention has been devoted to understanding the underlying *psychology* of murder.

One thing we are not generally mistaken about is that murder is a pernicious problem. According to FBI statistics, 16,503 officially recorded murders were committed in America in 2003, 16,229 in 2002, and 16,037 in 2001.[2] The last figure does not include the 2,992 murders from the horrific tragedy of the 9/11 terrorist attacks. Conservatively, over a million people were murdered in the United States in the twentieth century, not including another million Americans killed in the dozen major wars America fought. Comparable murder figures from many other countries are less reliable and often absent, so it's difficult to calculate worldwide statistics. A conservative estimate would put the worldwide figure at a minimum of a hundred million murder victims in the past century, with the true figure likely being double or triple.

For several reasons, even these alarming statistics grossly underestimate the magnitude of the problem of murder. First, they do not take into account the more than a million Americans who become "missing persons" each year. Although 99.5 percent are eventually found, that still leaves roughly five thousand who are not. Some have probably simply skipped town and are living in hiding, but an unknown number are murder victims. Second, some murders result from assaults that lead to the victims' death only days, weeks, or months after the attack. In such cases, the police do not always go back and change the crime classification for these killings from "assault" to "murder," and so some of these cases never make it into the official FBI homicide statistics. In addition, ambulances and modern medicine currently save the lives of many intended murder victims who would have died in times past; and for every "successful" murder, there are more than three attempted murders that fail because of successful medical intervention.[3] There are also nearly a million recorded cases of aggravated assault in America each year (e.g., 911,706 in 2000 and 909,023 in 2001), and an unknown number of these are "attempted murders" in which the killer's deadly mission failed.

These are only the reported attempts; there are an unknown number of attempted murders in which the victim successfully evades a killer entirely without injury and never reports the incident. One example occurred to a friend of mine while camping with a friend in Colorado. He awoke at 4 A.M. to discover an intruder breaking into his car. He wakened his friend, and the two of them went after the robber, pulling out a knife in an effort to dissuade and subdue him. But the robber suddenly lunged at my friend and wrestled the knife away, and then attacked with intent to kill. My friend saved his own life only by grabbing the knife blade with both hands and holding on for dear life, causing a deep gash, all the way through to the bones of his fingers. The attacker finally let go of the knife and ran. My friend never reported this to the police. Nor will we ever know how many murderers are thwarted when potential victims are careful not to put themselves in life-endangering situations to begin with. The threat of murder, in short, is many times more pervasive than the official body count recorded in the annual FBI statistics.

Misconceptions abound in public perceptions of murder, in part because of the types of murders that command media attention. Serial killers attract a wildly disproportionate share of media attention, but they actually account for only 1 to 2 percent of all murders in America.[4] In one study of the types of murders newspapers cover, the most common types were serial killers such as Ted Bundy or Charles Manson; mass murderers such as Charles Whitman, who shot forty-five, of whom sixteen were killed, from the University of Texas Tower in 1966; gang killings; professional mob-hit killings; murders of or by prominent people; murders that have bizarre characteristics; and killings linked to key political issues such as whether the criminal-justice system is operating effectively. Collectively, all these types add up to a mere 5 percent of all murders, so it's natural that people come away with a distorted perception of how and why most murders occur.[5] The Hillside Stranglers, John Wayne Gacy, Jeffrey Dahmer, John Hinckley, and Eileen Wuornos are outliers, not representative of most murderers. Nonetheless, people's fascination with these kinds of murders also results from our evolved homicide-prevention psychology. As we will see, the rare and unpredictable murders trip specialized defenses designed to deal with uncertainty. Gang killings activate our psychology of coalitions. And murders of prominent people have dramatic consequences for shifts in power, status, and reputation.

Another misconception is that murders are committed mostly by hardened criminals. David Lester, one of the leading scholars on murder, concludes that "this view is completely wrong."[6] In one study of murderers who were paroled, for example, only 6 percent were subsequently rearrested for committing another murder.[7] Although there clearly are some career criminals who have committed repeated murders, most murderers kill only once.

Yet another misconception is that murderers are insane or in some way psychotic. Some clearly are. An autopsy revealed a tumor in tower sniper Charles Whitman's brain, which may have triggered his killing spree. Jeffrey Dahmer, the serial killer who enjoyed cannibalizing his victims and kept body parts in his freezer, was clearly deranged. Nonetheless, our own study of Michigan murderers found that only 4 percent had a diagnosis of psychosis or some other disorder sufficient to qualify for the insanity defense.[8]

When we start to look more deeply into what the statistics reveal about murder, we discover some striking patterns in the data, some of which are quite surprising. One of the most salient observations that emerges is that murder is a male-dominated phenomenon. Year after year, the percentage of murders in the U.S. that are committed by men hovers right around 87. It may be surprising that men are also much more often the victims of murder. Of murder victims in any given year, on average, 75 percent are men—a percentage that has remained quite stable over the years, with 74 percent in 1964, 77 percent in 1974, and 75 percent in 1984. It's also interesting to look at how many murders by men are perpetrated against men. On average, 65 percent of all murders involve males killing other males. By comparison, 22 percent of murders involve males killing females. As for murders by women, 10 percent of all murders, on average, involve females killing males, and a mere 3 percent of murders involve females killing other females.[9]

If we look at the complete set of same-sex killings—male killing male and female killing female—we find that more than 95 percent involve men killing other men. These patterns show a remarkable consistency across cultures. In statistics compiled from thirty-five different studies representing a broad span of cultures, the vast majority of same-sex killings were committed by men: 97 percent in Brazil, 93 percent in Scotland, 94 percent in Kenya, 98 percent in Uganda, and 97 percent among the people known as the Tiv in Nigeria.[10]

We can read these statistics and simply conclude that men are much more inclined to violence, which is true, but that doesn't explain why they get violent, when, or with whom. We will find that there are compelling explanations for these striking gender differences in the patterns of murder. In fact, a host of personality variables on which men score higher than women correlate with criminality and delinquency in general. These include *impulsivity* (acting without deliberating), *sensation seeking* (taking risks to achieve novel experiences), *childhood aggressiveness, lack of empathy,* and *deficient moral reasoning*. None of these personality variables, however, have been shown to predict homicide specifically.[11]

Another striking pattern regarding who gets murdered and who commits murder concerns age. The highest rate of murdering occurs between the ages of twenty and twenty-nine, though murder rates start rising by the time males reach fifteen and continue to remain high into the thirties and forties.[12] Most murder victims also fall in their twenties, with a similarly wide age distribution. The murder rate per hundred thousand per year in the United States is only 1.6 between the ages of ten and fourteen, but it rises to 10 per hundred thousand in the fifteen-to-nineteen age bracket, and 17.8 in the twenty-to-twenty-four age bracket.[13] Then it gradually drops to 16.3 in the twenty-five-to-twenty-nine age bracket; 13.9 in the thirty-to-thirty-four bracket; and 12 in the thirty-five-to-thirty-nine bracket. What these numbers reveal is that murder increases dramatically as males enter the years of reproductive competition.

One of the interesting and counterintuitive aspects of murder is that, as crimes go, it is often easier to identify the perpetrator. In fact, of all crimes, murder has the highest "clearance" or solve rate, which is based on the number of people arrested and charged with the crime and turned over to the courts for prosecution, or offenders identified by the police when there is enough evidence to gain a conviction but, for reasons beyond the powers of the police, they can't actually arrest the perpetrator (e.g., the perpetrator goes into hiding, flees the country, or ends up getting killed). Whereas the clearance rate for burglary is only 14 percent, arson 15 percent, and larceny-theft 20 percent, the clearance rate for murder typically hovers around 69 percent.[14]

The high solve rate is due to another feature of murder that popular perceptions tend to underplay. In addition to the greater effort expended on solving murders than any other crime, a key reason for the high solve rate is that murderers so often know their victims. Murders by acquaintances, friends, and family are much more common than murders by strangers. Hence friends and relatives are often important witnesses or can provide instrumental clues about who had a motive to murder.

Nevertheless, a disconcerting 31 percent of all murders are *never* solved. Killers often take painstaking efforts to plan their murders, create alibis, and cover up their kills—highlighting how many murders are strategic, as opposed to irrational, crazed, spur-of-the-moment outbursts.

THE PSYCHOLOGICAL PUZZLE

If most murders are not committed by serial killers, hardened criminals, or the insane, how can we explain why people kill? One of the surprising things I discovered when I scoured the scientific literature is that virtually no theories have been formulated specifically to explain why people murder. Instead, scientists have mostly proposed theories designed to explain *violence and criminality in general*. Murder, in these theories, is viewed as merely an extreme manifestation on a continuum of violence or criminality.

This is one reason for the theories' inadequacy, since murder is qualitatively different from all other forms of violence. Unlike with other forms of violence, murder victims are gone forever. When you kill someone, you not only take away everything they have, you take away everything that they ever could have in the future. Murder is often a highly orchestrated act with a dead body as the outcome. Moreover, the motives for murder turn out to be vastly different from the motives for other forms of violence, such as beatings, robbery, or rape. Finally, murder is not a single homogeneous phenomenon; different types of murders require different types of explanations. Wife killing, same-sex rivalry killing, infanticide, stepchild killing, and mass slaughter in war, for example, differ vastly in motive, perpetrator, and method. General theories of violence simply cannot explain the differences we find among the many forms of murder.

Before we dismiss them, however, we should delve a little into the major theories so that the specific ways in which they fall short are clear.

Social-environment theories have been the most frequently invoked explanation for violence. A popular variant is the social-learning theory of Albert Bandura, which proposes that people acquire social behavior by observing and imitating others—behaviors for which they are either rewarded or punished, which then shapes their subsequent behavior. This theory has been proposed to explain the fact that men kill more than women. As leading aggression-researcher Leonard Berkowitz argues: "Think of all the ways in which *modern western society* . . . teaches children that fighting is far more appropriate for men than women. Popular literature and the mass media consistently show men but not women fighting. Parents buy toy weapons for their sons and dolls for their daughters. Parents are more likely to approve of and reward aggressive behavior in boys than in girls. Again and again, directly and indirectly, youngsters learn that males are aggressive and females are not. . . ."[15]

One glaring shortfall of this theory is that it cannot explain why even in cultures without these media influences men kill much more often than women, why sex differences in murder are universal across cultures, not unique to modern Western culture. Also, this theory does not account for the fact that we are exposed to many different models of behavior and taught many things. The models range from nice men who perform heroic deeds, to evil, sneering bad guys who get punished for having been violent. And we are taught from an early age that murder is wrong and that crime doesn't pay. Nothing in the theory can explain whom we will choose to imitate from the vast array of models to which we are exposed.

Pathology theories of criminality and violence have also been invoked to explain murder.[16] According to these theories, killing is caused by brain damage and major psychological dysfunction, stemming from factors such as child abuse, alcohol damage, or faulty genetics. Some proponents invoke damage to the amygdala, an area of the brain that is implicated in controlling social emotions such as jealousy and rage. Others invoke damage to the frontal lobes, which causes flatness of feeling and indifference to the suffering of others. Brain pathology or major psychological disorders undoubtedly are involved in some homicides, but, as I've already mentioned, our study of Michigan murderers revealed that the vast majority of those killers had neither. Furthermore, the types of homicide most likely to be produced by brain damage are those that are either random or senseless, or involve highly bizarre and unusual elements, as opposed to accounting for the vast majority of more "normal" killings. Furthermore, as neurologist Jonathan Pincus notes in his book *Base Instincts,* "only a small minority of people with brain damage ever become violent."[17]

Sociological theories of criminality have also enjoyed popularity in attempting to explain murder. These usually invoke features of the larger society, such as capitalism, poverty, or economic inequality. Capitalism, for example, is said to make people greedy. Poverty and economic inequality are said to force people into a life of crime. As such, the types of criminal activity these sociological theories are most appropriate for explaining are robbery, mugging, and perhaps the behavior of drug gangs—crimes committed to obtain economic resources. Though poverty per se is not a powerful predictor of crime, economic inequality is. In regions where there is great income disparity, where some people are wealthy and others dirt-poor, the rates of both property offenses and violent crime tend to increase.[18] Yet there is absolutely no evidence that murder or any sort of crime is more prevalent in capitalist cultures than in socialist cultures, according to criminologists Lee Ellis and Anthony Walsh.[19] And, unfortunately, no studies have examined whether the pressures of income inequality are linked with the many different types of murder that clearly do not involve economic resources. They also fail because they do not specify why our psychology would react to income disparity with violence and murder instead of leading us to do something else. Thus, the sociological theories are of limited value in our understanding of why people murder.

Evolutionary theory has occasionally been used to explain why people kill, but as we will see, the previously proposed evolutionary theories are also inadequate to explain the many types of murders considered in this book. Several evolutionary scientists, such as John Tooby, Leda Cosmides, and Richard Wrangham, have advanced compelling evolutionary theories of warfare or coalitional killing.[20] Tooby and Cosmides, for example, argue that men go to war primarily for access to women. This accords well with my own theory, and we will touch on war briefly in chapter 9. Nonetheless, the evolutionary war theory does not explain, nor is it intended to explain, the majority of murders, which are perpetrated by killers who mingle among us.

The overriding problem with all of these other theories is that they fail to delve deeply into the underlying psychology of killing to understand the ultimate causes of murder.

CRIMINAL PROFILING

It is important to distinguish my goal of delving into the deep psychology of murder from the excellent work of criminal profilers such as former FBI agents John Douglas, Roy Hazelwood, Ann Burgess, and Robert Ressler, forensic scientist Brent Turvey, and forensic psychologist David Cantor. Criminal profiling, although done informally for more than a century by psychologists and psychiatrists aiding the police, became formalized at the Behavioral Sciences Unit of the FBI at Quantico, Virginia. Key FBI originators Howard Teten and Pat Mullany began the process in 1970; it was further refined by John Douglas and Robert Ressler in the late 1970s and early 1980s. The primary goal of behavioral profiling is to collate a variety of sources of evidence—crime-scene analysis, victim characteristics, criminal modus operandi, autopsy data, and so forth—to come up with a distinctive profile or "signature" of the potential perpetrator, in order to reduce the pool of potential suspects and ultimately catch and convict the actual perpetrator.

One of the key contributions of the FBI group was to classify crimes into two basic types, either organized or disorganized, categories still used today. *Organized* crimes usually involve planning, the targeting of a stranger, and hiding the body. The perpetrators of organized crimes are said to be average or above average in intelligence, and socially competent; they often use alcohol in the context of committing the crime, and enjoy following the crime in the news or media. The perpetrators are often sociopathic—they lack a conscience and normal feelings of empathy, are interpersonally exploitive, are pathological liars, have a grandiose sense of self-worth, and pursue a manipulative strategy of conning others. *Disorganized* crimes are more often spontaneous, betraying little evidence of planning; victims are known to the perpetrator; violence is sudden; the body is left in view; and sex acts are often committed after death. The perpetrators of disorganized crimes are often psychotic—severely disturbed individuals who often experience delusions, hallucinations, and other breaks in contact with reality. Forensic psychiatrists such as Brent Turvey argue convincingly that the organized-disorganized dichotomy may be too simplified, and the FBI profilers now recognize "mixed" or intermediate types.[21]

Criminal profiling, which often involves combining a mixture of statistical information, profiler experience, and intuition, is primarily directed toward apprehending unusually problematic and elusive serial killers or serial rapists. Using the organized-disorganized classification system, and identifying the unique "signature" of a criminal—the kind of car he is likely to drive, the modus operandi, the likely age and race, the marital status, skill level, and personality characteristics—profilers can be invaluable in catching serial killers. Criminal profilers are typically brought in on high-profile cases such as the Green River killings or the Atlanta child murders. These unusual cases, as noted before, account for only 1 to 2 percent of all murders. My primary goal is to understand the deep psychological foundations of the majority of killers, the murderers next door. We need to get into the minds of murderers.

MURDER IN MIND

The great movie director Alfred Hitchcock frequently trafficked in murder. His classic *Strangers on a Train,* based on a book written by Patricia Highsmith, points to a possible function of homicidal fantasies. In one scene, the primary villain poses a parlor game at a society party—he suggests that everyone imagine how he or she might carry out a murder. One party guest immediately launches into the spirit of the game: "I read a case once. I think it would be a wonderful idea. I can take [my husband] out in the car and when we get to a very lonely spot, knock him on the head with a hammer, pour gasoline over him and over the car, and set the whole thing ablaze." She laughs at her vision as it unfolds, causing a horrified reaction from the other party guests. Later, on a train, the villain uses the vehicle of hypothetical fantasies to lure a stranger into a diabolical plot of double murder. Without knowing it, Hitchcock and Highsmith exposed one of the most important psychological circuits installed in the killing brain— homicidal scenario building.

As I contemplated the homicidal fantasies we recorded, I wondered, could the thoughts, fantasies, daydreams, internal dialogue, planning, and scenario building about destroying someone afford a crucial benefit to us in solving life's problems, one that has been overlooked entirely by social scientists?

In our research on homicidal fantasies, involving thousands of individuals from all walks of life across six different cultures, we discovered how they are used to build and work through scenarios of killing; how they help channel murderous intentions into other means of seeking redress; how they can also be used to simulate and rehearse carrying out a murder; and how particular passions come into play in evaluating whether or not to turn a fantasy into reality.

Homicidal fantasies are sometimes fleeting, but they are often quite detailed and elaborate. They commonly involve constructing and rehearsing surprisingly specific scenarios of murder, contemplating various means, carefully calculating consequences, and evaluating costs and benefits. As I studied more and more of these fantasies, I realized that they are not merely the emotionally driven venting of dangerous passions, though strong emotions do almost always accompany them, often shockingly strong emotions. Rather, close study of these fantasies reveals that our homicidal thoughts follow specific patterns. Men, for example, fantasize about killing for a quite different set of reasons than those of women, and people's fantasies reveal again and again a set of specific reasons for wanting to kill. They are triggered by a well-honed set of circumstances that are not at all random and that emanate from deep psychological motivations for murder. Our homicidal fantasies are not just irrelevant reveries about acts that we would never really consider committing.

The patterns that I discovered in the triggers of homicidal fantasies support a radical new theory of murder—that all of us house in our large brains specialized psychological circuits that lead us to contemplate murder as a solution to specific adaptive problems. That is why we found that homicidal fantasies are so common. That is why most of us have experienced thoughts of killing at some point in our lives. And that is why homicidal fantasies are not isolated among the insane, the depressed, or the career criminal.

Consider this interesting fact. The human brain constitutes only 2 percent of the average human's body weight, but it consumes roughly 20 to 25 percent of the body's calories. This reveals something important about thinking—cognition is metabolically costly. Energy devoted to solving one problem precludes energy available for other problems. The costs of thought, however, extend beyond calories. Time spent processing information about one problem preempts the cognitive work on other problems—"opportunity costs," in the language of economics. When we think about problems at work, we can't simultaneously think about problems with our mates (unless mating is interfering with work, or work is interfering with mating!). The nature, content, and duration of private reveries furnish critical clues about the pressing problems our minds have evolved to solve. Homicidal thoughts inhabit the minds of most normal people at certain times in their lives; even people we consider "nice"—the kindly co-worker, the dedicated husband, or the patient high school teacher—will sometimes contemplate committing murder.

To understand why thoughts dedicated to entertaining the option of murder might be part of the human psychological design, consider cognitive activity devoted to another important concern most of us grapple with quite a bit in our lives—sex. Sexual thoughts occur before, but do not invariably lead to, sexual deeds. Indeed, the vast majority of sexual thoughts are not acted upon. Fortunately! But sexual scenarios played out in the privacy of our minds serve many extremely useful functions. They allow us to evaluate what turns us on and what turns us off. We can visualize having affairs without actually engaging in them. Sexual fantasies afford the opportunity to scrutinize the consequences of our sexual actions before they occur. They allow us to play out some disastrous sexual scenes before we make the mistake of acting them out. They also sometimes motivate us to go ahead and make a move we've been too shy to try.

Homicidal ideation also allows us to fashion alternative scenarios and evaluate the extended costs, benefits, and consequences of each. Consider this homicidal fantasy by a woman in our study, age twenty-three, who thought about killing her rival:

> My boyfriend was cheating on me with this girl. She was a real bitch to everyone. My boyfriend was going to dump me for her. I hated her for taking my boyfriend, plus she treated him like crap. I thought about strangling her or chopping her head off.

When we asked what prevented her from carrying out this fantasy, she said that she knew that she would be caught and did not want to spend her life behind bars. We asked what could have changed to cause her to carry out the murder, and she replied, "If I knew I would not be caught." Spinning scenarios allowed her to evaluate the effectiveness and feasibility of alternative courses of action. In this example, she chose to spread malicious gossip about her rival, telling others she was a slut.

Think about it for a moment. Have *you* ever thought about killing someone, if only fleetingly?

People have hundreds of homicidal thoughts for every one that is acted upon. Though homicidal thoughts usually precede murder—as we found in the case files in the Michigan study of murderers—they do not invariably, or even very often, lead to murder. In fact, most fantasies help to put the brakes on murderous impulses, inhibiting the intent to kill, because we usually appraise the costs as too high and choose more effective, less risky solutions.

That's not to say, however, that they aren't "real" expressions of murderous intent. Indeed, homicidal ideation almost invariably precedes carried-out kills.[22] Although the graphic details of a killer's thinking prior to a murder are rarely available, a case from our study of Michigan murders illustrates the ideation that most often goes on prior to murder.

Two weeks before killing his wife, in a conversation with his boss, Charles W.* mentioned that he felt like killing her. He asked his boss, "Have you ever had a similar feeling?" The day before the murder, Charles W. visited a friend and reported that he was "going to beat Susan's* ass or hire someone to kill her." According to other observers, "the defendant made threats concerning his wife, saying he knew where she was and was angry enough to kill her." The back story reveals why. Two weeks before these remarks, Charles's wife had left him. He told the interviewer that he loved his wife and that she was going to divorce him for no apparent reason. On the day of the killing, he left work to go home to feed his children. Indeed, he said, "I love my sons a lot. . . . I was very proud of my sons. I loved 'em and I knew they loved me."

After feeding his children, he got into his car and went looking for his wife. He went to her place of employment, posing as a private investigator, showing workers a picture of a woman he was tracking down for supposedly committing fraud. He went to a bar he knew his wife frequented, using the same ruse. He then drove to the house of one of his wife's friends, who later told police that he was quite polite to her and said she noted nothing unusual about his speech. When he finally found out where his wife was staying, he drove back to his house and picked up a scope rifle and shells specifically for that rifle. He then drove to where she was staying, parked the car a block away, and approached on foot the house containing his wife. He cut the telephone wires to the house. From outside the window, he got his wife in the crosshairs of his scope. Then he fired. He later claimed that he did not intend to kill her, and only looked through the scope to determine if it really was his wife sitting by the window, and the gun

*Throughout this book, names and certain details have been changed to protect the identities of the individuals involved. An asterisk (*) follows the names that have been changed.

mysteriously went off. He said he didn't plan on using the gun, and had brought it "just to scare her into coming home, to show her that I meant business. . . ."

When asked why he shot his wife, he said: "It's kind of a long story. It's not simple. It started from the time that she first left 40 days before the shooting. I came home from work, and she ran up to me and gave me a big kiss and she was shaking. She was acting like she was scared. I saw fear in her eyes, and it made me suspicious. Something was not quite right. She had been fucking around, I knew. Then she left and I didn't know where she went. I thought she had gone to a women's shelter or something. Well, she finally called the house one day and she told me she had filed for divorce. . . . It was a little over two weeks after she left. Well, my heart sunk. I suspected she might do it, but I didn't think she really would because I knew she still loved me. I loved her and all this time I was just hoping to get her to come back home. I had lost my job, and now she was divorcing me." He also noted that he suspected that another man he knew "would eventually be trying to get into her drawers, especially once he knew she was divorcing me." All of his actions, comments to his boss and friends, and subsequent accounts of the murder to the forensic psychiatrist betrayed several weeks of homicidal thoughts—enough for the charge of premeditated murder.

In our case files of Michigan murderers, we found that 72 percent contained explicit evidence of homicidal ideation prior to the murder. Consider the years of homicidal ideation and careful planning that must have gone into the September 11 murders. The terrorists' diaries reflect what a recent study of serial killers revealed—86 percent had *vivid* and *recurrent* homicidal fantasies that preceded carried-out kills.[23] Homicidal ideation, of course, need not involve days, months, or years. It can be hours, minutes, or even seconds. In one case from our study of Michigan murders, the killer said: "Somebody rubs and picks on you, and you laugh with them. But inside you want to punch them and kill them. He saw something in my eyes, I guess, and started to leave. I called to him, saying 'it is okay,' but it didn't work. As he ran away, I pulled out my gun and shot him in the head." Whether they last seconds or months, thoughts of killing almost invariably precede deeds.

It was the realization that homicidal fantasies were so pervasive, combined with the explanatory inadequacy of existing theories of murder, that prompted me to develop a deeper and more comprehensive theory of why people kill. The core of my theory is that humans have evolved powerful psychological adaptations that impel us to murder as a means for solving specific problems we encounter during the evolutionary battles for survival and reproduction. We can think of these adaptations as psychological circuits in our minds, activated in a quite specific set of circumstances in order to solve particular adaptive challenges. There is an evolutionary logic at work in the vast majority of killings. This theory does a powerful job of explaining the patterns revealed in the statistics of murder that other theories don't account for, such as why so many murders are committed by men, and why so many victims are men. It offers a compelling explanation for why women kill when they do, and explains even the most perplexing kinds of murder, such as when parents kill their children.

A crucial point about this evolutionary theory of murder is that I am *not* arguing for "genetic determinism." I am *not* saying that we are lumbering robots with blind killer-impulses that inevitably get expressed. I am also *not* saying that we have no choice in the matter of whether or not we go to the extreme of actually killing someone. The mere existence of psychological adaptations that lead us to murder in certain circumstances does not mean that we are *inevitably* driven to kill. Murder is one strategy on a menu of solutions to a predictable set of adaptive problems that were frequent in the lives of our ancestors and, fortunately, most of the time people use non-lethal means of solving these problems.

THE EVOLUTIONARY-PSYCHOLOGY PERSPECTIVE

My theory is anchored in the exciting new interdisciplinary field known as evolutionary psychology, which is producing a scientific revolution in the understanding of human behavior. According to this understanding of human nature, we have evolved many psychological adaptations that contribute to our behavior, and those that might drive us to kill under certain conditions are only one set in that complex mix. We've also evolved adaptations, for example, for cooperation, altruism, peacemaking, friendship, alliance building, and self-sacrifice, among many others.

Before the development of evolutionary psychology, the dominant explanation of human nature was what's known as the "blank slate" argument.[24] This old paradigm holds that we have no essential nature when we are born, aside from a general capacity to learn. The content of our characters gets written onto this "blank slate" as we develop, so that our nature is shaped by outside forces: parents, teachers, peers, society, media, and culture. When it comes to explaining why we would kill, this perspective has pointed to a range of pernicious shaping effects "out there" in the world, such as bad parenting, poor socialization, media messages, cultures that glorify violence, and the ills of society.

Evolutionary psychology, by contrast, contends that we come into the world factory-equipped with a mind that is designed to solve a range of adaptive problems our ancestors grappled with throughout human history. This psychological equipment helps us to handle challenges of survival and reproduction—the adaptive problems—that have confronted generations of predecessors going back into deep time. People do not spring from the womb, of course, with these adaptations fully formed. Men are not born with beards and women are not born with fully developed breasts. They develop later on to help solve problems during the reproductive phase of our lifespan. Similarly, our psychological adaptations appear at the appropriate time over the course of our development.

As evolutionary psychology matured, it began to produce a remarkable range of new insights into human nature. The field offered compelling explanations about why people are so attracted to beauty even though we are taught that looks are only "skin-deep." It came up with answers about why people cheat on one another so much, even when they are in love with their mates, and about why men and women think so differently about having affairs.[25] It discovered that having a stepparent in the home is the single greatest risk factor for child abuse. It led to the discovery that women are better than men at a phenomenon known as spacial location memory—

remembering the positions and sites of things they have previously seen. And it explained for the first time why women's sexual desire varies over the course of the ovulation cycle.[26]

Evolutionary psychology has been successful in providing compelling explanations for many facets of human nature. So as I thought about the surprising prevalence of homicidal fantasies and how mesmerized people are by murder, I began to contemplate the disturbing possibility that humans have evolved adaptations to kill. I realized that murder might be an astonishingly effective strategy for dealing with some of the evolutionary challenges we face. Could it be that murder conferred powerful benefits over the eons of our evolution, that all of our minds contain mechanisms that motivate murder?

THE COMPETITIVE LEGACY OF OUR ANCESTORS

Every breath we take we owe to our ancestors—an unimaginably long and unbroken line of forebears who managed to survive all of the Darwinian "hostile forces of nature." We tend to think of evolutionary competition as the "survival of the fittest," as the struggle of animals to survive the challenges presented by a harsh environment. Those who failed to find food or avoid predators, those who succumbed to disease or became riddled with parasites, bit the evolutionary dust. This much is obvious.

What is less obvious is that the process of evolution by natural selection is played out through generations, and the key to the long-term outcome is *reproductive* competition. The winners in evolutionary terms are not only those who themselves survive, but those who manage to reproduce most successfully: those who have the most heirs who are healthy and go on to have heirs of their own. This competition to reproduce successfully is a key driving force in our lives, and the competition can be quite fierce. In each generation, there are a fixed number of reproductively viable women and men available to mate with. The dating market makes it quite clear that some mates are much more desirable than others. As the saying goes, all the good ones are taken. Each man and woman is ultimately in competition with other men and women for "shares" of the ancestry of the next generation.

We are all obviously descendants of those who succeeded in this reproductive competition. As the descendants of those who succeeded, we modern humans carry with us the remarkably beneficial components of body and designs of mind that helped our ancestors prevail.

The fierce evolutionary competition that has shaped us leads, if we will follow, to a theoretical insight both subtle in nature and profound in implication. Analysts of human nature have either failed to recognize it or have recoiled from its disturbing implications. In the intensely competitive game of reproductive competition, through the eons murder has been a remarkably effective method of achieving evolutionary success. Of course, as we became civilized, all human societies developed laws against murder, and in our contemporary lives, murdering carries the threat of harsh punishment. So murder is now a more costly strategy for defeating mating rivals than it must have been in our distant past. Through the long years of human evolution, however, killing would have been a highly effective means of vanquishing rivals and ensuring that the mate we selected passed on our genes and not another's. From a man's perspective, killing a rival's mate strips him of an invaluable and possibly irreplaceable reproductive resource. Killing his children can snuff out his genetic future entirely. Vanquishing an entire group of rivals through mass murder or genocide opens new vistas for the killers and their children to flourish.

It may seem coldhearted to talk about killing as adaptive or murder as advantageous, but if we consider the nature of reproductive competition humans have faced over the long time spans of our evolution, then we can appreciate just what an edge in that evolutionary competition killing would have provided. The benefits of killing, in an evolutionary sense, must be momentous and manifold, because, on the other side, the negative reproductive consequences of being killed are so profound.

No newspaper is likely to carry the headline "Scientists Discover That It's Bad to Be Dead." We know this. Getting murdered, however, turns out to be far worse, evolutionarily, than we have probably realized.

Bear with me as I play out the many aspects of this critical insight. To start with, being killed cuts off all avenues for the unfortunate victim's genes to be passed on. Never again will a male homicide victim court, attract, or seduce another woman. Never again will the victim make love with his wife. All potential sexual encounters with strangers, all potential liaisons with mistresses, are forever terminated. Every future act of mating, and hence every future opportunity for reproduction, is permanently extinguished. But that's merely the beginning.

The victim's wife, if he has a partner, now becomes eligible for mating with other men. No longer can the dead man fend off former friends or current enemies who attempt to charm her. Another man may now sleep in his bed, caress his wife's skin, and impregnate her. All of his mating losses become potential reproductive gains for other men. But the costs of getting killed get worse still.

The homicide victim's children now become frighteningly vulnerable. The victim is no longer around to help raise them and see them through life's countless hurdles. He can no longer protect them from beatings, sexual abuse, or homicide at the hands of strangers or stepfathers. His children also risk losing his wife's parental attentions if she remarries, which may get rechanneled to children she has with her new husband.

To compound these costs, given the calculus of evolutionary competition, the murder victim's losses become potential gains for eager competitors. His elimination from the status hierarchy opens a niche for a rival to ascend. The children of his antagonists will thrive in competition against his children, who now become hampered by their father's death. His entire kin group is weakened and made vulnerable by his death. In short, the costs of getting killed cascade to one's children, grandchildren, great-grandchildren, and the victim's entire extended family. Simultaneously, the victim's costs become his rival's benefits in this ruthless competitive struggle. The eternity of darkness that comes with premature death may be accompanied by the abrupt end of an entire genetic line.

If this view of the competitive motives behind human nature seems severe, consider the following story from a study of the Ache Indians of Paraguay, South America, one culture that may provide a glimpse into what our ancestral culture was like.

Among the Ache, meat is a scarce and prized resource. Although gathered berries, nuts, and plant foods are shared only within families, the Ache share meat from the hunt communally. Hunters deposit their kill to a central "distributor," who then allocates portions to different families, based largely on family size. Good hunters enjoy great status, and groups strive to keep good hunters happy, but, surprisingly, skilled hunters do not garner a larger share of the communal meat. They benefit from their greater-than-average contributions in two ways. First, the group provides extraordinary health care and solicitude to the children of good hunters. These children enjoy being groomed and tended—group members take the time to feed them, remove splinters from their feet, and nurse them to health when ill. Second, skilled hunters are highly attractive to Ache women. It's not uncommon for an accomplished hunter to indulge in a mistress or two on the side. These benefits, however, cause conflict.

One day a fight broke out between two Ache men, a skilled hunter and an average hunter. The conflict arose over a woman—a sexual infidelity discovered by the less adept man, who challenged his rival to an ax fight. The husband lost; he ended up dead, felled by the blade of his more athletic rival. Within a matter of days, the group convened to decide the fate of the dead man's thirteen-year-old son. The fact that he now lacked a father meant that he would be a net drain of resources on the group. The group made a decision. The dead man's son must die. The death of the father, in short, caused the group to kill the son. There's a lesson here—dead men can't protect their children. This case starkly demonstrates the costs of murder for the victim's kin.

So it's astonishingly bad to be dead. And on the flip side, it's also astonishingly advantageous to get a rival out of the way. Consider just a few of the specific benefits our ancestors *could* have secured by killing other human beings:

- Preventing injury, rape, or death to oneself, spouse, or kin
- Eliminating a crucial antagonist
- Acquiring a rival's resources or territory
- Securing sexual access to a competitor's mate

- Preventing an interloper from appropriating one's own mate
- Cultivating a fierce reputation to deter the encroachment of enemies
- Avoiding investment in genetically unrelated children (stepchildren)
- Protecting resources needed for reproduction
- Eliminating an entire lineage of reproductive competitors

Of course, many of us never come close to killing someone, and that's true for several reasons. One is that, as we've become more civilized as a species, we've developed more and more effective deterrents against murder, both through our legal systems and through our cultural conditioning—though, as we found in our study of homicidal fantasies, most of us do contemplate the idea of murdering at some point in our lives. Another force inhibiting us from committing murder comes from our evolutionary heritage. As the motivations to murder evolved in our minds, a set of counterinclinations also developed. Killing is a risky business. It can be dangerous and inflict horrible costs on the victim. Because it's so bad to be dead, evolution has fashioned ruthless defenses to prevent being killed, including killing the killer. Potential victims are therefore quite dangerous themselves. In the evolutionary arms race, homicide victims have played a critical and unappreciated role—they paved the way for the evolution of antihomicide defenses.

Thanks to these antihomicide defenses, it's often far too costly to kill. In attempting to kill, you become vulnerable yourself. The intended victim's friends and relatives might rush to his defense. From the killer's perspective, even if he survives and succeeds in carrying out the kill, he risks ostracism or banishment. We usually don't want killers in our midst, and neither did our ancestors, although in a confrontation with a hostile group, killers come in quite handy.

That we have such a rich repertoire of defenses against killers actually provides compelling evidence that murderers have been among us for a long enough time to have sculpted the human mind. Just as our prominent fears of snakes betray an evolutionary history in which snakes posed a hostile threat to survival, our well-honed defenses against murderers reveals an evolutionary history in which homicidal humans have threatened survival.

Because of the deterrents and the dangers involved with murder, most potential killers opt for alternative solutions in contending with a rival. One strategy is to form alliances with others in a group—a tribe, a social group, at the workplace—attempting to form a critical coalition to oust the rival. A second is to befriend the rival, currying his favor, making him part of your coalition. A third is to denigrate the rival to others in an attempt to lower his reputation in their eyes, weakening his position and making him more vulnerable to displacement. A fourth strategy is to lie like a snake in the grass, biding your time until a rival stumbles, and then making your move. And as you bide your time, a rare opportunity may arise. You may suddenly find all the stars aligning in a unique configuration. The costs of killing unexpectedly dwindle; the benefits abruptly loom large. Perhaps you happen upon your rival alone and unawares. Perhaps you can kill without being discovered. Perhaps you can actively arrange to create all of these conditions. You suddenly find yourself with the means, the motive, and the opportunity. And you seize the moment. Your psychological circuits for homicide become engaged.

Let's step away from our own species for a moment so we can be more objective, and examine our close primate cousins the chimpanzees. Chimps and humans diverged from common gorilla ancestors roughly seven million years ago. Nonetheless, humans and chimps share roughly 99 percent of their genes. This means that, of the three billion base pairs strung out on the strands of our DNA, as many as ninety-nine out of every hundred are exactly identical. The differences, of course, are as important as the similarities. Humans are bipedal and have evolved language, and women have relatively concealed ovulation. Chimps brachiate (travel from branch to branch through trees) and communicate without language, and the females have periodic estrus with bright red genital swellings visible from a hundred feet. Nonetheless, because they are our closest primate relatives, observing their behavior can sometimes shed light on our own.

Consider an observation by anthropologists who were following a chimpanzee troop around the jungles of Tanzania.[27] One sunny afternoon, eight chimpanzees, all males but one, roamed the border of their home range. Although they usually stayed within their home range, perhaps the chimps felt emboldened by the size of their group, protection afforded by numbers. Not far across the border, they detected a lone male. A chimp named Godi sat peacefully beneath a tree, eating ripe fruit in solitude. Godi, a member of the Kahama community, usually traveled with his group of six other males. This day he happened to be alone.

The second he saw the rival group, a jolt of adrenaline surged through his veins. He dropped his food, sprang to his feet, and bolted through the forest in the direction of his Kahama comrades. But the surprise ambush gave his attackers a timely advantage. His pursuers gave chase and surrounded him. In a flash, Godi was captured. Humphrey, one of the lead chimps, grabbed Godi's leg, yanked him to the ground, and pounced on top of him. Using his full weight of 110 pounds, Humphrey pinned him to the ground. Godi struggled, but was no match for Humphrey and his six male compatriots, each of whom carried the strength equivalent of four Olympic athletes at the peak of conditioning. With Godi rendered helpless on the ground, the others now launched an assault. In a frenzy of screaming, they bit, pounded, and jumped on their helpless victim.

After ten minutes that seemed like an eternity, the attackers finally stopped. They left behind a body battered and bleeding from dozens of wounds. Godi did not die immediately, but he was never seen alive again. The killer chimps had seized a rare opportunity, perhaps one that would not come along again for many months.

We often think of human warfare as formal battles between declared enemies, but in traditional foraging societies, killing more often takes the form of a raid not unlike that witnessed among the chimpanzees. Anthropologist Napoleon Chagnon, who spent years observing the lives of a group of native peoples in Venezuela called the Yanomamö, observed one such raid.

The night before the raid, a man named Kaobawa stirred the men into an emotional frenzy. He began to sing, "I am meat hungry! I am meat hungry!" Another man screamed, "I'm so fierce that when I shoot the enemy my arrow will strike with such force that blood will splash all over . . . his household."[28] At dawn the next morning, the women presented the raiders with a large cache of plantains as food for their raid. The men covered their faces and bodies in black paint for concealment. The mothers and sisters of the warriors offered parting advice, such as "Don't get yourself shot up."[29] The women then wept, fearful for the safety of their men. The trek to reach their enemies was long and took several days. At night, the raiding party built fires to keep warm, but on the last night, this luxury had to be eliminated for fear of alerting the enemy.

Back at the home camp, the women grew nervous. Unprotected women risk being kidnapped by neighboring tribes, and even allies cannot be trusted.

The raiding party broke into two groups, each consisting of six men. This grouping allowed them to retreat under protection: two men from each group would lie in wait to ambush potential pursuers. They struck. The attacking party managed to shoot one of their enemies with a poison-tipped arrow. The raiders then fled. One of the raiders was wounded as they escaped to their home camp, but he survived to go on a future raid. The foray had been a success. They killed one member of the enemy group and escaped with their lives, just like the chimps of Tanzania.

Killing, of course, is ordinarily not a first-line solution, even when your own life is on the line. When threatened by a weapon-bearing intruder who has broken into your home, you would be as likely to hide or flee as to go on the attack. The ancient phrase "fight or flight" captures two of the most important defenses available to us. The shields we've developed to stop killing have evolved alongside the mental mechanisms that provide the impulse to kill. Unfortunately, the process of coevolution, whereby new adaptations have developed to counter those defenses, has created a vicious cycle from which there is no escape. Even as we've developed defense mechanisms, we've also developed ever-more-effective means of killing.

Typically, coevolutionary arms races occur between two different species of which one is predator and the other prey, or between parasites and hosts. As predators pick off slower and less agile prey, the remaining prey and their descendants evolve to be faster and more skilled at evading capture. Then the prey's improved evasion abilities create greater selection pressure on the predators—the slow predators fail to eat and so die off, and the faster ones give birth to a higher percentage of speedy progeny. Each increment in the skills of one species leads to increments in the abilities of the other. The two species are locked in an endless escalating cycle from which neither can escape.

Coevolutionary arms races also occur within a single species, and this remarkable process has occurred in our species with the evolution of homicide strategies and murder-prevention defenses. As natural selection fashioned defenses against getting murdered by other humans, it simultaneously created more intricate killing strategies to evade these defenses. As potential victims evolved to detect homicidal intentions, potential killers evolved the ability to deceive and surprise victims, to disguise their homicidal designs. Our ancestors evolved to live in groups that afforded defense against marauding males. At the same time, they evolved recruitment tactics designed to increase the size of their killing coalitions.

One time-honored recruitment tactic for increasing coalitional size that we've read about in the news lately is to exploit men's desire for women. Mohamed Atta, one of the main architects of the 9/11 terrorist attacks, was unlucky in love. His recruiters instilled in him the belief that he would spend his afterlife surrounded by "women of Paradise" (from an assassins' manual found in Atta's luggage), "youths of never-ending bloom," and "companions with big beautiful eyes like pearls within their shells . . ." (from the Quran, about the rewards of becoming a martyr). The promise of prestige and the pledge of young women are powerful methods of coalitional recruitment. From the inner-city gangs of New York and Los Angeles to religious jihads, men are motivated to kill to gain these rewards. A relentless coevolutionary arms race in the human struggle for life, liberty, and the pursuit of progeny continues today.

Can this evolutionary-competition theory of murder really account for the motivations for murder in our present times? As I will reveal in the rest of the book, this theory does a remarkable job of accounting for the statistical patterns we find in who kills whom and for the multiple motives for murder. The more I analyzed the psychology of killing in cases of actual murder and in homicidal fantasies, the more striking was the realization that so many murders follow from the intense pressures of mating—a topic explored in the next chapter.

Three

THE DANGEROUS GAME
OF MATING

—◆—

"One sin, I know, another doth provoke; Murder's as near to lust as flame to smoke." —WILLIAM SHAKESPEARE, *Pericles*[1]

The Texas Cadet Murder. *In the fall of 1991, Diane Zamora and David Graham begin training to become cadets for the Civil Air Patrol, an auxiliary of the air force, in Tarrant County, Texas.*[2] *In August 1995, Diane and David started dating. The next month, they publicly proclaimed their true love. They announced to their families their intention to marry as soon as they both graduated from the military academy four years hence. They envisioned a ceremony embellished by the crossed swords of two flanks of cadets.*

A bump in their road of romance occurred on David Graham's return trip from a track meet held in Lubbock, Texas. He parked his car behind a public school and had backseat sex with Adrianne Jones, a track teammate. David could not shake his feelings of guilt over his betrayal. On December 1, he owned up to his infidelity, and Diane Zamora went ballistic. She screamed. She wept. And, finally, she insisted that he prove his love with an ultimate test of loyalty—by killing her sexual rival.

They planned the crime together, according to their original police confessions. Graham lured Jones into a late-night date. Unbeknownst to Adrianne, Diane Zamora was concealed in the car's hatchback. When they arrived at a remote lake road, Diane sprang into action, attempting to break Jones's neck. Adrianne Jones, however, proved more resilient than they had expected. In frustration, Zamora then grabbed a dumbbell and began to beat Jones repeatedly over the head. Somehow, Adrianne escaped and fled on foot. She was not fast enough for David Graham. He tracked her down and proceeded to shoot her dead. Zamora and Graham stripped off their bloody clothes and hid them miles from the crime scene.

A farmer discovered the body the next day, but Adrianne's murderers escaped detection for nine months. In August 1996, Zamora boasted to her new roommates about the depth of her love for Graham and his for her. They had proved their love, she gloated, by killing for each other. The roommates tipped off the police. Graham and Zamora were arrested. Although they initially confessed to the murder, they both later recanted. During separate trials, in which Graham and Zamora blamed each other, each was convicted of capital murder. They received life sentences.

How could two apparently normal young adults, with solid careers ahead of them, commit such a heinous crime, and in such a coldly calculating way? In his confession, David Graham himself expressed surprise at his actions: "We were both shaken and even surprised by the nature of our actions. Neither Diane nor myself were ever violent people."[3] He also expressed remorse: "I regret it now, for never did I imagine the heartache it would cause my school, my friends, Adrianne's family, or even my community. I guess I just shut it all out of my mind that instant when I convinced myself that Diane was even worth murder. After Diane gave me the ultimatum, I thought long and hard about how to carry out the crime. I was stupid, but I was in love."[4] Diane also confessed to the murder, but later recanted, placing all the blame on David. Despite her vows of lifelong love for David, Diane recently became engaged to another prison inmate. But it may be fifty-eight years before she'll be able to consummate her new marriage.

In the aftermath, many people expressed horror and outrage about their actions. One person said: "I think David and Diane deserve to live in misery for what they did to AJ. No one deserves to die like that and no one should even ask another to assist in something like that. I hope you both of you get beat up repeatedly in jail. Maybe, then you'll experience some real pain for once."[5] Not everyone agreed. Astonishingly, another person said: "I think that what Diane did was not wrong. She was hurt by the love of her life and she wanted to get the whore back. AJ deserved what she got. And I don't think that Diane deserves to be in jail. She did it for love. I think Diane should be freed."[6]

Our examination of the thousands of murder cases and murderous fantasies we pored over emphatically revealed just how central to so many murders is sexual rivalry. Consider these examples of fantasies that express such vehemence about sexual rivals.

CASE #14, *female, age 23. In a social setting she tried to dominate and manipulate the best available male companions within our group using nauseating tactics such as obviously fake laughter to enrapture a given male's attention, behaving like a whore, such as sitting on their laps, lifting her shirt to display her nipple piercing, what not. I think what was most irritating was the men—they liked it (assholes). . . . I fantasize about beating the shit out of her kung-fu style for an offense she commits which is obviously wrong to all present (this way the men agree with the reasoning of my brutal attack, which is delivered with such finesse as to gain their awe and arousal). . . . [What did you actually do?] Talked shit about her to my male companions. They agree with me, but they still enjoy her company. Men!*

CASE #124, *male, age 32.* [Who did you think about killing?] *A man who slept with my wife . . . He was her ex boyfriend. . . . My wife had talked about how much she used to care for her ex boyfriend and that she wanted to remain friends with him. They broke up because he went into drug re-hab. When he got out they remained friends but rarely saw each other. We became involved after this. About a year later is when she had sex with him. He came over to my apartment to visit with her and they had sex on my couch. Of course I was very angry and hurt and wanted to take my emotions out on him. Even if it meant beating him to death.* [What could have pushed you over the edge to actually kill him?] *Maybe if I had walked in on my wife and him having sex.*

CASE #P273, *male, age 24.* [Who did you think about killing?] *My ex-girlfriend's current boyfriend, who is 28 years old. He was fucking my girlfriend when I was still going out with her.* [How did you think about killing him?] *Choked him, pummeled his face till he became unconscious, and then kicked his head in.* [What prevented you from killing him?] *I didn't see him for a few months.* [What could have pushed you over the edge?] *If I had seen him, and if I was drunk and he had provoked me.*

CASE #P2366, *male, age 19.* [Who did you think about killing?] *Another guy. He slept with my girlfriend. I found out my girlfriend was sleeping with him when I saw his car in the driveway. I keyed the car and beat him up really bad, pummeling him with my fists until I was exhausted. I would have killed him if I had a bat or something. It would have been the wrong thing to do, but I was insanely enraged.* [How did you think about killing him?] *I thought about beating him repeatedly with a baseball bat.* [What prevented you from killing him?] *I did not have a bat.* [What could have pushed you over the edge?] *I was already there.*

The key to understanding why sexual rivalries lie behind so many murderous thoughts, and also so many actual murders, is that, in the evolutionary competition of life, the highest stakes involve whether or not we successfully find a mate—and not just any mate, but a reproductively valuable mate. So much about who commits murders and why they do relates to this central truth. As discussed in the last chapter, one of the most striking facts about murder is that so many more men commit murders than women: 87 percent of all murderers are men. We can consider that statistic and simply conclude that men are just a good deal more violent than women, but this doesn't explain why.

After all, the sentiments expressed by the women in the fantasies quoted above are every bit as aggressive as those expressed by the men. We could surmise that women are not generally as strong as men, and so over time violence wasn't a smart strategy for them, which might well explain some of the difference. If violence had been a more effective strategy for women, however, selection could easily have favored women who were larger and stronger, and there wouldn't be such a large difference in physical strength between men and women today. Then there is the fact that so many men kill other *men,* accounting for 65 percent of all murders. Deeper mental processes are at work, and those processes have to do with the specific challenges of the mating game.

THE HEATED COMPETITION OF SEXUAL SELECTION

Sexual rivalry pervades famous plot lines from Shakespeare to Nabokov. It saturates the love songs sung by Al Green and the rhymes rapped by Eminem. From the presumed gossip of our early ancestors around the campfire to that around the modern office printer, the dramas of sexual competition mesmerize us for a reason. In the high-stakes game of mating, we need to know the ins and outs of the rules of what Darwin called sexual selection, the process whereby men and women express preferences for certain potential mates over many others and simultaneously compete for the desirable mates.

Human attention, in principle, can be drawn to anything, even to the speed of grass growing. But it's not. Our minds evolved to be fascinated by social events of profound adaptive significance to our own lives. By paying such close attention to the fate of other people's romantic affairs, we learn invaluable lessons about which strategies work and which fail (though of course we aren't always able to deploy that knowledge successfully in our own romantic pursuits).

In any given social group, by keeping track of others' relationships we learn who is ascending the social hierarchy and who is slipping down the ranks. We learn which potential mates others are most attracted to, and we also hear about potential mates' flaws. By voyeuristically watching how others attract their mates, we learn what strategies we might use, and we also learn about tactics rivals might deploy to destroy our relationships.

The key to understanding why sexual rivalry has become such a fierce force in our lives, and why it underlies so many murders, is that in the mating game some people have great advantages over others. The playing field is not level, and not everyone is destined to find a lover, or to be able to keep a mate. According to the cold calculus of evolution, merely having children as a means for passing on our genes isn't sufficient in the long run. It's the progeny who inherit the best set of genes for meeting life's challenges who will have the best chances of themselves being able to pass their genes on. For this reason, deeply ingrained in our minds is the mandate not only to find a mate but to find the *right* mate, the best possible mate we can hook up with and hold on to. That has made all the difference.

Imagine how much simpler our lives would be—though also a good deal more boring—if we didn't have to compete to find lovers. Not all species reproduce sexually; many reproduce asexually. Just think about it. Members of asexual species do not have to search for a mate; they don't have to compete for that mate and go through the pain and anguish of being rebuffed; they don't have to engage in the intricate and often vexing dance of lovemaking in order to successfully have intercourse with that mate. Individuals in asexual species still face their challenges: they have to obtain the resources they need to live from their environment, fend off the predators that want them for dinner, and produce identical replicas of themselves. But they don't have to date.

The evolution of sexual reproduction, which made its first appearance on earth 1.2 billion years ago, radically complicated life, and introduced a great deal of strife into it. We tend to think of "survival of the fittest" competition in terms of the struggle against nature's threats and assume that some of us are better equipped to contend with those threats than others. Sexual reproduction added a whole new element of competition, that of members of the same sex vying to hook up with the most appealing potential mates. That intense competition opened the door for murder.

One of Darwin's most important discoveries concerned the central role in evolution of sexual selection, the process whereby some characteristics are favored—such as the classic case of the male peacock's elaborate tail—not because they provide a survival advantage to their bearers, but because the opposite sex prefers them. Those who possess the desired characteristics attain a mating advantage. Interestingly, the characteristics that are preferred do tend to have some sensible basis for being preferred, for they are generally indicators of a mate's likely reproductive fitness. In the long-term game of evolution, Darwin realized, the successful search for a mate required more than merely locating any random opposite-sex individual; individuals had to be selective, identifying a mate who was fertile rather than infertile, healthy rather than riddled with parasites. Over time, certain characteristics that were associated with health and fertility—in humans such things as a clear complexion, a strong physique, and proportionate breasts—were selected for, and mating competition centered on the quest to pair up with mates who displayed the most desirable characteristics.

Darwin emphasized the choosiness of females, because he noticed that the females of many species exercise a great deal of choice about whom they mate with. He even called this component of sexual selection female choice, but we now appreciate better that the choosiness goes both ways. Men are quite picky too.

Sexual selection opened up an entirely new arena of within-species conflict that never previously existed in the history of life on earth—intense rivalry with members of one's own sex for access to the most desirable members of the opposite sex.

Two stags locking horns in combat is the prototypical example of same-sex or intrasexual rivalry, and we've tended to think of males as being the ones more given to this kind of competition—which is true, but not exclusively so. The victor gains sexual access to the female, while the loser hobbles off wounded, with a broken antler, and psychologically defeated. But the most important consequence, in evolutionary-competition terms, is that those who are vanquished end up mateless. A male who is defeated in such a competition may well go on to find another mate, but his job has been made more difficult; in human life too, his status has been lowered, he can become "damaged goods."

Choosiness about mates has had a great deal of influence on how species have evolved. If females prefer males with brilliant feathers or elaborate nest-building skills or more expansive territories, those able to possess and display these qualities become lucky in love and their progeny develop even more brilliant feathers and elaborate nest-building skills. This is the theory about why male peacocks have such elaborate tails. Those lacking the desired qualities get ignored, shunned, and ultimately banished from breeding. Over time, species become more heavily populated by those who possess the more desirable qualities. Of course, as the qualities that lead to victory become more prevalent in a population, the competition becomes that much more fierce. The arms race escalates.

The pressures of sexual selection have introduced a great deal of tension in our lives, as we strive to make ourselves more appealing. If over the course of human evolution most women valued men who held territory, showed good hunting skills, or had the physical prowess to vanquish other men, men were forced by the desires of women to compete with one another on those terms. In more primitive cultures today, we still see that men will indeed stumble all over one another to demonstrate that they are superior on those terms. They will scramble for territory, spend days trying to take down a bear or a bison, and cultivate their combat skills.

In the developed countries, this competition is more likely to play out through men vying to elevate their status, acquire money, own impressive properties, and drive impressive cars. As for women, if men desire younger women who are healthy and physically attractive, then women will compete with one another to enhance the physical qualities men desire. Of course, women spend a great deal of time and money doing just that. Members of each sex, in essence, become willing victims to the whims and desires of the opposite sex. Those who don't compete often go to bed alone.

The most ruthless form of competition we face is the competition against one another to find and keep preferable mates, which is why this is such a preoccupation in our lives and in popular culture. The competition for mates plays itself out in two basic ways: we end up competing directly with our same-sex rivals—men against men, and women against women, often furiously—and we also end up spending a great deal of time trying to make ourselves appealing to the members of the opposite sex.

HOW MATING PREFERENCES RELATE TO MURDER

Much about sex differences in violence—and about when and why men commit murder, as well as when and why women do—can be explained by the differences in evolutionary pressures faced by men versus women based on differences in what men and women value in a mate.

Consider the issue of male violence. In the long human history of male competition against other males, dangerous strategies were often advantageous, even if they sometimes led to early death, as long as they conferred a mating advantage. Large-game hunting, for example, is a dangerous way to acquire food. In the process of trying to take down a bison, you may be injured or killed by the bison instead. But since women preferred men who brought home meat, men evolved hunting adaptations, even if some of them got injured or died in the process. Unfortunately, in mate competition men have had many incentives to be violent. Violence for men can be a means for vanquishing rivals, but also a desperate strategy for avoiding total matelessness. For one thing, women desire men who have the physical prowess to protect them, and men's displays of strength through violence have served as demonstrations of that prowess. By contrast, women did not have so strong an incentive toward violence against their female rivals. The qualities men have most desired in mates, such as beauty and fidelity, are not demonstrated through violence. And given the importance to women of caring for their children, violence proved more costly to women in the currency of reproductive success since they would risk injury or death that would damage their chances of seeing their children through to adulthood.

To understand how differences in evolutionary pressures for men versus women go such a long way to explaining the motives of so many murders, we have to look more deeply into the differences between what men and women look for in mates. Of course, both men and women favor a certain basic set of attributes, but beyond those, their preferences diverge greatly, and the ways in which they do so explain a great deal about the patterns we see in who murders whom and when.

WHAT MEN AND WOMEN WANT

The most massive cross-cultural study ever undertaken documented mating desires among 10,047 individuals in thirty-seven cultures, residing on six continents and five islands.[7] Many of the most desired characteristics in a romantic partner are valued by both men and women. Everyone expresses the strong desire for a mate who is kind, understanding, dependable, and intelligent. The adaptive value of these qualities is fairly transparent. Kindness signals a mate who will be a good and devoted mother or father, cooperative in spirit, and altruistic in nature. Dependability signals a spouse one can count on, who won't abandon or desert, and who will ensure that the children are fed well, socialized properly, and put to bed on time. Intelligence signals a collage of positive qualities, but skill at solving the daily adaptive problems each family faces is foremost among them. Both men and women want mates who will be good with children, cooperate with their kin, and able to get along with their friends. Both sexes are drawn to mates who are good at getting along and getting ahead, with a flare of personality and sense of humor to keep life interesting.

But there are three key qualities that men universally value more than women. They place a higher premium on good looks and on youth— meaning they prefer women who are young—and they place a great stress on sexual faithfulness in women. Women, on the other hand, express much stronger preferences for mates who possess financial viability, good job prospects, and social status. Men's desires for beauty, youth, and fidelity figure heavily in motives for murder. So do women's special desires for economic success and high status in men. If we look at these preferences in terms of the evolutionary-competition pressures faced by men versus women, we find that there are quite good reasons for what men and women want.

Though men's greater emphasis on physical beauty and youth in potential mates is often considered superficial, there are deeper reasons for their infatuations with these qualities. A common belief among social scientists over the past century is that standards of beauty are superficial, largely arbitrary, and highly variable from culture to culture. The past decade of research, however, turns this long-standing conventional wisdom on its head. Attractiveness turns out *not* to be merely skin-deep. The qualities men find attractive—clear, smooth, unblemished skin; lustrous hair; good muscle tone; symmetrical features; and a narrow waist and full hips that make a waist-to-hip ratio of .70—are clear markers of both health and youth, and hence of fertility.

These standards of female beauty are remarkably consistent across cultures, with a few notable exceptions, such as a preference for slimness or plumpness. Ancestral men who happened to desire fertile mates left more descendants. Over the course of evolution, men who mated with older, postmenopausal women sired no offspring. Those who mated with women who showed visible signs of bad health, such as open sores or lesions on the skin, left fewer descendants because their mates died earlier, didn't have as many children, or transmitted survival-impairing diseases to their children. Iterating this process over thousands of generations led to the evolution of finely honed male desires for women who display the critical signs of peak fertility. Beauty, in short, is in the adaptations of the beholder.[8]

The high value that men place on fidelity in their mates relates to another aspect of the special evolutionary pressures on men. Men who are cheated on can't know whether or not their children are really their own (or couldn't, that is, until very recently, with technologies such as paternity testing). The fact that human fertilization occurs internally, with an egg that is inside the woman's body, has meant that, whereas women have been 100 percent sure of their maternity—no woman has ever given birth and wondered whether the child was her own—men can't be so sure. A man who wasn't sure his mate was faithful to him risked diverting decades of his time, energy, effort, and resources to the children of a sexual rival.

Men who were indifferent to the sexual contact that their wives might have with other men ended up raising their rival's children more often than men who didn't tolerate their mates' indiscretions. So modern men have descended not from these indifferent men, but from men who strived, and succeeded more often than not, to maintain exclusive sexual control of their mates. As we will see, a great many of the murders of women by men are related to this desire to maintain sexual control. Quite a few of the murders committed by women against men are also due to the excesses of male "mate guarding," as we'll see in chapter 5.

Women are of course well aware, if perhaps more subconsciously than consciously, of these special preferences of men, and they work vigorously to satisfy men's desires. In general—for both men and women—there are two basic strategies you can follow when competing against the members of your own sex. You can either increase your own desirability by acquiring or displaying the qualities your potential mate seeks, or you can render your rivals less desirable. Women all around the world pursue both strategies. The seventy-billion-dollar makeup and cosmetic-surgery businesses are driven primarily, although not exclusively, by women's attempts to increase their allure. Women can also be quite determined in their methods of rendering their rivals less appealing.

Most commonly, women denigrate rivals verbally. Since men prize fidelity, women do battle with other women both to display signals of fidelity and to disparage their rivals by impugning their fidelity. In my studies of derogation of competitors, I found that women can get quite vicious about derogating other women on the sexual-fidelity dimension—calling their rivals whores, sluts, slags, tarts, and tramps.[9] Some women get quite creative, declaring a rival to be a mattress-back, fast-fanny, gift-box, spread-eagle, strumpet, chippie, hotpot, hussy, pox-box, or stump-thumper. Some are more subtle, implying that an adversary has entertained numerous past boyfriends, engages in frequent mate switching, or carries sexually transmitted diseases.

Because men so highly value beauty, many of the derogation tactics women use are focused on rivals' physical attributes. We discovered that women, far more than men, attempt to humiliate their sexual rivals by calling them fat, unattractive, and ugly. They might draw attention to particular physical features of a rival, such as sagging buttocks, a bulging waist, heavy thighs, or thick ankles. These tactics are often quite effective. Although one might expect men to evaluate women's appearance solely with their own eyes, uninfluenced by comments of others, research shows that social comments can indeed influence our perceptions of attractiveness.[10] Drawing attention to an imperfection amplifies its importance in a man's attentional field, and literally changes the way he perceives the woman's level of beauty. This women-versus-women rivalry can go well beyond verbal tactics.[11] In some cultures, such as in Kingston, Jamaica, women sometimes splash acid on the faces of their rivals, transforming beautiful women by scarring them hideously for life.[12] The following striking account from our study of homicidal fantasies reveals that women may also be driven to contemplate killing a rival in the fierceness of this competition.

> CASE #89, *female, age 19. I had known her for a couple of years and we were friends but the more I got to know her the more evil she seemed to be. She would get a kick out of _making fun of my body_ which I was really insecure about at the time. She did this almost daily until I just could not take it anymore. Also the examples I gave before played a part in my thoughts about killing her. . . . The way I wanted to kill her was to hit her in the head with a large object until she was dead.*

As we'll see in later chapters, although actually killing a rival woman is quite rare, the pressures women face because of the fierceness of mating competition do account for many of the circumstances in which women kill. So now let's turn to the issue of what women want in mates puts pressure on men in the mating market, and explains so much about why men murder.

HOW WOMEN'S PREFERENCES DRIVE MEN

How do women's preferences translate into the ways in which men compete, and why is killing actually a tactic of competition for men?

Though women also clearly value good looks in their mates, they express an even stronger preference for men who are successful and high-status. The reason women focus so much more on a man's success is not that women are superficial or greedy. Rather, women throughout human evolutionary history have confronted a radically different suite of adaptive problems from those men have had to solve. Key to the differences is the magnitude of investment: it's women who must carry a baby for nine months and it's women who give birth.

Because women invest so heavily to bring children into the world, they have a trump card that gives them enormous bargaining power in the game of mating. Someone who will carry your child inside her body for nine months, devote surplus calories to channel nourishment to the embryo through her placenta, and even leach calcium from her bones for the benefit of your baby—this someone offers you reproductively valuable resources indeed, and men are well aware of this. Those possessing such highly valuable resources do not give them away indiscriminately. So our ancestral mothers evolved to be extremely choosy and quite discerning in their choice of a mate.

Women's reproductive success has historically been limited not by the number of mates they can accumulate but, rather, by the genetic quality of a single mate, by his ability to accrue resources, and by his willingness to funnel those resources to her and her children. All modern women have inherited these mating desires from their successful maternal ancestors.

This fundamental difference in reproductive biology cascades throughout the entire mating system. For one thing, it accounts for why males throughout history have devoted far more energy to what evolutionary biologists call "mating effort," which includes chasing, attracting, and courting mates, as well as engaging other men in competition. Women rapidly reach diminishing returns, in the currency of reproductive fitness, from a fanatical expenditure of effort toward mating. Once a woman has found a man she's happy with, she wants to settle down more readily. This is because her fitness depends more on the quality of a single male and his investment in her children. For most women, adding additional sex partners does not increase, and may actually decrease, their reproductive success (although there are important exceptions, such as if her mate is infertile, if she's looking to leave the relationship, or if she can garner superior genes through an affair).[13]

A crucial point about women's preferences is that they judge men on the qualities known to correlate with *future* resource-acquisition capacities. Since status is linked with resources, men high in social status become imbued with a steamy aura of sexiness. Henry Kissinger captured this insight by noting, "Power is an aphrodisiac." He also noted, "Now when I bore people at parties, they think it's *their* fault." Although there are individual exceptions, this is why most women in every culture around the globe place a premium on a man's prestige.

A particularly stark example of the mating cachet of status comes from a study of the Siriono people of eastern Bolivia. One man, an unskilled hunter, had lost several wives to men who were better hunters. His status plummeted. But when the anthropologist A. R. Holmberg began hunting with this man, taught him how to kill with a shotgun, and gave him meat that he could claim as his own, the hunter's status rose dramatically. He began "enjoying the highest status, had acquired several new sex partners, and was insulting others instead of being insulted by them."[14]

One especially interesting finding is that, although men do not compete as strenuously as women to be physically attractive, men's attractiveness is far more influenced than is women's by the prestige of his clothing and other external accoutrements. When anthropologist John Marshall Townsend conducted a study in which the same men were dressed in Burger King outfits and caps or, alternatively, in designer shirts coupled with a Rolex watch, women judged the stylish men to be far more attractive. Women who looked at these photographs stated that they were unwilling to consider dating, having sexual relations with, or marrying the men in the low-status clothing.[15] Although this may seem intuitively obvious, analogous findings were not found for men viewing women clothed differently. Indeed, men seemed virtually impervious to clothing context, judging the same women to be nearly equally attractive regardless of the prestige of the clothes they wore.

As a consequence of this female preference, men devote more effort than do women toward the goal of getting ahead in the status hierarchy. They are more monomaniacal in singular devotion to work, favoring occupations that pay well despite being physically arduous and requiring fanatically long hours. Men more than women are likely to choose a job that pays well, even if it means living in a more polluted city with statistically elevated health risks.[16] As psychologist Jacqueline Eccles has shown through her research, men show a "single-minded devotion to one's occupational role" and an "excessive concern over one's work to the exclusion of other concerns."[17]

Our studies of the tactics men use to attract women also reveal that men tend to focus on displays of status and resources.[18] When men try to impress women, they are likely to boast about their accomplishments, talk about how important they are at work, flash money, drive expensive cars, exaggerate their prestige, and drop hints about their luminous career prospects. Men also derogate their rivals on precisely these dimensions. A man is more likely than a woman to scoff at a rival's achievements, indicate that his competitor lacks ambition and drive, point out how poor the rival's job prospects are, and denigrate the quality of a rival's car, house, stereo system, or TV size.

Among the many differences between sexual rivalry among men and that among women, there is one other hugely significant disparity. Men are far more likely to turn violent in the mating game. They are more likely to beat up a rival who "disses" them or humiliates them in public, resulting in a loss of status. Men lacking jobs are far more likely to murder than men whose careers are rocketing skyward. Men are far more likely than women to "go postal" when they lose their jobs, taking revenge by shooting a boss or rival co-workers who they blame for their demise. And men have had stronger incentives to make displays of violent force as a means of besting mating rivals. But the primary reason men are so much more given to violence, and specifically to the violence of murder, is that the stakes of the mating game are so much higher for men than for women, because there is much more *variability* among men than among women in reproductive success.

Despite the popularization in recent years of the stories of women desperately seeking elusive mates, studies show that most women in most generations across most cultures eventually find a mate and have children.[19] In contrast, more men in every generation are shut out of mating, because other men gain sexual access to multiple women, whether those women are mistresses or affair partners, short-term opportunistic sex partners, or even multiple wives in polygynous societies. For every man who monopolizes several women, there are other men forced to sleep by themselves. High reproductive variability dictates more intense and ferocious intrasexual competition—competition for which killing has entered men's arsenal of strategies.[20]

In fact, the greater variability in reproductive opportunity among men holds the key to an array of critical sex differences. It explains why men are larger and stronger than women, because they've competed more on the basis of physical prowess. It explains why men mature sexually two years later, on average, than women—to beef up for the intensity of intrasexual competition rather than enter the fray before they are ready. It explains why men expose themselves in larger numbers to dangerous recreational sports— to display their courage. It explains why men die seven years earlier on average than women, as a cumulative consequence of dangerous competitive activities originally engaged in to show off their physical prowess. And, most important, it explains why men have evolved adaptations to carry out extreme violence in specific circumstances involved with mating competition, including murder. Many, many murders can be explained by the evolved psychology of reproductive competition—an explanation more powerful than the others that have been offered to account for the high rates of male violence.

Extreme violence, attendant with blood, oozing wounds, bone fractures, spilled guts, and dead bodies, can be sickening to witness. My own experiences of poring over homicide case files for weeks on end, replete with color photographs of lifeless victims, nauseated me. Surely those who caused these bodies to be so disgustingly mutilated must be fundamentally deranged. Their brain circuits must be fundamentally corrupted, deformed by environmental trauma, distorted by the accumulation of toxic substances, or warped by some genetic defect. Killing must be a sickness, a dysfunction, or a pathology. Understanding murder would be easy if this were so.

Unfortunately, the pathology explanation simply won't work. Although a small percentage of wildly violent men do have organic defects, the majority do not.[21] Even for those cases judged to be legally insane, the presumed pathology does not belie the fact that sexual rivalry still resides at the heart of many murders. As Shakespeare noted in *Hamlet*, "Though this be madness, yet there is method in't."[22] Those with certain forms of pathology can indeed be less inhibited about venting their murderous rages, acting on psychological circuits that are already factory-installed. But their pathologies do not explain why humans have homicidal circuits to begin with.

Although there is little doubt that alcohol reduces inhibitions against aggression, more than two-thirds of all murders and other violent crimes are carried out stone cold sober.[23] And although it is true that in Western society we are all exposed to more images of men committing violence than of women, the media-exposure theory fails to explain why men in cultures entirely lacking in media exposure—the !Kung San of Botswana, the Yanomamö of Venezuela, the Ache of Paraguay, the Gebusi of West Africa, the Inuits of Alaska—show precisely the same sex differences in violence. The proposal that men are more violent than women because they are larger and stronger might partly explain why men can get away with violence toward women. But it fails to explain why the vast majority of extremely violent acts are perpetrated by men *against other men,* who are also large and physically formidable. Furthermore, invoking physical size as a cause fails to explain why men are larger and stronger to begin with—why evolution has fashioned male bodies to be so much more physically formidable than women's bodies.

Even more telling, these nonevolutionary explanations pale when we look at the broader spectrum of primate and mammalian species, where we find analogous sex differences in physical violence. When we witness two male hamadryas baboons going at it tooth and claw, two male elk crashing antlers, or two male sea lions attempting to gore each other to death, invoking "pathology" or "media exposure" or "parenting practices" obviously doesn't get to the core of the matter.

How do the pressures of mating competition that men face account better for the patterns of male violence? Consider the case of a man who holds few resources and little social status, so he is utterly unappealing to women. Because he lacks what women want, he's headed down the road to a reproductive dead end. He's got nothing, so he's got nothing to lose. Violence becomes an alluring means to improve his prospects.[24] In the lexicon of economists, he becomes highly risk-prone or risk-seeking. He may pull a gun and rob a store, or challenge another man to fight to increase his status and reputation. Violence gives him a chance to change paths. If over the course of evolutionary time resorting to violence afforded men a measure of resources or respect and assisted them in attracting mates, even if only temporarily, evolution would have favored adaptations to carry out violent strategies. This is one good explanation for why, throughout human history, warriors, adventurers, and explorers come disproportionately from the ranks of men who had few alternative strategies for acquiring the perquisites of status and resources.[25] And it explains why men occupying the bottom rungs of the reproductive ladder more often resort to violence.[26]

Risky strategies have historically also held out the prospect of dominant status for men. Consider this observation by the feared conqueror Genghis Khan (1167–1227), who deployed killing as a strategy to rise to the top. He explicitly relished the great sexual access he attained from the conquered tribes: *"The greatest pleasure is to vanquish your enemies, to chase them before you, to rob them of their wealth, to see their near and dear bathed in tears, to ride their horses and sleep on the white bellies of their wives and daughters."*[27]

Murder, of course, rarely gets a man to the top in modern Western civilization, given our tough criminal penalties and expertly trained police forces. Men did not evolve, however, in a modern environment with penal codes. Our psychology was forged in the furnace of an evolutionary environment in which aggression sometimes paid astonishingly well.

Killing to get to the top has been one effective strategy in the male competition of mating across cultures and over deep evolutionary time. Sexual benefits historically have flowed to victorious killers, as we can see throughout recorded history, from Biblical texts on. One example is this verse from the Old Testament: *"Now kill every male dependent, and kill every woman who has lain with a man, but spare for yourselves every woman among them who has not lain with a man."*[28]

One might think that killing would be a great turnoff to women, but apparently that's not the case. As Gore Vidal noted: "Women are always attracted to power. I do not think there ever could be a conqueror so bloody that most women would not willingly lie with him in the hope of bearing a son who would be every bit as ferocious as the father."[29]

Amazingly, even today convicted murderers remain highly appealing to some women. Scott Peterson, recently convicted of murdering his wife and unborn child, has been bombarded with hundreds of love letters and marriage proposals.[30] Serial killer Ted Bundy received thousands, and actually wedded one woman while in prison. Multiple murderer Charles Manson continues to attract women.

Killing to achieve status is not the only murderous strategy men have employed over time to try to get a leg up in the mating game. Murder is also one means of keeping a rival from winning away a mate, and a means of getting a rival out of the way. As we will see in later chapters, all of these motivations show up in the patterns of murder committed by men.

The great variability in mating success among men, recurring generation after generation over deep evolutionary time, selected for violent strategies both to avoid the bottom rung of matelessness and to reach the summit of mating success. The pressures are intense for both men and women, but men have the stronger incentives to engage in violence, and fewer evolved inhibitions against violence.

That the pressures of mating competition are such powerful motivators behind so many murders provides a compelling explanation for the patterns we've observed earlier in who kills whom and when. It explains why so many murders are of men killing men, why murder victims are often men in their peak reproductive years, and why so many murders are committed by men in these years; and it explains why so many murders are committed by people known to the victims. It also explains, ironically, why so many murders are committed for love, a topic we'll explore in the next chapter.

Four

WHEN LOVE KILLS

———

"If you're not going to live with me, you're not going to live at all."

—Phrase uttered by a male partner
of a woman shortly before he murdered her.[1]

O N THE EVENING OF July 24, 2002, in the thriving city of Houston, Texas, Clara Harris, age forty-four, got into her silver Mercedes-Benz sedan and killed her husband, David Harris, a forty-four-year-old orthodontist, in the parking lot of a hotel.[2] Using her car as her weapon, she ran into him once. Her anger still not placated, she circled the lot and ran over him again. Witnesses differ on precisely how many times she backed up and crushed her husband with the four-thousand-pound vehicle. One said five times, another four, and a third witness indicated only twice. Videotape from the hotel security cameras revealed that the correct number was three. And when she finally stopped, the Mercedes was parked on top of him. Some think that Clara Harris is evil and deserves to rot in jail for the remainder of her life. But some view the homicide as justifiable, or at least understandable.

David Harris had been having a torrid sexual affair with Gail Bridges, his former office co-worker. Clara Harris discovered the infidelity through Blue Moon Investigations, a private-detective agency she hired when she initially became suspicious. She confronted David. The morning of his death, David swore to Clara that he would end the affair. Later that night, Clara, along with her stepdaughter, Lindsey, began to search for David Harris. When they finally tracked him down at a hotel, according to Lindsey, "She said she could kill him and get away with it for what she's been through."

Indeed, Clara had gone to great efforts to win her husband back after she discovered his affair several weeks earlier. Clara was a former beauty queen, but after the affair was discovered, David and Clara sat down and he made point-by-point comparisons between Clara and his lover. David described his wife as overweight, his mistress as petite with "the perfect fit to sleep with, holding her all night."[3] David seemed obsessed with the ample size of his mistress's breasts, and described Gail as having a perfect body, although he conceded that Clara's hands, feet, and eyes were prettier. Clara vowed to make herself "real pretty so Dad would want her and not Gail," Lindsey said.

During the week before the murder, Clara Harris joined a fifteen-hundred-dollar-per-year fitness club, spent time at a tanning salon, and went daily to a hairdresser. She also consulted a plastic surgeon and agreed to pay a five-thousand-dollar deposit for liposuction and breast implants. By the day of the fatal murder, Clara had lost fifteen pounds, had her hair lightened, and begun wearing more sexually provocative clothing.

Clara's jealous rage may have intensified because her efforts had gone unrewarded. Or it may have been the fact that the hotel was precisely the one where Clara and David had been married a decade earlier, on Valentine's Day. When she saw her husband emerge from the hotel elevator hand in hand with his mistress, Clara Harris went ballistic. She screamed at her rival: "You . . . ! He's my husband!" She ripped the blouse off her rival's body and wrestled her to the ground. Although she clearly intended to do more damage, her husband pulled her off his mistress. According to one witness, he grabbed his wife's face and threw her back. Hotel clerks firmly escorted Clara out of the hotel. As she left the lobby, David shouted to her, "It's over! It's over! It's over!"

It was then that Clara Harris became strangely calm, according to her stepdaughter, Lindsey, who accompanied her out of the hotel. Clara silently stepped into her Mercedes. Her tears had stopped flowing. David Harris walked toward his Chevrolet Suburban in the parking lot, and everyone thought the conflict was over. Clara was cool and composed as she suddenly stomped on the accelerator and, with tires squealing, rammed her car into her husband. She then circled the parking lot and ran over her husband again. And then circled and ran over him yet again. Her stepdaughter tried to get out, but had to wait until Clara stopped the car. "You killed my dad," Lindsey said when the car finally stopped.

According to one witness, Clara got out of the car. With David Harris lying pinned under the front tire, she apologized and told him that she loved him. During the trial, Clara Harris maintained that she still loved her husband. In light of the circumstances, many in Texas do not judge Clara's horrific deed as evil. Some think David Harris got exactly what he deserved. The judge and jury did not agree. They sided with the prosecutor, who argued, "If the man is cheating on you, you do what every other woman in this country does—you take him to the cleaners. You don't get to kill him."[4] They sentenced her to twenty years in prison and fined her ten thousand dollars. On December 16, 2004, a Texas state appeals court upheld her conviction.

The jealous emotions that drove Clara Harris to attack her sexual rival in the hotel lobby are not unusual. Nor was her experience of murderous rage toward her husband upon the discovery of his betrayal. Nor even was the fact that the couple lived an upper-middle-class life, with a white brick house valued at more than six hundred thousand dollars that included a circular driveway and a swimming pool. Women of all classes react with jealous rage when they discover their husbands are cheating. But most women do not act on such homicidal passions. Far more men do—and in this chapter we will explore the reasons.

Murder mysteries and crime dramas on TV, not to mention the nightly news, have popularized the notion of a crime of passion—when a man or woman kills a romantic partner, or the "other lover," the man or woman with whom their partner is having an affair. The motives in these cases may seem obvious—jealousy, or vengeance, or the desire for retribution; the murder is payback for being jilted. Surely those emotions usually accompany these crimes, as the accounts by murderers who have committed them dramatically confirm. One man from our study of Michigan murderers who killed his girlfriend said: "I was deeply in love with her and she knew that. It infuriated me for her to be with another guy." Another man in our sample of murders erupted in a jealous rage when he and his wife were having sex one night and she asked him, "How does it feel to fuck me right after someone else has?" He put his hands around her throat and strangled her on the spot.

Yet, on deeper reflection, we have to ask ourselves why those passions would drive someone to kill the person who is the object of such intense affection. Why would someone want to see that person dead? Perhaps the explanation is simply that love has turned to hate, and yet, as many of the cases we studied revealed, the murderers are generally still in love with the people they kill. Consider this excerpt from the confession to the police of a thirty-one-year-old man after he stabbed his twenty-year-old wife to death. They had just been reunited after a six-month separation.

> Then she said that since she came back in April she had fucked this other man about ten times. I told her how can you talk about love and marriage and you been fucking this other man. I was really mad. I went to the kitchen and got the knife. I went back to our room and asked: Were you serious when you told me that? She said yes. We fought on the bed, I was stabbing her. Her grandfather came up and tried to take the knife out of my hand. I told him to go and call the cops for me. I don't know why I killed the woman, I loved her.[5]

As we studied the data regarding these murders of mates, and pored over the case studies of actual murders and the homicidal fantasies people recounted in which they conceived of killing the mates they loved, we discerned patterns that indicate the deeper psychological "logic" at work. One such striking pattern is a remarkable difference between the sexes. From the revelations of the previous chapters, we'd expect that more men kill the women they love than women kill the men they love, which is true. Not only that, but the percentage of the total murders of women that are committed by their lovers is staggeringly high.

In the United States between 1976 and 1984, 4,507 women were murdered annually on average.[6] The FBI statistics don't reveal the underlying motives, but detailed studies of particular regions reveal that the majority were killed by men who loved them deeply. One study of female murder victims during a five-year period in Dayton, Ohio, found proportions typical of such studies: 19 percent were murdered by their husbands, 8 percent by current boyfriends, 17 percent by estranged husbands, and 8 percent by prior sex partners. These total to an astonishing 52 percent of all the women murdered in Dayton during that time. In sharp contrast, in a typical year, only 3 percent of male murder victims die at the hands of a female lover.

In a massive study of homicides committed within the United States between 1976 and 1998, more than a third of the women were known to be killed by an intimate partner—surely an underestimate, given that in nearly a third of all cases the perpetrators were never found. In contrast, only 4 percent of the murdered American men in this study were killed by wives or lovers.[7] Similar statistics are pervasive worldwide, from the Australian Aborigines to murder among the Munda of India.[8]

In one of the most detailed studies conducted in the 1950s, criminologist Manfred Guttmacher published an analysis of thirty-one spousal homicides.[9] This study had the excellent feature of containing consecutive cases of intrafamily homicides in the city of Baltimore. Twenty-five of these cases were motivated by what Martin Daly and Margo Wilson call "male sexual proprietariness."[10] A majority of fourteen of these murders were triggered by the woman's outright abandonment of the husband for a new sexual partner. The remaining eleven murders were attributed to the woman's promiscuity (five cases), "pathological jealousy" on the part of the husband (four cases), suspicion of adultery (one case), and discovery of the wife in the act of carnal embrace with another man (one case).

When women kill their romantic partners, male sexual jealousy often plays a key role as well. Women frequently kill to defend themselves against men who are enraged by the woman's infidelity or defection. The following case illustrates this common theme.

> *. . . a man who had constantly harassed his ex-wife returned many times to the house to violently accost her months after the divorce. She eventually bought a gun to protect herself, keeping it in her bedroom. In an account verified by her adolescent children, the ex-husband came again to the house, was let in by one of the children, and chased his ex-wife to the bedroom, where she locked herself in. He broke down the door and moved toward her, even though she had the gun in her hand and warned him she would shoot. He continued to advance toward her. She shot once into the floor but that did not stop him, so she then shot and killed him. The woman was convicted of voluntary manslaughter and sentenced to 20 years in prison.[11]*

In another study of all wife killings, technically called uxoricides, occurring in a Canadian city over a twenty-two-year period, female-initiated separation from the romantic partner proved to be the critical motive in 63 percent of the cases.[12] In a study of wife killings in New South Wales, Australia, during the nineteenth century, almost half of the wives murdered were separated from their husbands when they were slain.[13] Another study, of twentieth-century wife killings in Australia, revealed that 45 percent of the 217 victims had dumped their husbands or were in the process of extricating themselves from the marriage when they were killed.[14]

Our own study of 429,729 homicides from the FBI database we obtained provides less detail about motive but powerful circumstantial evidence for precisely the same pattern.[15] From this large sample, 13,670 were cases in which a husband killed the woman to whom he was legally married. Of the cases that contained some information on the circumstances of the uxoricide, the most frequently cited condition was what the FBI codes as a "lovers' triangle." Although the crudeness of this category does not enable us to identify precisely what was going on in each case, the majority were due to either the woman's leaving her husband for another man, a sexual infidelity on the part of the woman, or both.

A study in North Carolina of 293 women killed by lovers or boyfriends between the years 1991 and 1993 revealed that 43 percent were killed after they left their mates, tried to leave their mates, or threatened to leave their mates.[16] A study conducted in Ontario, Canada, found that, of the 551 intimate-partner murders, 32 percent were killed in the context of estrangement or separation, with an additional 11 percent killed over suspected or discovered sexual infidelity.[17] These figures underestimate the true rates, given the absence of information about circumstance and motive in many police reports. Some experts believe the true percentage of women killed by a romantic partner lies between 50 and 70.[18] Based on the entire body of empirical research, it's clear that a wife's desertion is an even more powerful motive for getting killed than is her sexual infidelity. For some men, in the cruel currency of differential reproduction, the loss of a mate, especially to a sexual rival, is an adaptive problem for which murder is perceived as a sensible solution.

Cross-cultural evidence is scant, but several studies from Africa corroborate this motive. In a study of ninety-eight consecutive homicides among the Basoga, a tribe residing in Uganda, forty-two cases involved men killing women. In nearly all the cases, the victim was a wife or former wife. In thirty-two of these cases, the police ascribed a motive to the killer—a third because of adultery, a third because of wife abandonment or sexual refusal, and a third because of a variety of other causes such as arguments.[19] In a study in the Belgian Congo, male sexual jealousy was the cause invoked by investigators in fifty-nine out of 275 convicted killers. Of these fifty-nine, sixteen men killed wives who were unfaithful, thirteen killed wives who had divorced or threatened to divorce, and three killed the new mates of their ex-wives.

My evolutionary theory of murder can explain why the killing of a lover is so common. We tend to think about why we love someone in quite particular terms, focusing on their specific attributes, or how complementary their attributes are to ours. We love them because they are who they are, because we like their sense of humor, even temper, dazzling personality, and physical appeal. The alchemical process by which any two individuals fall in love remains a mystery even after years and years of expert study. But the study of love in the field of evolutionary psychology has produced some robust results that reveal general underlying motives and patterns behind why we fall in love and with whom. These findings have quite a bit to say about why love sometimes turns deadly. One of the profound, if somewhat disturbing, findings of evolutionary psychology about love is how much it is governed by the mandates of sexual selection.

THE EVOLUTION OF LOVE

Contrary to common myths disseminated in the social sciences in the twentieth century, love was not invented by Western European poets a few centuries ago. Evidence points to the opposite conclusion—love is a cross-cultural universal, and probably has been since the emergence of long-term pair bonds back in the history of human evolution. From the Zulus in South Africa to the Inuits in Alaska, people report experiencing the obsessions of mind and passions of emotion that those in the Western world link with love.

In a survey of 168 diverse cultures, anthropologist William Jankowiak found strong evidence for the presence of romantic love in nearly 90 percent.[20] For the remaining 10 percent, the anthropological evidence was too sketchy for definitive conclusions. As one !Kung woman from Botswana expressed it, "When two people are first together, their hearts are on fire and their passion is very great. After a while . . . they continue to love each other, but in a different way—warm and dependable."[21]

Not only is romantic love a human universal, but, despite the impression given by the proliferation of dating services, dating-advice books, and dating TV shows, we're quite good at finding people to fall in love with—though actually hooking up with them and staying hooked up with them are surely more problematic. Sociologist Sue Sprecher and her colleagues interviewed 1,667 women and men in Russia, Japan, and the United States. They found that 61 percent of the Russian men and 73 percent of the Russian women reported being currently in love. Comparable figures for the Japanese were 41 percent of the men and 63 percent of the women; among Americans, 53 percent of the men and 63 percent of the women.[22]

Love is such a wonderful thing. It's a powerful drug. But it's also a heartbreaking thing. And when it goes wrong, it can become a scorching, devastating nightmare. It may seem odd to ask why we have this emotion. But if you think about it, love is rife with turmoil and often inflicts such heavy costs in our lives. It's a good question to ask why, over the course of our evolution, such intense love has been an advantage. If love is a universal human emotion, why did evolution install it in the human brain? The answer to that question will bring us to the underlying motives that lead lovers to kill their soul mates.

One of the major developments along the way in our evolution from our early primate ancestors was that the timing of a woman's ovulation became hidden. This proved a strong motivator for long-term coupling, as opposed to the short-term mating that almost certainly characterized our prehuman ancestors, and currently characterizes so much of the animal kingdom (with notable exceptions, such as lovebirds and other avian species). If you can't tell when a woman is ovulating, then another system will have to develop to instigate mating. Although there might be subtle physical changes in women—a slight glowing of the skin, or an almost imperceptible increase in her sexual desire—there is no evidence that men can easily discern when women ovulate. This contributed to our ancestors' having more continuous sex throughout the female ovulation cycle than is found in most of the animal world.

This development must have been a key to the evolution of long-term pair bonding, but also to the heavy investment of both men and women in their offspring. Among most mammals and primate species, the fathers do little or nothing to feed, raise, or nurture their offspring. At some point in human evolution, however, men began to make substantial contributions to raising their children. The meat obtained from the hunts went to provision children. Men's long-term devotion of time, resources, and protection to their own children came at the express *cost* of not seeking a proliferation of mates to impregnate. Given fixed time and energy budgets, most devoted fathers don't have the psychological resources to chase additional women. Men are acutely aware of the tensions of these trade-offs—in the terms of evolutionary biologists, parental effort comes at the expense of mating effort.

We must take a step back to realize how extraordinary these changes are—and also to appreciate the costs involved, in evolutionary terms, of long-term committed mating and the devoted raising of progeny. Some women began allocating their entire reproductive careers to a single man, rather than to whoever happened to be the reigning alpha male when they were ovulating. Men began to guard their partners, fending off rival males who might be tempted to lure away the men's mates. Surplus resources that in many species go to the female as an inducement for an immediate copulation now were channeled to the wife and children. Indeed, this gave men extra incentive to acquire surplus resources, especially in the form of hunted meat, containing valuable amino acids and rich protein.

The evolution of long-term mating required a set of psychological circuits designed to ensure a reproductive payoff to allocating all of one's resources to a single partner. Elementary economics tells us that those who hold valuable resources do not give them away indiscriminately. Evolution ruthlessly discriminated against those who squandered reproductively valuable resources in long-term mateships that produced no genetically related offspring. People required some means for determining that one particular mate, above all other potential mates, would be there through thick and thin, through sickness and health. They required, in short, a solution to the problem of commitment—to ensuring that a woman would remain faithful and a man would continue to devote his best resources to a woman's kids.

Love is the tie that binds us to that commitment. My own empirical studies on the close link between love and commitment converged precisely with a theory proposed by evolutionary economist Robert Frank. He also contends that the emotion we call love is the evolved solution to the problem of commitment.[23] If a partner chooses you for purely rational reasons, he or she might leave you for the same rational reasons: finding someone slightly more desirable on all of the "rational" criteria. If your partner is blinded by an uncontrollable love, however, a love for only you and no other, then commitment should be strong even when you are sick rather than healthy, when you are poorer rather than richer. It's the emotion that signals to your mate that you are willing to commit emotional, economic, and genetic resources over the long haul.

The experience of love also provides a pleasing psychological rush when we solve the problem of commitment successfully. It's a brain opium that tells us the challenges of the mating game have been met with triumph.[24] People in love literally experience a flood of dopamine, adrenaline, and serotonin—brain chemicals that simultaneously produce euphoria, psychological intoxication, and ideational obsession. These psychological rewards keep us performing activities—having sex, investing in romance, giving to children—that lead to successful reproduction.

Unfortunately, that's not the happy end to the story of the evolution of love. Evolution is utterly indifferent to the reprehensibility of the tactics it favors. It ruthlessly favors whatever strategies work in the retention of reproductively valuable resources, even if that means inflicting costs on others by those strategies. And when it comes to mating, evolution has equipped us not with a single strategy but, rather, with a menu of strategies. Even as it has provided the motivations and mechanisms for falling into committed love, it has also given us strong incentives to cheat, and to fall out of love. There are snakes in the garden, troubles in emotional paradise.

As we are all too aware, once the desire for love exists, it can be exploited and manipulated ruthlessly by both sexes. Men deceive women as to the depth of their loving feelings, for example, just to gain short-term sexual access.[25] As Ovid noted hundreds of years ago, "Love is . . . a sexual behavior sport in which duplicity is used in order that a man might win his way into a woman's heart and subsequently into her boudoir." Women, in turn, have coevolved defenses against being sexually exploited. They imposed a longer courtship process before consenting to sex, attempted to detect deception, and became better able to decode nonverbal signals. And women sometimes deceive too. A woman may let a man believe that she remains in love with him, for example, while taking his resources but secretly planning her exit strategy. The coevolutionary arms race between deception and the detection of that deception continues with no end in sight.

Another problem is that what comes up often comes down. People fall out of love as crashingly as they fall in love. We can't predict with certainty who will fall out of love, but recent studies provide some critical clues. Just as the fulfillment of desire looms large when one is falling in love, violations of desire portend conflict and dissolution. A man who was chosen in part for his potential wealth and ambitious goals may get dumped when he loses his job. A woman chosen in part for her youth and beauty may lose out when a younger model beckons the woman's partner. An initially considerate partner may turn cruel. And a couple's infertility after repeated episodes of sex may prompt either to seek a more fruitful union elsewhere.[26]

The most crushing blow to long-term love comes from the harshness of the mating market. A mated couple initially equal on overall desirability may experience a widening gap over time. Consider an entry-level professional couple. If the woman's career skyrockets and the man gets fired, it puts a strain on both, because their market values now differ. When actress Meg Ryan's career surpassed that of her husband, Dennis Quaid, she had an affair with rising star Russell Crowe. Sudden increases in status open up new mating opportunities. A "9" who was previously out of reach now becomes accessible. We may admire a woman who stands by her loser husband. But few of those who did are our ancestors. Modern humans descended from those who traded up when the increment was sufficient to outweigh the manifold costs people experience as a consequence of breaking up.[27]

WHY WOMEN HAVE AFFAIRS

One mid-night Sukhu Munda heard three persons calling his wife from outside for illicit relations. Sukhu tried to stop her but she insisted on going. Thereupon Sukhu assaulted her with a Dawli (a sharp cutting weapon) and she succumbed to her injuries. Sukhu was acquitted by the court on the ground of being insane.[28]

Why would a woman, after going through the exhausting process of selecting and attracting a mate, securing his long-term love, and making vows of commitment, suddenly decide to risk it all for a fleeting moment of sexual pleasure—a transient delight that can put her life in peril? This question has baffled scientists for decades, but we now have the fundamental outlines of the answer. Mating, like murder, has multiple motives.

The first motive is an unconscious attraction to men who possess good genes. To understand this requires penetrating the reproductive logic of the mating market. The average woman is able to attract a far more desirable mate for a short-term sexual encounter than for long-term love, because highly desirable men are willing to consent to sex with a woman of lower mate value as long as the liaison does not come burdened with entangling commitments. A man who is a "9" on the mating market is often willing to have sex with a woman who is a "7." Successful athletes, such as the basketball star Kobe Bryant, and successful movie stars, such as Jude Law or George Clooney, suffer no lack of willing women. That's fine and good for the successful man, in the currency of reproductive fitness, because he's able to secure sexual access to a fertile woman at little cost. But the woman's husband, based on the law of assortative mating, is typically on roughly the same level as she—he's a "7" as well. Her infidelity with a more desirable man gives her husband a motive for murder.

By mating briefly with a more desirable man than her husband, the woman increases her odds of acquiring a critical resource that is relatively deficient in her husband—superior genes that can be transmitted to her children. Better genes come in several flavors. One is genes for good health. Many indicators of good health are obvious and observable, such as clear skin, lack of open pustules, sores, and lesions, quality of hair, and firmness of gait. My colleagues have discovered a more subtle marker: symmetry. Humans are bilaterally symmetrical. If you draw a line from the middle of your forehead straight down your body, the two halves are roughly mirror images of each other. But not exact mirror images. Injuries, parasites, malnutrition, and other environmental insults while growing up can cause one side to look different from the other. Some individuals are more genetically susceptible to these environmental insults. Others are more resistant to them, or manage to avoid them altogether. Those who are resistant have better genes for health, or, in the lexicon of biologists, are more "developmentally stable," than those whose developing bodies are easily perturbed.

Evolutionary psychologist Steve Gangestad and evolutionary biologist Randy Thornhill have been pioneers in exploring the potentially profound consequences of symmetry for human mating.[29] They used calipers to measure the precise length and width of different body parts on each side of participants, from index fingers to earlobe length. They obtained a difference score for each part, signifying the degree to which the body part was asymmetrical. By summing the difference scores, Gangestad and Thornhill obtained an overall index of individual differences in asymmetry. Among American cultural icons, Lyle Lovett would lie on one end of this dimension, Brad Pitt on the other.

With this health indicator securely measured, they then explored the links between symmetry and mating. In a study of 203 heterosexual couples, they found that women mated with men measured as asymmetrical were more likely to have affairs than women mated to symmetrical men. Women who have affairs choose affair partners who are more symmetrical than their regular partners. Indeed, symmetrical men report that they engage in substantially more mate poaching than asymmetrical men, suggesting that many of the sex partners of symmetrical men are women already in committed relationships.

A study I conducted with my colleague Heidi Greiling found that women's mate preferences shift dramatically when they are considering a long-term committed partner versus a short-term affair partner.[30] We found circumstantial evidence that women go for "sexy son" genes for short-term flings. In contrast to the qualities they desire in a regular mate, women are especially attracted to love buddies who are sexy, highly desirable to the opposite sex, physically attractive, and good-looking. The benefit, in the currency of reproductive success, is not that such women have more offspring. Rather, they increase their odds of producing "sexy sons." These are males who are highly attractive to women in the next generation. So women, at least historically, increased their reproductive success through an increased number of grandchildren obtained by the sexual successes of their sexy sons.

Studies of sexual variations across women's ovulation cycles found even more startling support for the "good genes" motivation for women's affairs.[31] When ovulating and therefore capable of conception, women in committed romantic relationships report flirting more with other men, feeling more sexual desire for other men, and experiencing more sexual fantasies about men other than their regular partners. These effects, however, occur only if the woman is mated to a relatively asymmetrical partner. Even more shocking, women having affairs appear to time sex with their affair partners to coincide with the time they are ovulating, acting on their lust for other men, whereas they time sex with their regular partners to coincide with when they least fertile! Women are obviously not thinking, "Now that I'm ovulating, I had better go out and secure good genes." Rather, modern women have evolved desires for other men that lead them to have affairs when they are maximally fertile, and these desires historically had the effect of creating children who carried the genes of the affair partner rather than the humble, committed, regular mate who had the misfortune to be born with a lower complement of good genes.

If good genes provide one explanation for why women have affairs, there are at least three other powerful motives—access to resources, mate insurance, and trading up. The explanation for resource attainment is straightforward. Although a few dinners might not provide much of an incentive in the modern environment, food shortages over deep time produced evolutionary bottlenecks. Those who managed to gain access to scarce food made it through these bottlenecks; those who didn't left no descendants. This may explain why our studies show that women place a premium on men who show extravagant displays of resources primarily in short-term mating contexts.[32]

In the modern world, many people take out car and house insurance to guard against the unfortunate event of an accident or a fire. In the ancestral world, people sought an equivalent with their long-term mates. In mating, having a backup mate, one who could step into the void, would have been a tremendous advantage. Backup mates should possess special qualities. They should indicate their availability and attraction to the woman. They should be able and willing to provide resources. They should be powerful enough to protect her from sexual aggression from other men. Our studies found that women prized precisely these qualities in an affair partner—

those who were protective, showed athletic prowess, displayed strength and muscularity, and were physically fit.[33] We also discovered that one function of flirting is to cultivate backup mates. Furthermore, one reason women cultivate opposite-sex friends is to fill a potential void if a mating vacancy opens up in their lives.[34]

Last, but not least, a fourth function of women's affairs is to trade up to a better mate. There are several circumstances in which mate switching would be advantageous. First, if a woman's regular partner plummeted in desirability, became a slacker, failed to bring home resources, started abusing her, or began an affair of his own that siphoned off resources, his value to her would dip relative to that of an alternative mate. Second, if her own level of desirability increased, perhaps because of an ascent in status or a new blossoming of beauty, she would then be able to attract a man of incrementally better mate value. Third, if a new mate became available who had not previously been present, thanks to migration or perhaps the loss of his own mate, she might benefit by trading up. Finally, if she shed her own encumbrances, as might happen with the death of her child, she might become suddenly more attractive to men who were previously beyond her reach. All these changes might create the ability and willingness to trade up in the mating market.

In sum, a bounty of benefits flow to women who have affairs. They can secure superior genes for their children. They can gain access to additional resources. They can cultivate a backup replacement mate, a form of mate insurance should something go awry in their primary relationships. And they can use the affair to leverage themselves into a better mateship, trading up to a partner of higher quality. But as we explore below, it's dangerous to create a liaison with another man.

Men also have affairs as a strategy for trading up, and in some respects, it's easier for them to do so. Since resources and status are so critical to what women want, men who experience a rise in status or a windfall in resources become suddenly attractive to women who were previously out of reach. But for many men, cheating is simply an evolved strategy whose function originated in producing more numerous children by gaining sexual access to multiple women. Men, of course, do not think to themselves, "I'll have a fling in order to increase my reproductive success." Rather, they simply find other women attractive, and if given the opportunity and the risks are low, they often go for it. As comedian Chris Rock noted, "A man is only as faithful as his options." Studies that compare men's and women's motives for affairs invariably find that "sex," pure and simple, is a more dominant motive for men. It doesn't necessarily mean they don't love their wives.

THE DANGERS OF A BROKEN HEART

Falling out of love has many dark sides. "Love's pleasure lasts but a moment; love's sorrow lasts all through life," wrote the French fabulist Celestine. The crash is psychologically traumatic for both sexes, and is all too often physically dangerous for women. Hearts broken from love lost rate among the most stressful life events a person can experience, exceeded in psychological pain only by horrific events such as the death of a child. Men who get rejected by the women with whom they are in love often abuse them emotionally, and sometimes physically. Some men stalk their exes with repeated phone calls, unexpected visits, and threats of violence. Victims of stalking experience psychological terror, disruption of work, and interference with new relationships. In our recent studies, as I'll describe in detail later in this chapter, we found that an alarming number of men who are unceremoniously dumped begin to have homicidal fantasies, and too many proceed to act on those fantasies.

The following case, from a systematic compilation of all homicides that occurred within one year in the city of Houston, Texas, is chilling:

Case No. 191 begins as a domestic quarrel. A 37-year-old White woman and her 42-year-old husband were drinking and quarreling. The woman first ran next door to her sister's apartment but only found her 11-year-old nephew awake. She left her sister's house to seek assistance from a neighbor. Her husband intercepted her as she crossed their driveway, a further argument ensued, and the woman shouted for help as she walked away from her husband. The neighbors found the woman lying bleeding on the sidewalk and called an ambulance. The husband told police that the whole thing started because his wife did not love him anymore. . . . [This] led him to pull out a pocketknife and stab his wife in the chest.[35]

But the pain that jilted men feel does not adequately explain why they kill the women who have cheated on or left them. The killing of a mate poses a serious puzzle. How could this bizarre form of behavior possibly have evolved? After all, killing a mate destroys a key reproductive resource. Evolution by selection should favor preserving, not destroying, vital reproductive resources. Mate killing seems outrageously counter to self-interested reproductive survival.

To solve this puzzle, we must remember that evolution operates by differential reproduction, and in certain circumstances, selection can favor strong motivations for killing an unfaithful mate. Let's explore this logic in more detail. First, in most cases, killing a mate who has been unfaithful *would* have been detrimental to the killer. An unfaithful woman might still be a valuable reproductive resource to her husband. If she *continues* to be his sexual resource, then killing her would be damaging his own fitness, an instance of futile, vengeful spite. As Margo Wilson and Martin Daly correctly observe, "Murdered women are costly to replace."[36] If the woman has borne him children, then killing her hurts his children's chances to survive and thrive, dramatically. Finally, by killing her, the cuckolded man risks retribution. The woman's brother or father might be motivated to exact vengeance. For all these reasons, killing a mate is usually a remarkably ineffective solution to the problem of cuckoldry.

But sometimes the elements in the cost-benefit equation become rearranged. In certain circumstances, the benefits of killing can statistically outweigh the costs. To understand how this is so, we must explore why a woman's infidelity is so damaging to men.

THE COSTS OF CUCKOLDRY

A man's loss of a woman's love carries with it the loss of the largest reproductive bounty he has ever had. If he has been genetically cuckolded and is
unaware of this, he risks investing years or decades of his time and resources
in a rival's children, a double-barreled disaster from the perspective of his
reproductive fitness. The risk of genetic cuckoldry is not merely hypothetical. Estimates from modern populations based on blood and DNA-
fingerprinting studies conducted over the past thirty years estimate the rates
to be between 9 and 13 percent.[37] This means that roughly one in ten people
was sired by a man who was not his mother's regular partner at the time.

Historically, mistaken paternity would have inflicted staggering costs on
a man. First, all of the effort a man devoted to selecting, courting, and
attracting a woman would go down the fitness drain. Second, all of his
effort to guard and maintain the relationship—from vigilance to violence—
would now be lost. The resources he provided to his partner and her children become wasted when she becomes a reproductive vehicle for his rival.
Third, the cuckolded man suffers opportunity costs—lost mating opportunities with other women that are irretrievable. By investing in his unfaithful
wife, he forgoes the chance to mate with other women, either for brief sexual liaisons or for more committed romantic involvements.

The costs of genetic cuckoldry run even deeper. Not only does the victim risk channeling his parental efforts to a rival's children, but all of his
partner's parental efforts, which would have benefited his children, now
benefit his rival's children. If the cuckolded man already has biological children, or will have them, then the new child, the product of the infidelity,
becomes a half-sibling rather than a full sibling of these children. This creates genetic conflicts of interest, so that this own children will suffer. Half-
siblings have less genetic stake in each other's welfare.

The costs of cuckoldry do not end there. The esteem in which the man is
held by others, the reputation that is so critical to the social animal we call

humans, can suffer enormous damage. Consider the reaction in Greek culture to cuckoldry:

> The wife's infidelity . . . brings disgrace to the husband who is then a
> Keratas—the worst insult for a Greek man—a shameful epithet with
> connotations of weakness and inadequacy. . . . While for the wife it
> is socially acceptable to tolerate her unfaithful husband, it is not
> socially acceptable for a man to tolerate his unfaithful wife and if he
> does so, he is ridiculed as behaving in an unmanly manner.[38]

Ridicule of cuckolds is not limited to the Greeks. The following murder occurred in France, one of the cultures that is most tolerant of sexual infidelity.

> The murder took place in the city of Orléans, located on the Loire
> River. Yvonne Chevallier was having trouble with her husband, Dr.
> Pierre Chevallier, a politician and former war hero. Dr. Chevallier
> was going places, rocketing to the top of the political hierarchy, mov-
> ing in elite circles, enjoying a social success he had never known.
> Yvonne remained at home alone much of the time. Meanwhile, Dr.
> Chevallier began an affair with a married woman, Jeannette Perreau,
> wife of Roger Perreau.
>   Yvonne Chevallier discovered the infidelity via a note she found
> in her husband's coat pocket, which read, "Dear Pierre, Without
> you, life would have no beauty or meaning for me, . . . Jeannette."
> Yvonne got a gun, a huge 7.65mm automatic with the power to stop
> an elephant. When applying for the gun permit, she explained that
> her husband's prominence in politics made precautions necessary.
> Yvonne Chevallier then confronted her husband with her suspicions
> of his infidelity. Seizing the opportunity, he announced his intention
> to divorce her. She shot him four times, after which she took her son,
> who had witnessed the shooting, downstairs to be tended by a ser-
> vant. She then went back up and fired a fifth shot into her husband.

With two shots to the head and three to the body, he did not stand a chance.

The reaction of the public to the testimony of Roger Perreau, beleaguered husband of Jeannette, proved fascinating. People who filled the court laughed at him openly, making the cuckold sign of horns behind the head as he walked by. The ridicule reached a crescendo when he told the court that he knew his wife had been having an affair and had made the decision to tolerate it. He confessed that his wife had had previous affairs, and that each one he had managed to "chase away." After all, his wife was widely viewed as a stunning beauty, with "long red hair under a jaunty beret, wide-set eyes and sensuous lips."[39] But her affair with Dr. Chevallier, for some reason, he did not find objectionable. He drew more derision from the crowd. And when he said, "No . . . it may seem strange, but I found him likeable. I got on with him very well," the courtroom erupted with mockery.[40] In an ironic twist to this story, Yvonne Chevallier was judged not guilty on all counts of the murder. France has a separate category of murder, the crime passionel, *for which killers get a special discount and sometimes, as in this case, outright exoneration.*

Indeed, cuckolded men are *universal* objects of disrespect and derision. Their reputations often suffer catastrophic damage. A person's reputation is not a mere social nicety. It's something extraordinarily valuable. Reputations lost can sometimes never be repaired. Protecting a reputation is something that some people consider worth killing for.

A damaged reputation endangers a man's current social position. It hinders his future ascension in the social hierarchy. It impairs his ability to attract future mates. Women smirk. Men scoff. The cuckold acquires a reputation as easily exploitable once it becomes known that he has been exploited. Women assume that he lacks the ability to prevent other men from encroaching. Perceptions of his desirability on the mating market plummet. All these factors add up to formidable fitness costs of being cuckolded.

Unfortunately, a man who murders a mate who has cuckolded or deserted him sometimes salvages his status and reputation, or at least would have in the small-group living conditions in which humans evolved. Killing her sends a signal to everyone in the group that he's not a man whose interests can be infringed upon without retribution. It eliminates the physical reminder that he's a cuckold who can't hold on to his partner, warning other wives (if he's polygynous) or future mates that they will pay heavy costs for cheating or deserting. His violence sends a threat to other men to back off, deterring future attempts they may make to poach on his mates. By curtailing his slide in status, he can recover a measure of reputation that might otherwise be irretrievably lost. Simultaneously, the murder deprives his closest rivals of access to a reproductively valuable resource that he no longer possesses anyway, giving the murderer a leg up in the ruthless game of reproductive competition. As disturbing as the idea is, mate killing under certain conditions would have been reproductively advantageous, leading to the evolution of psychological circuits for mate murder.

The conditions, of course, would have to be highly specific. First, if she lacked a father or brother in the vicinity, the killer would be less likely to suffer violent retribution from her kin. This would have been quite common in traditional tribal societies where marriage is exogamous—where women migrate away from their own kin group and move in with their husband's kin group when they marry. Second, if he had not reproduced with her, killing her would not jeopardize the survival of his children. Consequently, I predict that mate killing will occur more often when the couple does not have existing children. Third, if his social reputation became so severely damaged by his wife's infidelity or desertion that his status would fall irretrievably, undermining his ability to attract another mate, killing her might be beneficial in stopping the slide. Fortunately, it's usually too costly to kill an unfaithful or deserting mate, and most men don't. But men's homicidal circuits are attuned to those rare circumstances in which the benefits outweigh the costs, triggering predictable forms of mate murder.

Consider for a moment the logic of the argument outside the context of mating. If you have just killed a game animal to feed yourself and your hungry family, and a scavenging animal comes along and steals it before you can eat it, you suffer a loss. But if your rival steals the meat, the loss becomes compounded in the currency of evolutionary fitness, since selection operates on the principle of *relative* reproductive success. Your loss becomes a gain for your immediate rival, whose children survive and thrive while yours go hungry or perish.

The same logic applies to mating. If your mating loss bestows a sexual gain on your immediate rival, then the fitness costs of being cuckolded become compounded. This theory leads to a counterintuitive prediction: the younger, healthier, and more attractive the woman, the greater the loss to the cuckolded man and the greater the gain for the rival who now sleeps in her bed. This leads to a disturbing prediction of the theory—the more good-looking, healthy, and fertile the woman, the more motivated the man will be to kill her upon discovering a sexual infidelity.

Does the actual evidence about when and why men kill their mates back this theory up? In our own studies, we found that outright estrangement, in which a woman leaves the relationship, and a woman's infidelity are by far the two most powerful predictors of men's recurrent, persistent thoughts about killing their romantic partners. Here is one example:

> She accused me of cheating on her. I got mad and broke off the relationship, even though I still loved her. She then decided to start fucking my best friend. I was pissed off because she said I was the only one for her. She is a bitch, and unfortunately has to be pretty. I want her to be gone and I want my best friend to die too. . . . We are on her boat and I start talking to her. She asks to leave and starts getting nervous, so I tie her hands and feet together and strap her to the steering wheel, where I proceed to fuck her brains out. Then I make her drink a lot of alcohol so she can't think straight. I jam the steering wheel so that she is on a one way push to the cliffs that are in front of her house. That's where I jump off and watch the boat explode. [What prevented you from killing her?] I'm a sane human being and I realize that she is just a stupid bitch, and hopefully will become fat and ugly when she gets older. [What would have pushed

you over the edge to kill her?] *If I would have caught her fucking around with my best friend while we were still going out.*

Two elements in this fantasy warrant note. First, the victim is both young and pretty, signifying that she is highly reproductively valuable. Second, she has sex with the man's best friend, who has now become a rival.

The intensity of love a man feels for a woman is often mirrored in the intensity of his homicidal thoughts, as shown in the next case.

CASE #145: *I knew her for five years and shared the best times of my life with her. . . . I screamed and yelled and broke all the pictures of her and beat the shit out of the guy she cheated on me with. . . . My girlfriend of 1½ years who I had been friends with for over 5 years started hanging out with some cocaine addicts and started calling me less and less. Now she is a "coke head" and having sex with these fucks that she met. I tried everything I could to help her out but I eventually gave up. . . . I wanted to grab her by the throat and lift her in the air and just scream into her face all the horrible acts she had committed and how I felt about it. I then wanted to shoot her and the assholes that got her hooked. . . . Sometimes my bare fists, sometimes a gun . . .* [What prevented you?] *My conscience and my being connected to reality. I know that there is really no reason to take a loved one's life. I realize that there is a consequence to every one of my actions. . . . The fact that I loved this girl more than anything I had ever loved in my entire life. I would have happily died for her and would have married her in a heart beat. Because of this she hurt me more than I had ever been hurt in my life. I didn't want to live and I didn't want her to live.*

Precisely the same themes emerged in our study of Michigan murderers. One man suspected an infidelity, brought a gun to his girlfriend's workplace, but left it in his car. He confronted her with his suspicions, and she confessed. He then returned to his car, retrieved the gun, and shot her dead.

He told our interviewer: "I loved her. I was deeply in love with her and she knew that. It hurt me for her to be with another guy." Another man had divorced his wife but continued to have a sexual relationship with her, and still considered her to be "my woman." When he suspected that she was cheating, he tracked her down at a motel. He stabbed her five times with a knife, although she was smaller and unarmed. Despite this, he told the interviewer: "I love her. . . . I didn't mean to kill her." A third man killed his girlfriend, who had recently jilted him, and explained, "She was the most beautiful woman I ever made love to in my life."

Real murderers and men in our homicidal-fantasy studies show an amazing psychological similarity. They both mention the physical beauty of wives or girlfriends. They both talk about the depth of their love. And the rage of both groups of men stem from their dismal prospects for finding a mate of equivalent value. They differ in only one respect—the men in our homicidal-thought studies have not, to our knowledge, actually acted on their fantasies. The Michigan murderers have.

WHICH MEN MURDER THEIR MATES

Most men do not kill mates who cheat on them or abandon them in a one-sided breakup. Many attempt to hold on to the women with positive inducements—they promise to change, they shower them with gifts, and they declare their undying love. Some turn belligerent, threatening harm if the women do not return. Some begin to stalk their exes, interfering with any attempts the women may make to hook up with other men. Some men lick their wounds and move on, go back on the mating market, and remate, until, eventually, the emotional calamity following the breakup recedes to a distant if painful memory.

If we could predict in advance how men react—which ones beg and plead, which threaten, which stalk, which go away, and which kill—then we could save much anguish and many lives. We can't. Because homicide is a relatively rare event, predicting when, where, and who will kill proves to be extraordinarily difficult. But we have been able to identify the circumstances in which a woman's life is in particular danger, conditions that increase her likelihood of being killed.

One obvious predictor is the man's catching the woman in the act of intercourse with another man, as already indicated by the frequency of mate killings that occur in our sample of Michigan murders, FBI statistics, cross-cultural studies, and in male homicidal fantasies. Unfortunately, this clue does not lend itself to prevention. Although women go to great lengths to conceal their infidelities, men have coevolved defenses to discover them.[41] The rage inspired by witnessing a partner in a naked coupling with another unhinges most men.

A second predictor is alcohol consumption. In one study conducted in Australia, slightly more than 50 percent of spouse killers had consumed alcohol in the hours before the killing.[42] Alcohol, of course, is a known releaser of violence, lowering inhibitions against venting emotions ranging from sexual lust to jealousy-induced rage.[43] One study conducted in Sweden, for example, found that as per-capita alcohol consumption increased the homicide rates countrywide also increased.[44] On the other hand, nearly 50 percent of the spouse killings occurred without prior consumption of alcohol.

Even in those cases in which alcohol is consumed, the killing cannot necessarily be attributed solely to intoxication. Indeed, one coping strategy that men use when discovering a mate's sexual infidelity is to go out and get drunk. Infidelity in these cases may cause drinking, which then changes men's assessment of the costs and benefits, lowering the perceived costs of killing and therefore increasing its likelihood. Alcohol selectively disinhibits our evolved murderous mechanisms.[45] It increases men's perceptions of their own power and prowess.[46] When intoxicated, men are more likely to think they can get away with murder. Alcohol changes how men perceive the risks and rewards of killing. It is thus best viewed as a substance that facilitates the activation and implementation of our evolved homicidal circuits. Interestingly, however, the vast majority of women who kill their mates tend to be quite sober: only 24 percent have consumed any alcohol prior to the murder.[47]

Age of the man is another predictor of mate murder. In one representative study, 81 percent of men who killed their partners were between the ages of twenty and forty-nine.[48] This age distribution contrasts with that for other sorts of violent crime, such as armed robbery or gang warfare, which are heavily concentrated among men between sixteen and twenty-four.[49] Once men hit fifty, the rates of mate murder sharply decrease. Whereas men in their forties represent 23 percent of all mate murderers, men in their fifties account for only 7.7 percent. A fascinating finding, however, is that women who kill their mates are almost invariably young. The vast majority of women who kill their partners, 79 percent, are in the prime of their reproductive years, between sixteen and thirty-nine. As we will see in the next chapter, this difference provides a critical clue to a sex difference in the motivation to kill.

The rate of mate murder starts to rise again after men hit their sixties, representing 11 percent of mate killings.[50] This increase can be explained by two factors.

First, many are mercy killings. Clearly, cases in which the motive is compassion, not rage over infidelity, cause this spike in frequency. In one case from our study of Michigan murders, a man age seventy-two came up behind his seventy-four-year-old wife and dealt a fatal blow to her head with a lead pipe. His wife had been suffering greatly from cancer. He reported that they had talked about it for a long time, and on the night of the murder, he had thought about it a great deal before doing it. He said he couldn't bear to see her in pain anymore, wanted to put her out of her misery, loved her very much, and was sorry that he had killed her.

Second, older men married to younger women, the so-called May–December marriages, kill their partners at a higher rate than similarly aged men married to partners closer to their own age.[51] Sexual infidelity is often the cause of these murders. Younger women, being more attractive and fertile, have more mating alternatives and are targeted more frequently by mate poachers. Furthermore, older men married to substantially younger women will generally have greater difficulty replacing them with women of equivalent desirability. My study of married couples confirmed that sexual infidelity and intense mate guarding increased with the age discrepancy between man and wife.[52] Older men married to younger women get both more vigilant and more violent. In one study of all homicides that occurred in Houston, Texas, during an entire year, thirty-two were spousal homicides. Of these mate killings, 25 percent showed an age disparity of ten or more years.[53]

The killing of *Playboy* Playmate Dorothy Stratten by small-time hustler Paul Snider exemplifies the logic of mate value discrepancies. Snider met Dorothy when she worked at a Dairy Queen. She was seventeen, he twenty-six. After a brief period of intense courting, they became a couple. He convinced her that she had a perfect body and a gorgeous face, and that they could achieve fame and fortune together through *Playboy*. He photographed her in the nude, sent pictures off to Hugh Hefner, and received a reply within two days.[54]

She moved into the Playboy mansion, with Paul Snider insisting on tagging along. She made Playmate of the Month in 1979, won Playmate of the Year, and was being considered for Playmate of the Quarter Century. Readers and viewers of *Playboy* became captivated by her young translucent skin, her wholesome well-proportioned body, and her innocent girl-next-door eyes. Hefner despised boorish Snider and eventually banned him from the Playboy mansion. Snider remained unemployed. In the meantime, Hefner introduced Dorothy to Hollywood players, including Peter Bogdanovich, the renowned director of movies such as *Paper Moon* and *The Last Picture Show*. Paul Snider, the smarmy hood from Vancouver, remained an outcast, but continued his involvement and proposed marriage. She agreed to marry him because she felt she owed him for her success at *Playboy*, but then fell hopelessly in love with Peter Bogdanovich. Despite efforts from friends to convince her to break off all contact with Snider, she agreed to meet him one last time, at his insistence. She felt she owed him the courtesy of this final meeting.

On August 14, 1980, she met with Snider to break off the relationship for good. She had a thousand dollars in her handbag, a gift that she hoped would smooth over the breakup. Snider killed her with a shotgun. Homicide detectives found her body, smeared with blood. The innocent face that beamed from millions of magazine covers was totally destroyed. They found two of Snider's bloody handprints on her buttocks, and evidence that he had raped her. Dorothy Stratten, whose mate value far exceeded that of the small-time, unemployed Snider, was dead at age twenty. Ironically, on her *Playmate* fact sheet, she listed "jealous people" as one of her turnoffs. The Stratten murder contained all the ingredients for women's highest risk of being murdered by the men they reject—when they are young and attractive, when they are mated to men substantially older, during the first few months of the breakup, when a rival has gained sexual access to her, and when the man's prospects for replacing her with a woman of equivalent mate value approach nil.

In general, young women are in special danger from those who profess to love them. From Australia to Zimbabwe, the younger the woman, the higher the likelihood that she will be killed as a result of a sexual infidelity or leaving a romantic relationship.[55] Women in the fifteen-to-twenty-four-year-old bracket are at the greatest risk. For women aged twenty-five to thirty-four, the risk drops by 25 percent. And the risk continues to decline with age. Why would the youngest women be more at risk?

The answer lies in the cluster of related facts. Young women are more fertile, more reproductively valuable, and hence represent a greater reproductive loss for the man. From the man's perspective, his loss is compounded by the increased odds that his young former mate will remate or remarry, so his loss becomes a rival's reproductive gain. In the cold-blooded game of differential reproductive success, killing a young estranged wife inflicts greater costs on a rival than killing an older one.

Another key predictor is the *length of the separation*—the shorter the separation, the greater the risk. In one study of 217 estranged Australian women murdered by their spurned husbands, 47 percent had left the relationship within the past two months![56] Another study from Australia found that the majority occurred within the first year.[57] A study of homicides in the city of Chicago found that 50 percent of wife killings took place within the first two months of the separation, and an astonishing 85 percent of these women were killed within the first year.[58] Just when women feel as though they have successfully escaped a bad marriage is precisely the time when their lives are most in danger.

It is likely that the key danger sign is not the length of time per se but, rather, when it hits the man's skull that she is inexorably lost and will never return to him. Evidence for this contention comes from the fact that for the few mate killings that occur a year or more after estrangement, it seems that the couple actually had sexual contact during that year even though she had moved out. The hope that she might return, as indicated by sex, offers a protective buffer, lowering the odds that he will try to kill her. But then when the sex stops, and he realizes she will never come back, her life is in danger. An example of this situation was described in our study of women's antihomicidal thoughts:

> He kept on calling me and telling me that he loved me and told me that he didn't know what he would do if I ever left him. . . . I thought that because he knew where I lived he would come to my house and kill me. [What did you do to prevent being killed?] I constantly begged and pleaded for him to leave me alone. I didn't know what else to do, and I didn't want to tell my parents. [What prevented him from killing you?] _Because he loved me so much and thought that there might be a chance for us to get back in the future._ [What would have pushed him over the edge to actually kill you?] _If I dated someone else._

Only when it really sinks in that she is lost for good, and likely going to a sexual rival, do the odds of murder escalate dramatically.

Another danger sign is a *mate value discrepancy*—when the woman is markedly higher in mate value than her mate. May–December marriages are one instance, but age is not the only variable; a man's lack of financial resources is another problematic source of discrepancy. A woman's greater desirability signals either that a man will not be able to replace the woman at all, or that the odds that he can replace her with a woman of comparable desirability are vanishingly low. Men who confront the problem of replaceability most poignantly are those who lack what women desire in a long-term mate. Men who are slackers, who can't hold a job, or who squander their money on drugs or gambling plummet in mate value in the eyes of most women. Thus, men who can't replace a mate are those who lack what women want.

In fact, a study that matched men and children based on seven blood types documented precisely how much more risk men lacking resources run of being genetically cuckolded.[59] Of men in the highest socioeconomic bracket, only 2 percent of the children had fathers other than the putative father. Among the middle class, the genetic-cuckoldry rate rose to 12 percent. And among the lower class, the genetic-cuckoldry rate rose to 20 percent. Since genetic cuckoldry can only occur when women have affairs, it's clear that men lacking resources experience more paternity uncertainty.

It comes as no great surprise, therefore, that men who are unemployed, and hence lack the resources that women want, will find it most difficult to replace a mate who has abandoned them. And these men are most likely to kill or try to kill when dumped.[60] Homicide statistics bear out this critical prediction. In one study, 64 percent of men who killed their mates were unemployed at the time of the killing.[61]

And it is also precisely these men who are most likely to get killed by their mates, who are often acting in self-defense against men who have repeatedly abused them, threatened to kill them, or tried to kill them. In one study, forensic psychologist Angela Brown interviewed forty-two women who had been charged with the murder or attempted murder of their husbands.[62] The women's partners tended to be from lower social classes than the women themselves were. The men's average level of education was lower. And many of these men showed marginal resource-providing abilities, with less than half being fully employed during the bulk of the relationship, and 28 percent only sporadically employed.

Though men with fewer resources and status are more likely to kill, many, many men who hold decent jobs kill as well, as the following case illustrates.

"Matthew and Karen were both in their early 30s. He was a success-ful medical practitioner and she was a business manager. They had one child and Karen was several months pregnant. Although there was no known history of domestic violence in this marriage, it was

reported that Matthew had been unfaithful a few years earlier. When
Karen discovered the affair, she threatened to leave the marriage.
Matthew had responded that he would kill her if she tried to divorce
him. She remained, but a few months before the homicide she began
an intimate relationship with another man. Matthew alleged that
three men broke into their home, shot Karen, and tied him up in the
boot of his car. However, the evidence that was gathered by the
police showed that he had in fact killed her and Matthew was found
guilty of murder."[63]

Although lack of economic resources increases the odds of mate infidelity and hence mate murder, spousal infidelity and related spousal killings occur across socioeconomic boundaries, as we saw earlier in the case of San Antonio millionaire Allen Blackthorne, who was convicted of murdering his ex-wife. Although a man's gainful employment lowers the risk that his partner will play around, women in such marriages are still sometimes motivated to stray, and in doing so risk death at the hands of the men who love them.

All men have an evolved psychology of mate killing that lies latent in their brains. For many men, the psychology never gets activated, because they never face the relevant adaptive problems of mate infidelity or desertion, or not in a way that triggers homicidal intent. Just as living in a friction-free world prevents the growth of skin calluses, living in a state of monogamy and lifelong love keeps men's mate-homicide mechanisms dormant. But when that psychology is activated, it can inflict such severe costs on women that evolution by selection has forged powerful defenses for women.

WOMEN'S DEFENSES
AGAINST MURDEROUS MATES

If men have more homicidal thoughts about partners' infidelity than women, and if men are more likely to translate murderous thoughts into deeds, we should expect that women would have evolved more defenses than men to prevent being killed under these circumstances. One of these defenses is terror of being killed in the precise circumstance in which a partner suspects or perceives a sexual transgression. Many women in our study of antihomicidal thoughts revealed this fear.

> **CASE #340, *female, age 26.*** [Who did you think might kill you?] *My boyfriend . . . I cheated on him with my ex boyfriend that was his friend. . . . He was really mad and did not know what to do for a few minutes. . . . I simply thought that he probably wanted me to disappear at the moment. . . . He did not try to kill me. I am sure he was so mad that the thought ran through his mind but he would have never actually tried to physically harm me.* [What prevented him from killing you?] *He calmed down and left the situation. I don't think that would ever actually happen.*

What's fascinating about this case is that the boyfriend gave absolutely no indication—no signs, no signals, no threats—that he wanted to kill her. The mere fact that he discovered her infidelity triggered the thought that he might want to kill her. A psychological circuit connects the woman's awareness of the boyfriend's discovery of her infidelity directly to thoughts that he might be provoked to a homicidal rage.

In the next case, the woman's infidelity alone was enough to trigger worry about her safety, even though the boyfriend had not discovered the affair.

> **CASE #543, *female, age 32.*** [Who did you think might try to kill you?] *My boyfriend. In reflection I don't think he would have hurt me but at the time the threat felt very real. At the very least I thought that he would physically injure me or my family. He never found out that I had an affair with someone else. He was extremely jealous and had told me before that he would do something awful if I ever did anything like that. <u>Fortunately, he never found out that I had an affair with someone else.</u>*

As we'd expect, the fear of being killed gets more intense when women are discovered being sexually unfaithful.

CASE #458, *female, age 21*. [Who did you think might try to kill you?] *My boyfriend. He had a very bad temper and all the males in the family were known for it. He was my boyfriend all throughout high school and the love of my life. He cheated on me, so I cheated on him. He didn't like that idea very much. He would push me or verbally make me feel like shit. And of course I took it because I loved him. One day at school he grabbed me by my neck. I thought he was going to strangle me. He squeezed hard, choking off my ability to breathe. I loved him. He realized he was hurting me I guess. I know he wouldn't have actually gone through with it. He just had a really bad temper. He realized what he was doing and I know he loved me and just couldn't do it.*

Women's antihomicide defenses can be exploited by men. One means of manipulation is to imply or threaten murder as a deterrent of infidelity. Many women who feared being killed by their mates discussed these implied or actual threats.

CASE #398, *female, age 24*. [Who did you think might try to kill you?] *My boyfriend. He is very jealous and has a problem with controlling his anger. We were in his car and he was drunk and started accusing me of cheating and the angrier he got the faster and more reckless he drove. I thought he wanted us to crash so I could die because he pointed out that there was only one air bag and it was on the driver's side. . . . When we were in his car he started to drive really crazy and fast and let me know that there was only one air bag and it was not on my side. . . . He didn't seem to care about his actions. He was like in some crazy mindset. And he was drunk, usually when he drinks he is very impulsive. . . . I thought he would purposely cause a crash on the passenger's side of the car to kill me. . . .*

[What did you do to prevent getting killed?] Well, first I put on my seat belt and then I talked to him to clear things up. He was under the impression that I was being unfaithful in our relationship so I had to convince him otherwise and calm him down. So I basically

*gave him a guilt trip for thinking that I would cheat on him. . . .
Because I noticed that I am proficient in guilt trips and they work
very well on him, they also calm him down.* [What prevented him
from killing you?] *My talking with him and convincing him that his
accusations were completely false and unrealistic.* [What would have
pushed him over the edge to actually killing you?] *If I had admitted
to cheating or said that I should because I was being accused of it
anyway.*

In contrast to the many women who feared being killed by mates jealous
over real or suspected infidelity, only one man in our study reported this
fear, and in this case it was compounded by his having dumped the
girlfriend.

CASE #307, *male.* [Who did you think might try to kill you?] *My
girlfriend. I cheated on her with another girl and then broke up with
her for the girl. After a week she threatened to kill me when I was
sleeping with the other girl. . . . She got angry fast and always had a
very intense demeanor. Also she was more physical with me.* [How
did you think she might kill you?] *When I was sleeping . . . with her
father's gun.* [What did you do to prevent being killed?] *I prayed she
wasn't serious. I locked my door. My gut feeling was she wasn't serious, but I didn't want to take any chances.* [What prevented her from
killing you?] *Her family and friends talking with her.* [What would
have pushed her over the edge to actually killing you?] *If I had
pushed her buttons with my new girlfriend around.*

Fewer men than women fear being killed by their mates, because the
adaptive problem of being killed by a mate has always been far lower for
men than for women. Women are more likely than men to forgive a partner's sexual indiscretion, especially if it was a single episode and not linked
with emotional or psychological involvement with the short-term lover. But
women too can turn deadly under certain circumstances, and we'll explore
the specifics of those in the next chapter.

Five

SEXUAL PREDATORS

——

To have and to hold from this day forward . . . till death do us part.

H ELL HATH NO FURY like a woman scorned" resonates with popular caricatures of the female temperament. Rudyard Kipling proclaimed that "the female of the species is more deadly than the male." The philosopher Friedrich Nietzsche asserted, "In revenge and in love woman is more barbarous than man." As we've just seen overwhelmingly in the previous chapter, however, Nietzsche was way off the mark. Men are much more murderous. In our FBI database of 429,729 homicides, for example, 378,161 were committed by men, versus 51,567 by women. When women do turn murderous, there are specific adaptive reasons, and these differ markedly from those that motivate men.

In contemplating how different women's motives for killing are from those of men, consider this statistic. Among the men who entertained thoughts of murdering their mates, fully 54 percent were triggered by the woman's ending the relationship. In contrast, among the women who contemplated killing their mates, getting dumped accounted for only 13 percent.[1] None-theless, of the roughly thirty-two thousand homicides committed by women between 1976 and 1994, fully 43 percent of them were cases in which a woman killed a husband, ex-husband, boyfriend, or ex-boyfriend.[2] As with men, mating and murder are closely linked among women killers. How-ever, a quite different set of circumstances have governed the evolution of women's psychology of murder and when it gets activated.

INTIMATE SEXUAL PREDATORS

Chilling accounts of women's fantasies of murder from our study highlight the kinds of specific issues that are involved in motivating women to kill their mates.

> **CASE #P2308,** *female, age 18.* [Who did you think about killing?] *An ex-boyfriend, Jeffrey. I met him through friends in high school; he's 21 years old. Throughout our relationship, my ex would verbally abuse me. Telling me that I was fat and would never amount to any-thing in my life. He would follow me places and not allow me to interact with my friends. He would also make me do things that I didn't feel comfortable doing, such as forcing me to have sex and making me do sexually degrading things.* [How did you think about killing him?] *Back in high school I knew some of the biggest gang-sters and had dreamed that they had beat my ex up until he was dead.* [What would have pushed you over the edge to killing him?] *I'm not one to kill a person, unless my life or my family's life is in danger. So, if I had felt that he was really going to hurt me or my family I would really consider it.*

Her boyfriend cut off her relationships with friends. He forced her into sex she did not want. He constantly undermined her self-esteem, and dero-gated one of the core dimensions on which women evaluate their own desirability, physical appearance. Although she managed to extricate herself from the relationship without resorting to murder, killing as a solution to the problems with her mate occurred to her, as it did to many women in our study.

> **CASE #P96,** *female, age 19.* [Who do you think about killing?] *Michael, my ex-boyfriend. I think the feeling occurred because of a year and a half of events, not just one single event. The things he did to make me think about killing him were as follows: try to control who I saw, what I did, where I went, when I went. He tried to control every aspect of my life once we came to college together. He would say mean things, call me names, make me feel worthless or like I couldn't find anyone else (even though I knew this was untrue, it still made me feel like I couldn't find anyone better). There were two main events that triggered my thought—1) he got in a huge fight with my mom, 2) he called me a whore.* [How would you kill?] *I never actually planned out how I would kill him. I just remember the feelings of wanting him dead (not necessarily by my hands) being much more intense than the others.* [What prevented you from killing him?] *I would never consider actually killing someone. I have morals and I am a Christian and don't believe it is my right to take someone's life. I think that it only helps imagining someone is being hurt or killed that hurt you.* [What might have pushed you over the edge to kill him?] *Nothing . . . Well, actually, if he would have ever hit me or started physically hurting me I would have considered it seriously.*

Again, we hear about the boyfriend undermining her self-esteem, making her believe that no one else would want her, and denying her access to the outside world. Despite her Christian values, and despite initially indicating that nothing would push her over the edge to kill, she concluded that physical abuse might have pushed the fantasy into a higher probability of reality. Interestingly, her homicidal thoughts reveal a fundamental sex difference throughout our scientific studies—women were far more likely than men simply to want the partner dead, often not wishing to do the killing themselves. But this is not always true. Some women do envision specific methods of killing abusive mates, as illustrated by the following case.

CASE #S483, *female, age 43.* [Who do you think about killing?] *My boyfriend, who was 47. I used to be a very cheerful and easy going lady. My easy going nature made me encounter this man who was being introduced by my friend. At first, things went well, but later I came to realize that I was under his control—it could be the black magic. I became very cowardly and he did not want me to mingle around anymore. At times, when I went back to see my relatives, my brother and sisters, he would throw big temper at me, throwing my clothes down from my flat, yelling and shouting at me in the public, hit and slapped me at times. There is even one day when he caught me with my elder brother, he raised his fist at him and they turned into a fight. He even threatened my brother that he will come back for more. From that day, I hated him more.* [How did you think of killing him?] *When working, my thoughts ran wild. I had this vision of putting poison in his food. My imagination started from the moment when he is back home, and went for his bath. I would put the dinner on the table and take out 2 separate bowls for the soup. One bowl of his will contain rat poison. Without suspicion he will finish the soup. Then I visualize him suffering stomach pain, then white bubbles come out of his mouth, and the next thing he collapses.* [What prevented you from killing him?] *I was afraid of being jailed.* [What would have pushed you over the edge to kill him?] *If he hurt my brother.*

This case highlights several important aspects of why, and how, women kill. One is that, in addition to damage to self-esteem, women, far more than men, mention damage to their genetic kin as a motive for murder. In this case, her mate insulted and threatened the woman's brother. In the prior case, the woman mentioned the boyfriend's fight with her mother. In many other cases that prompt thoughts of killing, the mate inflicts costs on a woman's children.

Another striking difference between men and women that this case points to is the methods of killing that are contemplated. Men are larger and stronger than women on average, so women must use different means of killing, and even in their fantasies—where one would presume they could do whatever they wanted—they conjure up different means. This woman, like many women in our sample, thought of poisoning the food of her partner. Among the means of actual murders, women are far more likely than men to use poison. In fact, only one man in our sample of more than five thousand study participants mentioned poison in his homicidal fantasies.

The following case, from a systematic study of killings of mates in Australia, illustrates just how closely mate killing by women follows the pattern of a man who becomes desperate and sees defection by his wife as a real possibility:

> "Sue and Don had been married for fourteen years and had two children. Apparently, the marriage had experienced _difficulties in the past few years due to financial hardships._ Don had also become quite abusive, verbally and physically. The latter included many types of humiliation, and being hit across the head regularly, being threatened with death, being locked in a closet, and _being forced to sit looking in a mirror while Don made derogatory comments about her._ On the night of the killing, Don held a knife to Sue's throat while threatening to kill her. He had also both locked her in a closet and urinated in her face. Later that night, after Don had gone to sleep, . . . Sue struck him with an axe to the side of the neck about three times. She then stabbed him in the stomach about six times with a large carving knife. Sue did not recollect the sequence of these actions clearly and was clearly emotionally distraught, requiring sedation, when the police arrived."[3]

Financial difficulties, in this case Don's failing to bring in sufficient money, are a potent statistical predictor of women's leaving a relationship. This accords with the evolutionary logic of what women look for in their

mates. In order to prevent her departure, Don resorted to increasingly desperate measures of mate guarding—belittling her appearance to lower her
perceptions of her own desirability, humiliating her by urinating on her
face, beating her up, and literally locking her up. Don had become a type of
sexual predator.

The following case, from our study of Michigan murders, also indicates
the special circumstances in which women's homicidal switches get tripped.
A woman in her late twenties had finally had enough. She had endured several years of beatings by her diabetic husband, and every time she tried to
leave, it got worse. She finally decided that she had to act. Interestingly, she
asked a boyfriend she had on the side to help her. Over a period of several
months, she discussed the situation with her boyfriend, and decided that
killing was the only way out. They secured a lethal dose of high-grade
heroin. On the day of the murder, she hesitated at first and didn't want to
go through with it. Her husband chose that day to backhand her across the
face. She made up her mind. It would be easy. She would simply mix the
heroin with her husband's regular shot of insulin, and it would look like a
heart attack. She killed her husband to escape the abuse.

The fact that so many abused women stay with their abusive mates is
utterly perplexing, and even infuriating to the families and friends of
abused women. But if we examine the appalling methods employed by abusive men, and consider the underlying psychological dynamics of long-term
mateships, we can understand why so many abused women stay, and also
why some of them eventually resort to murder.

In being dumped, men get cast out into uncertain mating waters, and
risk flailing around frantically to find another woman. As a consequence of
these costs, they often resort to desperate measures to prevent being
dumped, clinging to a woman to forestall the ominous consequences that
will follow from her departure. Psychological and physical abuse, paradox-
ically, are designed to hold on to long-term love.

The quaint phrase "domestic violence" and its typical analysis by psychologists fail to capture the cloaked reasons why men beat up their mates.
Wife beating is usually attributed to pathology, cultural values of macho
men, or patriarchal societies in which men are united in their interests with

other men to oppress all women. These explanations cannot be correct, for they utterly violate the logic of how evolution by selection designs men's psychology. Men cannot be united with other men in their interests of oppression, even in principle, for the simple reason that men are primarily in competition with other men.[4] Men do not desire to oppress all women, for they have sisters, mothers, daughters, and nieces whom they desire to protect and defend. Men do have adaptations to control and manipulate their own mates, and therein lies the horrifying bridge to abuse.

Men abuse their mates as a means of solving a specific adaptive problem. Abuse acts to damage a woman's self-esteem.[5] Self-esteem, in turn, is a woman's internal tracking device, monitoring her perceptions of how desirable she is in the mating market.[6] When it's low, she feels that she's worthless and ugly, that no man would want her. By undermining a mate's self-esteem, a man may convince a woman that she is profoundly fortunate to have the man she's with. No other man would deign to look at her, much less entertain her as a mating possibility. In their obsessive and possessive efforts to prevent partners from leaving, men typically attempt to cut off their mates' social ties to their families and friends, thereby curtailing social access to other potential mates. This effectively deprives women of access to countervailing information that could bolster their artificially damaged self-esteem. Abuse, intense mate guarding, and sequestering all serve the diabolical function of tethering women to damaging relationships.

Women are not, however, simply passive pawns in a male game of control. Even if abuse all too often works to maintain a man's control over his mate, evolution has created defenses in women that serve to protect them. Their first line of defense is to strive to maintain contact with family and friends. Women will also solicit flirtations from additional prospective mates as a means of accurately evaluating whether men find them desirable. And if the abuse becomes too costly, women will resort to desperate measures to extricate themselves. Sometimes they resort to murder. The psychological logic of killing in such an abusive situation has given legitimacy to the battered-woman-syndrome defense, which is more and more successful over time.

Women who kill in self-defense while their husbands are violently

attacking them are increasingly able to avoid jail time. The problem, however, is that women are typically weaker and smaller than their mates, and
have difficulty defending themselves in the midst of a violent attack. As a
consequence, many abused and battered women choose a time to kill when
their partner is more vulnerable, such as when he is drunk or asleep.
Because the laws typically state that a person's life has to be in imminent
danger to invoke self-defense, defense lawyers often have a difficult time
convincing juries that a battered woman who waited until her husband fell
asleep was actually acting in self-defense. The majority of such women end
up being convicted, typically receiving sentences that range from four to
twenty-five years.

The case of Sue and Don described above is a perfect example. Sue
received a prison sentence of five years for killing her husband. The judge
levied this sentence by invoking what a "reasonable man" would do under
similar circumstances. The reasonable-man standard—a fixture of legal
doctrines throughout the modern Western world—is geared toward determining what an "average person" would have done in similar circumstances. According to one summary of the "reasonable man," "he is not
impotent and he is not normally drunk. He does not lose his self-control on
hearing a mere confession of adultery, but he becomes unbalanced at the
sight of adultery, provided, of course, that he is married to the adulteress."[7]

Unfortunately, the law fails to recognize that "reasonable women" and
"reasonable men" face profoundly different adaptive problems, which call
for different adaptive solutions. Because of differences in size and strength,
a man abused by his wife does not face the same level or probability of
physical threat or forced sequestering. Men can more easily walk out the
door. Women sometimes cannot, as in the case of Sheila Bellush at the start
of this book. Thanks in part to research on the battered-woman's syndrome, the laws are gradually changing to recognize that there is no such
thing as a generic "reasonable person" when it comes to murder.

That defense did not help, however, in the case of Susan Wright, who
was convicted of killing her husband. Her case highlights a specific trigger
that most often motivates women to kill—a desperate attempt to escape
from a husband who had, in essence, become a sexual predator.

Susan Wright, an attractive blonde twenty-seven-year-old, stabbed her thirty-four-year-old husband 193 times in their Houston, Texas, home with a hunting knife on January 13, 2003, and buried his body in a hole in their back yard. Jeffrey Wright's murder stunned the state of Texas. Court TV nationally televised the trial, gripping millions of American viewers. Jeff was a charming and extroverted man, well liked by friends, family, and admiring women. He worked as a successful carpet salesman, and from all outward appearances, they had a happy middle-class marriage with two attractive children. This outward show, however, masked a much darker side of Jeff.

The couple met on a beach in Galveston, Texas, when Susan worked as a waitress. Just as Jeff had no trouble meeting women, Susan had no trouble meeting men. Earlier, she had worked in a strip club. Her beauty earned her high marks with the customers, but she quit after two months, not finding the work to her liking. The courtship of Susan and Jeff started out storybook-style. Jeff frequently bought Susan flowers and showered her with surprise gifts. He wanted what many want—a house, a nice car, a family, and a dog. But all was not as it seemed underneath the smooth façade of the happy marriage. Jeff continued to frequent strip bars, had affairs with other women, and, according to Susan, gave her herpes as a result of one of the affairs. Then everything changed.

After the birth of their first son, Bradley, Jeff became obsessively controlling. He called her multiple times each day to check up on her. He required Susan to notify him of her whereabouts day and night. He allowed her to leave home only for brief periods. If she stayed even a few minutes extra when visiting her parents or made an unreported stop at a store, he would fly into a jealous rage and accuse her of cheating. He insisted that the house be spotless, and yelled at her for the slightest departure from domestic perfection. Jeff began abusing cocaine, and his outbursts grew most violent when under the drug's influence. Several times he pushed Susan against the wall and then punched her in the chest. Susan's sister began noticing bruises on her arms and legs. Twice Susan showed up with black eyes. The intense mate guarding got worse after the birth of their second child, a daughter named Kaily.

On January 13, 2003, the abuse took a terrible turn. After returning from a boxing lesson, Jeff began hitting his son. Bradley went crying to Susan, and for the first time, according to her testimony, she decided that she could not live any longer with the violence against her or her son. Jeffrey's abuse compelled her to make a decision. She gave him an ultimatum—either he had to deal with the drugs and stop the violence or she would be forced to leave him. Her thoughts of leaving Jeff may have been partly fueled by economic factors—Jeff's cocaine abuse was leaving their family behind on bills, he started borrowing money from others to support his drug habit, and his work became sporadic. But the most likely motive was self-defense and a fear of what he would do if she dumped him. "I couldn't go on and I was afraid of him. I knew if I left him he would kill me. But I had to ask him to get help. And that was my big mistake."[8]

According to Susan's testimony, Jeff exploded in a rage, pushed her onto the floor, and began kicking her in the stomach. After repeated kicks, he dragged her up onto the bed and raped her—something he had done repeatedly in the past. Then, when she opened her eyes, she heard him say, "Die, bitch," and she realized that he held a hunting knife in his hand. In desperation, for preservation, and motivated by the added fuel of maternal protection, Susan kneed him in the groin and grabbed the knife as he doubled over in pain, according to her testimony. "I was terrified because he was gonna kill me," says Susan. "I knew the second that I stopped he was gonna get the knife back and then I was gonna be the one that would be dead."[9] She stabbed him repeatedly, stopped momentarily when Bradley knocked on the bedroom door, then, after assuring Bradley that everything was OK, closed the door and continued stabbing her husband, inflicting 193 separate wounds. "I stabbed him in the head and I stabbed him in the neck and I stabbed him in the chest and I stabbed him in the stomach, and I stabbed him in the leg for all the times he kicked me, and I stabbed him in the penis for all the times he made me have sex when I didn't want to."[10] Susan's sister Cindy confirmed this, testifying that she "understood why she stabbed him so many times. She said she stabbed Jeff for all the times he punched her in the chest. And she stabbed him in the penis for all the times he raped her in the middle of the night."[11]

Susan described being in a fog during the five days following the killing.

Although she dragged Jeff's body to the hole in the back yard and put dirt on top, she still felt terrified that he would rise up and kill her. Five days later, she told her mother what had happened. They contacted an attorney and brought in the police, who found the knife in a flower pot and the tip of the knife lodged in Jeff Wright's skull.

The prosecution argued for premeditated murder in cold blood. They contended that Susan was driven not by self-defense or to escape from a repeatedly abusing cokehead husband, but, rather, by greed. Jeffrey had a two-hundred-thousand-dollar life-insurance policy. The prosecution argued that Susan had lured Jeff into the bedroom with the promise of kinky sex, tied his arms and legs to the bedpost, and then viciously stabbed him to death. They argued that Susan was a devious manipulator, playing well the role of a wife frightened by an enraged husband. Susan claimed that she had no knowledge of the insurance benefit, and indeed Jeff kept her in the dark about many matters. In contrast, she became worried when Jeff decided that he wanted to take out a life-insurance policy on her. Several witnesses—Jeff's party buddies, Susan's sister, Susan's hairdresser, and the next-door neighbor—all corroborated her testimony about Jeff's cocaine abuse, Jeff's drug-induced violence, and the bruises and black eyes Susan suffered. In fact, he had previously been convicted of assaulting another woman, a stripper with whom he had carried on an affair on the side. In contrast, Susan, by all accounts, was a loving mother and had no prior history of crime or violence of any sort.

After five hours of intense deliberation, the jury returned their verdict on March 2, 2004. They felt that the 193 stab wounds, the pause in the killing while she attended to her son, and the intentional burial of the body in the back yard indicated premeditation, the ability to distinguish right from wrong, and the workings of a rational mind. The jury found Susan guilty of murder in the first degree. She received a twenty-five-year sentence, and will be eligible for parole after serving twelve. Susan Wright is currently appealing the conviction.

This case vividly illustrates how the design of the murdering mind differs between the sexes. Repeated physical, sexual, and psychological abuse are by far the most common triggers of women's homicidal fantasies, and also the leading predictors of when women kill their mates. Abuse of their children is an additional trigger, feeding fuel to the homicidal fire. And Susan's fear that her life would be in danger if she left Jeff highlights the danger women face when they decide to leave an abusive relationship. Although we don't usually think of husbands as sexual predators, an abusive husband who sequesters his wife, obsessively controls her sexuality, and rapes her has indeed become a type of sexual predator.

The main motives for murders committed by women, in short, are self-defense and a desperate desire to escape a dangerous marriage. Women who find themselves in such abusive relationships are not mistaken about the degree of danger they are in. Many women in similar circumstances who attempt to leave their mates are not as lucky as Susan Wright: at least she got away with her life.

WOMEN'S HOMICIDAL FANTASIES

That doesn't mean that no women are capable of wanting to kill their mates, or ex-mates, because they've been dumped. Such blows to status do come into play for women too, but not nearly as often. Other issues are probably also involved, as the following account of a vivid homicidal fantasy by one woman in our study points to.

> **CASE #F1,** *female, age 38. My ex-boyfriend. He's a liar, a cheat, and a sponger. (1) found condoms in his drawer; (2) three weeks later I met him in the street with his wife and daughter (this was about 350 miles away from where he said he was). [How did you envision killing him?] I hired an explosives specialist to blow him up in his car; the car exploded, blowing him up. [What prevented you from killing him?] It would be wrong and I could not afford it. [What would have pushed you over the edge to kill him?] Winning the lottery. [Over what duration did you think of killing him?] More than 270 days. [What did you actually do?] I reported him to Internal Revenue Service and arranged to have his property damaged.*

Notice that in this case it's not merely the infidelity that has provoked such intense anger. His deception fans the flames. And the fact that he's spending the precious commodity of time with another woman and her child seems especially vexing. Since she lacked the resources to hire a killer, she extracted her revenge in the place where it often hurts men most—his financial resources.

As our study of homicidal ideation showed, the average cognitive effort men allocated to thinking about killing women who rejected them was a great deal more intense than that devoted by women. During the temporal course of the fantasy, these men devoted nearly fifteen minutes per day to thinking about killing, often over periods of time that stretched to weeks and months. By way of contrast, women who thought about killing partners who had dumped them devoted only four minutes per day.

One indication of how infuriated both sexes feel when romantically rejected, however, comes from an analysis of whether torture was part of the fantasy. On this index, getting rejected and discovering a partner's sexual infidelity prove to be about equal for women and men, with 57 percent of the victims of each experiencing torture fantasies. Here are a couple of examples:

CASE #3217, *female, age 21*. *I wanted to make it as painful and degrading as possible; I wanted to expose him naked to the world and then hit him hard to finish him off.*

CASE #S507, *female, age 28*. [Who do you think about killing?] *Ex-boyfriend, my lover. He jilted me and broke my heart. I felt very dejected, like my life had no meaning anymore.* [How did you think about killing him?] *Ask him out as a friend. Go to bed with him to do sex. Stab him at the midst of doing sex.* [What prevented you from killing him?] *I still love him.* [What would push you over the edge to kill him?] *If I saw him with another girl.*

The key difference between the sexes is not so much in having homicidal fantasies about mates who have left them but, rather, in the likelihood of acting on them. Whereas men kill mates who have dumped them, women kill mates who sequester, abuse, and threaten them so heavily that they see killing as the only way out.

STALKERS AS SEXUAL PREDATORS

One of the main reasons women may feel they have no other option is that so many men who are scorned become stalkers—a different type of sexual predator. In the movie *Fatal Attraction,* the character played by Glenn Close stalked the character played by Michael Douglas. She left tape-recorded voice messages in his car. She spied on his family. She feigned pregnancy and claimed that it was his child. She boiled the family's pet rabbit. After *Fatal Attraction* became a big hit, it was rumored that there was an unusual increase in sexual fidelity among married men. Contrary to the Hollywood take, however, the overwhelming majority of persistent and dangerous stalkers are men, not women.

Although stalking is now illegal in all states in America and in most countries throughout Europe, our research has revealed that it's a surprisingly common strategy of human mating.[12] It emerged as an issue with astonishing frequency in our study of homicidal ideation about ex-mates.

Stalking is an unusual crime in that it is legally defined by the psychological impact it has on the victim. It consists of repeated forms of behavior—such as following, phoning, e-mailing, leaving gifts, threatening, or dropping by work—that *evoke fear* in the victim.[13] If these behaviors do not evoke fear, they do not legally qualify as stalking. Many of the behaviors are ordinary tactics of courtship, such as sending flowers, leaving notes, phoning, dropping by. If the overtures are welcome, it's courtship. If they are unwelcome and elicit alarm, they qualify as stalking.

The strange thing about stalking is that it sometimes works. Consider the following case from our study.

CASE #3998, *female, age 21. Stalker, ex-boyfriend. I broke up with him and he couldn't handle it. He felt like he owned me or con-*

trolled me and when I made decisions such as this [breaking up with him], he would just snap. I could not date anyone because he would get so mad and he would try to fight that other guy.

In this case, the woman reported that her ex-boyfriend would show up and threaten to beat up every man that she dated. All men withdrew, telling her that they really liked her but she should give them a call once she got rid of her stalker. After six months, she started dating her ex-boyfriend again, because she said that there were no other men around—he had scared them all away! In our studies of stalking, we found that 15 percent of victims of stalkers ended up dating their stalkers, and 6 percent ended up having sex with their stalkers.[14]

Stalking as a male mating strategy has a diabolically double-edged effectiveness. First, it inflicts costs on any man who approaches his ex-partner, often making it prohibitively dangerous to go out with her. Men sometimes fear ex-boyfriends precisely because they apprehend the level of rage and possessiveness stalkers feel about "their" romantic partners, even in the aftermath of a breakup. In the face of this kind of uncertainty, people tend to avoid the risk-prone options.[15] They often stop their romantic overtures, which is precisely the stalker's intended effect.

Second, stalking inflicts costs on the ex for any attempts to get romantically involved with others. The stalker makes it seem hazardous to be seen with anyone who remotely conveys romantic interest. Victims of stalkers often respond by backing off, curtailing their social lives, and terminating their romantic lives. Stalking ex-mates, in short, drives a wedge that prevents them from remating. The severe damage that stalkers inflict on their ex-mates creates a profound adaptive problem for the victims. Some women try to reason with their exes, a notoriously ineffective tactic.[16] Some try to avoid their exes by changing phone numbers, relocating, or altering their normal routines. In a few cases, victims of ex-mate stalkers are forced to change their names and move to a new city or country. So severe is the disruption to the victim's psychology and physical health, work productivity, and romantic life that some begin contemplating murder, as in the case below.

CASE #P2372, *female, age 20. Victim, male, age 23.* [Who do you think about killing?] *My ex-boyfriend.* [How did you know this person?] *We met through a mutual friend.* [What caused you to want to kill him?] *I met him in April and we dated through the summer. I broke up with him because he wanted to get married and I didn't. I thought things were going too fast. I had just moved into a new apartment with my friend at the beginning of the summer. So I couldn't bail out, nor did I want to. So, after I broke up with him, he moved into my apartment complex—just two doors down! After this, he began stalking me. He would watch my apartment and go outside EVERY TIME my roommate or I would leave. He left notes on my car and door. He would stand in his upstairs window at night and watch for me to drive up. Then he would come outside and try to talk to me. I started to hate him because he had made me a prisoner in my own home.*

[How would you kill?] *It started out as a dream. I dreamt that he came outside one night when I drove up, and tried to talk to me. I told him to leave me alone because I didn't want to talk to him anymore. And he wouldn't leave. He wouldn't even let me get out of the car. And I just couldn't take it anymore. I have no idea where I got it, but I had a gun in my backpack. I pulled it out and shot him. First in the stomach. And when he stumbled backwards, I shot him three more times. All in the torso area. I woke up when he hit the ground. After this, I thought about it two more times.*

[What prevented you from killing him?] *I am a Christian person. It took me a very long time to get past the hatred I felt for him. Even though I thought of it, I don't think I could actually kill a person unless they were about to inflict physical harm upon me, a family member or a friend.* [What could have pushed you over the edge to kill?] *Same as above.*

This woman is not alone in her contemplation of murdering a stalking ex.

CASE #P22, *female, age 20.* [Who do you think about killing?] *My ex-boyfriend.* [What caused you to want to kill him?] *I dated him for*

2½ years. He was jealous and obsessive and the longer we were together the worse he got. When I broke up with him, he went crazy. He acted like he was going to kill himself and anyone who ever came in contact with me. <u>*Even three years after we broke up, he still stalked me and the guys I dated.*</u> [What method did you think about using to kill him?] *I never thought about how I would do it, I just wanted him out of my life. I didn't really want to hurt him. So, probably poison or for him an accidental car wreck would have been the most realistic.* [What prevented you from killing him?] *I didn't want to hurt him. I'd rather he had gone to prison.* [What could have pushed you over the edge to kill him?] *If he would have actually hurt someone who was close to me, because he did threaten even my best friends. The odd thing is that he never threatened to kill or hurt me.*

The woman above had not even thought deeply about a method for murder. She clearly just wanted her ex to disappear. Some women, however, have more vivid homicidal ideation, working through detailed scenarios of how they would kill.

CASE #P5, *female, age 24.* [Who do you think about killing?] *Ex-boyfriend. We started dating and became boyfriend and girlfriend. Slowly I started to find out that he had been lying to me about different situations and he had stole from me. I finally broke up with him. He would not stop calling me. He would do things like keep in touch with my cousins, brother and sister so he could keep tabs on me. He had found out that I was dating someone else and started spreading ugly rumors. He would anonymously call me, and came by my job. This went on 3 years after I broke up with him.*

[What method did you think about using to kill him?] *I figured one day I would catch him coming to my job, and have someone follow him from my job and do a drive-by, since I know some people who are known for doing such things as drive-bys. The one thought I harped on was simply asking my cousins, since he constantly calls and talks usually with them. They got information on where he lives and works. Then I would scope him out and see what he does from day to day. Then when I realize there is a time he is by himself, come to him and act like I want him back, then lure him out of town and shoot him, dump the body.*

[What prevented you from killing him?] *My conscience for the most part. Aside from that, if they ever found the body I would probably easily become a suspect because people know I can't stand him up to this day.* [What could have pushed you over the edge?] *If he would have continued to be overly aggressive in pursuing me after we broke up. At first he was but then he mellowed out but he continued to pursue me.*

Although suffering through three years of stalking may seem like a lot, that length of time is merely a year over average: stalking by ex-mates can last as little as a few days or as long as a decade, and the average, according to our studies, is twenty-four months.[17]

Women have good reason to fear ex-mates who stalk. Among women killed by a partner they have separated from, a full 88 percent had been stalked prior to being killed. In one of our interviews with policemen, an officer recounted arresting a man who had stalked his girlfriend for eighteen months. The man said he was obsessed with his ex and hated her dating. He finally shot her with a handgun. "She was my girl and I won't let anyone else have her," he told the arresting officer. Although most stalkers do not kill their victims, most mate-killing men do stalk their victims. Stalking is one sign of danger that women should not ignore.

RAPISTS AS SEXUAL PREDATORS

There are other sexual predators who inflict great costs on women—male friends, acquaintances, dates, and strangers who turn into rapists. Indeed, a major trigger of homicidal fantasies for women, though much less frequently translated into actual murders, is having been raped. Many of those fantasies were recurrent and quite violent, vivid evidence of the tremendous damage rapists inflict on women. The stunning prevalence of sexual abuse of women was attested to in vivid terms in our study of homicidal fantasies in which the long-term and haunting effects of these attacks were made painfully clear.

CASE #86, *female, age 18.* [Who did you think about killing?] *A rapist. I met him at a fraternity party. It was the last day of finals of the fall semester. My girlfriends and I went to our guy friend's dorm to drink and party, since finals were over. I knew all of the guys and liked to hang out with all of them. About an hour later, the guy that I had thoughts of killing walked in and I had a weird instinctive uneasy feeling about him. Don't ask me why but I did. Anyway, as the night went on I had a couple of beers, I would say about three. I know my drinking limit and three beers is definitely not enough to make me black out. The attempted rapist had given me a drink which I think might have been drugged because about 30 minutes later after having that drink I cannot recall anything. With the amount of alcohol I had I should not have just blacked out, and out of all the times I have been drunk this was the only time that I cannot remember anything from that night.*

I woke up the next morning completely topless next to a guy I knew that was his fraternity brother, not him. I asked the friend to take me home immediately and did not ask questions. About two days later a girlfriend of mine called me up and asked me what had happened that night. I said I didn't remember but did wake up topless at another guy's apartment. She told me that the guy who supposedly had sex with me told all of his friends that "he had sex with a virgin" and word got back to my girlfriend and she told me. I was extremely upset not only because of the fact that he said this but also because I was a virgin. What also really bothers me is that I have no idea if this event actually happened or not. The gynecologist said there were no signs of trauma or bruising, but there is never any closure for me because I don't know what went on. I told my father and my father called him. I talked to him but did not press any charges because he moved out of town. I didn't plan out his death or how I would kill him. I just wished he hadn't ever existed. I wanted him dead only in the fact that I didn't want him to do this to other girls. . . . I am very cautious around guys now and my trust is gone in all of them. [What might have pushed you over the edge to actually kill him?] *If he tried to do this again.*

The woman in Case #86 was obviously psychologically devastated enough to describe this as her most vivid homicidal thought. However, the intensity of her homicidal rage is pallid compared with that of most women who have been sexually victimized, as the following case illustrates.

CASE #120: *I met a guy at a party. I was very young (13 yrs) and he was probably about 18. I was very drunk and he took advantage of me at a party even as I said no and demanded that he stop. After- wards I was humiliated and very angry. Many people found out about the situation. I had to go to school with him the following semester and saw him often. It was terrifying and humiliating. I was so angry I always thought of killing him. . . . I would humiliate him and beat him severely. I wanted to beat him to a pulp and make him suffer. Sometimes I would think of shooting him. . . . I had a lot of built up anger. I would have dreams of encounters I would have with him where I would tell him everything I ever wanted to say or would become violent with him and beat him . . . punching, kicking, with a bat, shooting him with a gun. . . .* [What would have pushed you over the edge to actually kill him?] *Probably if he or other people had really tortured me about it, like confronting me about it at school or teasing me about it.*

These are merely two among dozens of cases in our study that attest to the horrible frequency of rape and the enormity of psychological damage it causes. The psychological scars can devastate victims' lives. One woman, age twenty-one, thought about killing her grandfather:

He had been sexually perverted with me, coming on to me, trying to watch me dress, hiding in my room or bathroom, and touching me. I had just moved in with him and my grandmother. I was so terrified, since I was only a 15 year old girl. I felt disgusted with myself. I felt it was somehow my own fault. This continued over a period of more than a year, and I became severely depressed. I lost all ambition and gained 30 pounds to make myself unattractive. Then I totally lost it. The last straw was over an encounter where he wanted me to perform oral sex on him for money. I lost it and told him that if he ever touched me again I'd kill him and go to the police. I didn't care about living anymore. I already felt dead.

The magnitude of psychological devastation that is inflicted on women by rape attests powerfully, I believe, to the underlying female psychology designed to protect their reproductively valuable resources. Women fear rape to an intense degree because rape has been a recurrent threat over human evolutionary history. In fact, the frequency of women's fears of being raped is one of the most striking of the findings to come out of our study of homicidal fantasies. Just as with stalking, women's fears are well founded. Although estimates vary tremendously because of the differing definitions of rape and the tremendous number of rapes that go unreported, an estimated 13 to 25 percent of all women are raped at some point during their lifetimes.[18] Social class is no barrier. In one study of a representative sample of Los Angeles women under the age of forty, an astonishing 22 percent reported that they had been raped or sexually molested.[19]

One cause of women's fears of being raped is the fear of being killed by their attacker. This was a consistent theme in our study. Perhaps the media have contributed to some degree to the perception that rapists kill. Rape-murders are frequently played out in the movies and on TV, and many of the rapes that are reported in the media are cases in which the women were killed. But one of the strange truths about rape is that, in fact, very few rapists kill the women they attack. According to the FBI database *Crime in the United States,* only one woman out of every 1,596 reported rape victims are killed by the rapists.[20] Michael Ghiglieri estimates that if unreported rapes are put into the equation rapists actually kill fewer than one out of ten thousand rape victims in the United States.[21] The actual number of rape-murders, however, is difficult to determine, because in some cases the crime is merely reported and classified as a homicide without any notice of the relevant rape component.[22] Nonetheless, all experts agree that the numbers are extremely low, most likely accounting for fewer than 2 percent of all murders. In most of those cases, the motive for murder was quite clear—to leave no witness to the crime.

One perfect example occurred in our study of Michigan murderers. A twenty-seven-year-old man broke into his next-door neighbor's house with the goal of simple robbery. While robbing the house, he heard noises from the other room. He became quite startled, but was relieved to find that it was only the neighbor's wife, who he'd been attracted to for some time. Things escalated. On impulse, he raped her. And then, realizing what he'd done, he killed her to prevent being caught. What started out as a simple robbery turned into a rape-murder.

Another paradox about women's fears of rape that we found in our study is that the vast majority of women expressed the fear of being raped by a stranger. Yet many more rapes are committed by men that women know—stepfathers, sisters' boyfriends, acquaintances, and dates—than by total strangers. Interestingly, only 9 percent of the women in our study who expressed a fear of being raped and murdered worried that this would happen at the hands of someone they knew. A full 91 percent focused on strangers.

There are at least two plausible explanations for women's heightened sense of being in danger of murder by a stranger rapist. First, it is probable that stranger rape-murders were more prevalent in our evolutionary past than they are today. For thousands of years, rape of women by conquering warriors was the norm. Over the past century alone, thousands of women have been raped and killed in warfare contexts, as documented amply in Susan Brownmiller's classic *Against Our Will,* and more recently in *The Rape of Nanking,* which documented the rapes and murders of Chinese women by invading Japanese men during World War II, and *Rape Warfare,* which documented the rapes and murders of women in Bosnia-Herzegovina and Croatia during the 1992–95 wars.[23]

If being raped and then killed by strangers was a recurrent feature of women's evolutionary past, then women's fears of rape-murder may reflect an evolved defense mechanism designed to avoid strangers. This defense mechanism, adaptive in the past, has been transplanted into the modern environment. In the context of large-city living and geographical mobility, the modern world creates daily encounters with strangers of a volume and at a frequency unprecedented in the human past. As a consequence, women's anti–rape-murder defenses, so perfectly adaptive in the past, are somewhat hyperactivated in the modern world.

A second possible evolutionary explanation is that women's fears of rape-murder by strangers reveal what is called an "adaptive bias."[24] Recall that evolution favors avoiding the most costly of possible errors. In this case, there are two ways to err. A woman can err in believing that a stranger does not have designs to rape and murder her when he actually does. In that case, she is at grave risk of death. Or she can err by overattributing rape-murder intent to strangers, when in fact for many of them no such intent exists. Clearly, the first kind of error is vastly more costly. The second error, what I refer to as "adaptive paranoid bias," only results in the relatively trivial costs of avoiding strangers in lots of instances when it's unnecessary to do so. Even if women are wrong in attributing a rape-murder intention to strangers 999 times out of a thousand, evolution will favor the adaptive paranoid bias if it motivates women to avoid strangers and hence save their own lives in the one out of a thousand instances in which their lives truly are in danger.

These two explanations are not, of course, incompatible. Both factors may well be at play. Women may have evolved an adaptive bias to overinfer the rape-murder intentions of strange men, *and* this defense gets hyperactivated in the modern world, when women encounter many more strange men than they ever did in the past.

When uncertain about the intentions of an attacker, women sometimes assume the worst possible outcome from being attacked—murder. Unfortunately, some men exploit this adaptive bias in women's thinking order to facilitate the act of rape. They do this through convincing threats to kill a woman if she doesn't go along with him and then promising to let her live if she does. Indeed, many rape victims believe that they will be killed if they don't go along with the demands of the rapist. Ironically, this runs counter to the evidence on rape. Most rapists give up on attempting a rape without harming the victim if she puts up a huge fight. However, even if murder occurred in only a small percentage of the cases in which women resisted being raped over our evolutionary history, selection could have shaped women's antihomicide defenses to opt for the lesser of two evils in a lose-lose situation—to choose being raped over being murdered.

The rage that so many women feel after being raped comes through loud and clear in this quote from one of our interviews: "I was date raped at a party. I was a virgin. I have been affected so much. He actually came to my college last year, stayed with a guy two doors down in the dorm, and started saying bad stuff about me. . . . I thought about leading him up to a bed, pretending like I was going to have sex with him, and then shooting him in the balls."

Rape is the source of such rage not only for the women who have been attacked, but also for their mates, family members, and both male friends and girlfriends. We found that the people close to a rape victim also often report fantasies of killing the rapist.

One man who took part in our study wanted to kill his roommate and longtime friend because the "friend" tried to molest his girlfriend while she was asleep. Another wanted to kill the uncle of his ex-girlfriend, since she had been sexually abused by him earlier in life on several occasions, resulting in her attempting suicide. He wanted to "shoot him in the genitals," and said that he would have gone through with it if the uncle had abused her in front of his own eyes.

Here is an excerpt from the interview with a man contemplating killing someone who raped his female friend:

CASE #P2207, *male, age 18.* [Who do you think about killing?] *A 25 year old ex–army guy who was also a student. He raped a friend of mine. My girlfriend called me and told me in detail how our mutual friend had just been raped. Neither my friend nor the rapist, were under the influence of any substances. She was just walking him home when he raped her. Then he just drove her home as if nothing had happened.* [How did you envision killing him?] *I went to his apartment with some friends. We beat the shit out of him. Then we tied him up and waited for him to regain consciousness. When he did come to, I asked him why he thought what he did was okay. I shot him in his left knee. I asked him how he liked being treated as if he wasn't a person. I shot him in his right knee. I told him to think about what he had done and pray to his God for forgiveness. Finally, I shot him twice in the stomach and left him to die.* [What prevented you from killing him?] *1. My friend is filing a lawsuit against him anyway. If I killed him it would only make things harder on her. 2. He has a family somewhere who is innocent, I have no right to take him from them. 3. I am hoping he gets arrested and goes to prison so he can experience first hand how much he enjoys rape when he is on the receiving end.*

Another man, age twenty-one, fantasized about killing a man who had raped his female friend:

He gave her rohypnol, a date-rape drug, and then called her and bragged about it to her and his friends. I thought about pinning him on the ground as I put my knee on his throat, crushing his throat. My friend asked me not to hurt him, so I promised her I wouldn't. If he went unpunished he would probably rape again and by doing so would have pushed me over the edge to kill him.

Women friends of rape victims also experience vivid thoughts of killing sexual predators who prey on their female friends:

CASE #227, *female, age 23.* [Who did you think about killing?] *My best friend's father. Actually, he wasn't her real father, but he was her step-father. He molested my best friend for years. I saw him touch her, and it made me very angry. He looked at me the same way that*

he looked at her, and I remember thinking that he would do it to me
if I didn't kill him. This started when I was in 7th grade, my best
friend told me that her step-father had made her have sex with him
since she was 8 years old, and that she couldn't tell her mom,
because she thought that he would be mad. We slept with a knife
every night from then on when we would have sleepovers. I just
hoped and prayed that we could kill him. [How did you think about
killing him?] *He would come in during the night, and he would try*
to get her to go with him, but I would jump up out of the bed and
stab him and then she would get up and help me. [What would have
pushed you over the edge to actually kill him?] *If he had ever come*
into that room in the middle of the night, I think I would have
stabbed him out of fright more than anything else.

Several important themes emerge from this woman's homicidal fantasy.
First, she took actual steps to avoid becoming a victim of her best friend's
father—she obtained a knife and slept with it when she felt at risk. Second,
the psychological scars of her friend's victimization and her terror of
becoming a victim herself remain with her in adulthood. Third, stepfathers
are far more likely to molest and rape their stepdaughters than are men
who are the actual biological fathers of their daughters.[25] Although most
stepfathers, of course, do not sexually molest their stepdaughters, having a
stepfather in the home nonetheless increases the risk tenfold.

Although it is intuitively obvious to most people that sexual predators
inflict severe damage on rape victims, the reasons it is such a devastating
kind of attack for those who are not killed, and is considered one of the
great violations of our social rules, are worth closer examination. From an
evolutionary perspective, the costs of rape are enormous. The core element
of women's mating strategies is the free exercise of choice of a mating partner. Recall that, because women invest so heavily in children, and can bear
only a small number in their lifetimes, evolution has crafted a female psychology that puts great stock in the process of choosing a high quality
mate. The repertoire of women's choice criteria includes an elaborate menu

of mate preferences, close scrutiny over extended time of the qualities of potential candidates, and a deep evaluation of love and commitment.

In one brutal moment, a rapist shatters the sophisticated strategies women have evolved to select, attract, and retain precisely the right mate. A raped woman risks an unwanted and untimely pregnancy with a man she has not chosen—a man who imposes himself against her will, and a man who is almost invariably lower in mate value than she desires.

To compound the circumvention of female choice, a raped woman risks being blamed, punished, or abandoned by her regular mate, friends, and even family. Some may erroneously suspect that she was complicit, that the forced sex might somehow have been consensual, or that she had done something to bring the rape on herself. Indeed, many men whose partners have been raped express the feeling that they are now left with "damaged goods." They report that they cannot bear the thought of remaining with a woman who has been sexually violated by another man. According to one study, more than 80 percent of couples in which the woman was raped during their relationship end up breaking up.[26]

When we fully comprehend the staggering costs a sexual predator inflicts on his victim, her partners, and her kin—the malevolent interference with women's evolved strategy of exercising mate choice, the damage to her social reputation, the tarnishing of her mate value, the disruption and erosion of her mateship, the shunning by her kin—we can appreciate that evolution would fashion a powerful psychology to motivate killing as one solution to the complex adaptive problems posed by rape. Over the long span of human evolutionary history, women, their kin, and their mates had to defend against the manifold costs of sexual victimization on their own. In our evolutionary past, there were no laws, police, judges, juries, or jails. Justice remained in the hands of the victims, their partners, their friends, and their kin.

It would be shocking if evolution had *not* equipped women with defenses and counterstrategies to avoid incurring the costs of sexual predation, and to manage the costs in its aftermath. The pervasive fear of being raped is one of these defenses. Another is choosing "special friends"—that is, opposite-sex friends who care enough about a woman to protect and defend her, or whose presence deters potential rapists. A third defense women use is to surround themselves with kin who act as deterrents. A fourth is choosing men as mates who essentially act as "bodyguards," protecting them against sexually aggressive men.[27] Resorting to homicide is, of course, also one of these evolved defenses.

Homicidal psychology—thoughts about killing, threats of killing, and the actual killing of sexual predators—serves several key adaptive functions for women. First, such mechanisms motivate women to avoid circumstances in which they are at risk of rape. Second, they prompt women to arm themselves with weapons, as in the case of the girl who slept with a knife under her pillow when sleeping over at her friend's house. Third, they motivate women to enlist the aid of friends and family. Fourth, threats of death sometimes succeed in warding off a sexual predator, as in the case of the grandfather who finally stopped molesting his teenage granddaughter when she threatened to kill him. Fifth, killing rapists terminates ongoing sexual victimization. Sixth, it sends a strong signal to other males that the woman is *not* sexually exploitable and will not tolerate sexual trespass without violent retribution. Seventh, in principle, it helps to preserve her desirability in the mating market.

As with most instances of homicidal fantasies, few thoughts are translated into deeds. Most people work through cost-benefit calculations, figure out alternative means of solving the problem, and decide that the costs of killing are too high. Thoughts of murdering sexual predators, however, would not be so prevalent if women weren't prepared to follow through on them sometimes.

An illustrative case comes from our study of Michigan murders. Clarice,* age twenty-four, with a high-school degree, was hanging out with a friend named Mark* one evening in her apartment. At one point, Mark asked her for sex. She agreed at first. They lay on the couch, with him between her legs: "He was rubbing his penis against my vagina trying to get an erection. He was taking a long time. I was getting tired, and he was getting heavy, and it was irritating my vagina. So I asked him to stop." He refused, saying, "You are going to lay here and give me this pussy." She tried to push him off again, but he pinned her down. "I was trying to get him off me and get away from him. I finally pushed him off and jumped up. I was asking him, 'Mark, why are you doing this?' In the past, he would always stop when I asked him to stop. He'd say 'damn' or get upset but this night he did not want to stop. I don't know why, it just scared me. I saw a knife on the counter. He grabbed me and we started to wrestle. I turned around and started stabbing him. When I poked him I had to poke him a couple of times because he was still fighting and the more he was fighting the more I was poking him. He fell to the floor, and finally said 'I can't take it no more.' That's when I stopped." An autopsy revealed eleven stab wounds. According to the forensic examiner, Clarice was considered average in intelligence, did not suffer from any disorder of thought or mood at the time of the alleged offense, and had the capacity to distinguish right from wrong. She did not meet the criteria for the diminished capacity of legal insanity. She used enough force to prevent being raped, and ended up killing a sexual predator.

Clarice is not alone in using murder to stop a rapist. In July 2002, in the city of Albuquerque, New Mexico, a woman who wishes to go by the pseudonym of "Mira" awoke at 1:30 A.M. to find a man straddled on top of her. He had a flashlight focused on her face and a gun pointed at her chest. The man, Michael Magirl, fifty-one years old, had done this before. Indeed, he was a convicted sexual predator, having been convicted eighteen years earlier of criminal sexual penetration. He's listed on the New Mexico Web site of convicted sex offenders. This time, he preyed on a woman who showed great bravery. Mira was a single mom around thirty years old. She later said that she "acted only on instinct, and was driven by the desire to survive."[28] Mira thrust the gun away from her chest, but he threatened her life: "Do you want to die?"[29] Something in her mind snapped, and she later described her condition then as "a dream state." She suddenly lunged and managed to wrestle the .38-caliber gun from her assailant, push him onto the floor, and fire three shots into his prone body. Two met their mark, embedding themselves in his chest. Not knowing if he was dead or alive, she ripped the pantyhose mask from his face so she could later ID him, ran to a neighbor's house, and called the police. By the time the cops arrived, Magirl was dead. Mira killed to prevent being raped, and permanently stopped a serial sexual predator. The killing was judged to be self-defense, and Mira was not charged with a crime.

On November 18, 1998, a man wearing gloves and a mask, hunting knife in hand, broke into an apartment housing a University of North Carolina teenage college student.[30] His name was Adrian Cathey, and he had done this before. He prodded her with his hunting knife to awaken her, held a knife to her neck, and then prepared to rape her. Thinking quickly as he fumbled with his pants, she reached into her nightstand drawer and silently slipped a pistol into her hand. Her aim was true, and soon Adrian Cathey lay dead in a pool of his own blood. Subsequent DNA tests revealed that he was a sexual predator who had been linked with violent sexual assaults on four other students.

Farther south, in Pasco County, Florida, Maria Pittaras's story unfolded in a similar fashion. Maria awoke late one night in her own home to find a stranger sitting astride her body, his face concealed beneath a black mask. While he held a knife to her throat, she managed to pull a gun from her nightstand and shoot Robert Metz to death. The emergency center recorded her terrified call: "I just shot a man. A man was just in my house and tried raping me. . . ."[31] Police found Metz's inert body, a bullet hole in his neck, the knife still clenched in his fist.

In all of these cases, the young women could be considered fortunate, yet they all have to live with the terrible memory of their violent defensive acts. Killing their assailants prevented them from being raped, possibly saved their lives, and they were not charged with a crime. Véronique Akobe, a twenty-three-year-old immigrant from the Ivory Coast working in Nice, France, was not so lucky.[32] Ms. Akobe worked as an underpaid maid, putting up with small wages because she lacked working papers. Her wealthy boss, sixty-three-year-old Georges Scharr, and his son, twenty-two-year-old Thierry Scharr, raped her repeatedly. Véronique described them as holding her by the neck and cupping a hand over her mouth to prevent her from screaming. As one held her down, the other would rape or sodomize her. Father and son took turns. Her options were limited. After the third brutal attack, she decided to take action. She secured a knife and stabbed both father and son, wounding one and killing the other. Medical examination of Véronique revealed lesions consistent with forced anal sex. She told others: "They killed something in me, something of my true personality. I killed to wash my honor."[33] Without funds for a lawyer, she was represented by a court-appointed attorney who failed to base her defense on the repeated acts of rape that had been committed against her. Véronique Akobe was sentenced to twenty years in prison. After serving over nine years, she was officially pardoned.

It may seem unconventional to consider physically abusive boyfriends, sexually abusive husbands, stalkers, and rapists in a chapter entitled "Sexual Predators." But they are all tied together with a common thread—the use of violence to gain or maintain sexual access to a woman. Men use physical abuse to control and coerce their partners, preventing them from leaving, and thereby maintaining exclusive access to their sexual resources. Men who rape their wives use ruthless aggression to force them into unwanted and unconsenting sex. Stalkers, the spurned lovers who refuse to give up, relentlessly pursue their female victims in an effort to interfere with their former partner's new romances and regain the sexual access they once had. Rapists, whether strangers, acquaintances, dates, or even husbands, hunt their victims and brutally force themselves on women whose lives are forever changed.

Although many of the women who kill do so to defend themselves against men who turn into sexual predators, they may kill for other reasons as well, which we will explore along the way in subsequent chapters. One other kind occurs in the case of mate poachers—someone stealing away a romantic partner—which, as we will see in the next chapter, is a vexing problem looming over the evolutionary competition of the mating game.

Six

MATE POACHERS

—◆—

"Give me that man that is not passion's slave."

—WILLIAM SHAKESPEARE, *Hamlet*

ONE OF THE MOST terrifying displays of homicidal psychology I've personally witnessed happened at a friend's home. It occurred during a holiday. A group of friends and family were all staying at the friend's home for a long weekend of eating, drinking, talking, hugging, and having an all-around good time. Among the guests was a recently married couple, Amber* and Tony.* At one point, one of my friends, a tall, extroverted man named Richard,* put his arm around Amber and gave her a big hug. Since we were all being physically affectionate, no one thought twice about it. Except Tony. Half an hour passed, and a few of us migrated to the kitchen. I sensed that something was wrong, because Tony had grown suddenly silent. His eyes had become coal-black. Then he blurted out, "I've got to do something about Richard." I asked him what he meant. "I feel like taking a screwdriver and ramming it into his neck!" He was deadly serious. I took him to one of the back rooms to talk in private. As I tried to calm him down, he explained that he "knew" that Richard was coming on to Amber. He didn't like Richard touching his wife. I asked him if he wanted me to talk to Richard about it, which I did. Was Richard's hug of Amber an innocent gesture of friendly affection, or was he really trying to poach on Tony's mate? No one knew. By then word had spread among the group about Tony and his alarming desire to stab Richard with a screwdriver. Everyone's anti-homicide defenses were on hyperalert.

When Tony returned to the kitchen, he picked up a pair of scissors and began turning them over and over in his hands. Everyone eyed him nervously. Richard went outside for a smoke, people gradually dispersed, and the tension receded. But that night Richard and everyone else in the house made sure that their bedroom doors were locked tight. Everyone knew that Tony was a peaceful man, one who had never before shown any signs of violence. Now no one was quite sure what Tony would do. The next morning, everyone left. Fortunately, a crisis was averted and no violence occurred. But I realized that I had witnessed the frightening sight of a homicidal circuit switched on, triggered by the threat of mate poaching.

The earliest written record of mate poaching comes from the Bible, the account of King David and the alluring beauty Bathsheba. One day King David spied the stunning Bathsheba bathing on the roof of a neighboring house. She happened to be married to another man, named Uriah, but David was not deterred; his being king certainly didn't hurt. He succeeded in seducing and impregnating Bathsheba, and then he devised an ingenious solution to oust his sexual rival permanently. He ordered Uriah to the battle-front, and then commanded his troops to retreat, exposing Uriah to mortal danger. With Uriah safely in his grave, King David married Bathsheba, a union that bore the fruit of four children.

The poaching of another's lover is one of the ages-old strategies for getting the person you most want, and one that is both unnervingly effective and fraught with danger. The tactic has been bred into us through eons of evolution, and it pervades the animal world.

Among the elephant seals living off the coast of northern California, males compete for access to a harem of females. The fights are horribly violent, with rival males maiming and killing one another with their vicious tusks until one wins the position of alpha male, who has almost exclusive mating access to all of the females. The payoff is huge. Just 5 percent of the males secure 85 percent of all copulations within the harem. But maintaining this alpha status is costly. Defeated males who live through the battle continue to attempt sneak copulations with the females, and sometimes succeed. The reigning male must guard the harem with great vigilance and furious anger. Doing so takes such a toll that few elephant seals can maintain their position for more than a season or two.

Mate poaching is even common in the insect world, incredibly common. In fact, it's so pervasive that males have evolved a dazzling array of defenses to prevent it.[1] They will sometimes physically remove their mates from areas containing potential mate poachers. Others will produce signals that conceal or counteract the attractant signals emitted by their mates. Among crickets and katydids, males initially use noisy chatter to attract a female, but once they succeed in getting her attention, they switch to soft courtship chatter. Some insects take an approach more like that of the elephant seals. Male bark beetles, for example, will claim a territory and defend their patch vigorously against any intrusion by an alien male.

For anyone who has found his or her true love or "great catch," mate poaching remains a real threat. The most desirable mates are always in short supply compared with the large numbers of people who would like to be mated with them. People simply gravitate most strongly toward the handsome, the beautiful, the prestigious, the glamorous, and the sexy. The highly desirable tend to be removed rapidly from the mating pool. But that does not mean that they can't be lured away again. As many a jealous lover is all too well aware, mate poachers lie lurking, waiting for a lapse in mate guarding, a window of opportunity, a crack in the armor of the relationship.

Mate poaching is a disturbingly prevalent problem in our lives.[2] Evolutionary psychologist David Schmitt and I discovered that 60 percent of American men and 53 percent of American women admitted to having attempted to lure someone else's mate into a committed relationship. Although half of these attempts failed, half succeeded. For short-term sexual encounters, sex differences loom large. We found that 60 percent of men and 38 percent of women reported attempting to lure someone into a sexual liaison. Far higher percentages of both sexes report that *others* have attempted to entice *them* into leaving an existing relationship—93 percent of the men and 82 percent of the women for long-term love, and 87 percent of the men and 94 percent of the women for a brief sexual encounter. Lower percentages report someone trying to poach their own mates. This shows that many poachers are quite clever about plying their trade safely away from the prying eyes of unsuspecting victims or perhaps demonstrates that our mates like to keep potential back-up mates secret. Roughly a third of the sample reported that a partner had been taken from them by someone else.

Schmitt found similar patterns in the most massive study of mate poaching ever conducted—16,964 individuals from fifty-three nations from Argentina to Zimbabwe, from Botswana to Tanzania.[3] In South America, for example, 66 percent of men and 50 percent of women reported having attempted to lure someone away from his or her current mate for a long-term relationship. In Middle Eastern countries such as Israel, Turkey, and Lebanon, 67 percent of men and 44 percent of women reported having been lured into a sexual encounter while already in a long-term romantic relationship. The numbers were even higher for men in the pursuit of short-term affairs—70 percent of the men and 38 percent of the women. Peoples inhabiting the East Asian world region of Japan, Korea, and China report the lowest prevalence of mate poaching. But even there, 47 percent of the men and 34 percent of the women reported long-term mate-poaching attempts.

This international study also revealed a profound sex difference in patterns of poaching. Women are far more likely than men to be the targets of short-term mate-poaching attempts; in other words, men make many more attempts to lure women into brief affairs than women do with men. But women are far more successful than men in luring committed mates into casual encounters. The reason is that men are less resistant to having short-term affairs than women are. Men more often seek to have affairs, but when seeking them, women more often succeed. People in cultures all over the world display these sex differences. Men around the globe are more interested in short-term affairs. Interestingly, the situation is quite a bit different for long-term affairs.[4]

The frequency of luring someone who's already mated with the intent of starting a long-term romance is much more equal between the sexes. Worldwide, averaging across the fifty-three nations in Schmitt's study, 81 percent of both sexes report that they have successfully enticed someone away from a relationship and started a long-term relationship of their own with the stolen mate. Even in the Middle East, where, given the strict customs regarding women, one might expect few women to engage in mate poaching, roughly 64 percent of men admit having been successfully poached away from their partners for a committed relationship, as do 54 percent of women. When asked about their *current* relationship, 11.8 percent of men and 8.4 percent of women worldwide report that their partner was initially involved with someone else when they met. And 9.9 percent of men and 13.6 percent of women worldwide report that their current partners poached them from existing relationships. Interestingly, roughly 3 percent were double-poaches, in which both partners were already in committed relationships when they lured each other into their current relationship.

Personality characteristics play an interesting predictive role in who engages in a mate poaching, who is targeted for a poach, and who succumbs to poachers. Those who attempt to poach are typically more extroverted (sociable, gregarious), disagreeable (aggressive, mean-spirited), unconscientious (impulsive, spontaneous), and narcissistic (self-centered, grandiose) than their non–mate-poaching peers. It's the narcissistic party animals you have to watch out for.

Personality also factors into who is targeted for poaching. The objects of poacher's affection are disproportionately people who are extroverted and open to new experiences. Poachers also, predictably, target people who are physically and sexually attractive more than those who are less attractive. Poachers are keenly attuned to their task: those who succumb most readily to the allure of mate poachers do in fact tend to be more extroverted, open, and sexually attractive.

Cultures differ, of course, in the prevalence of mate poaching, but the most potent predictor of differences has little to do with the characteristics of the cultures. It has to do with the practicality of sex ratios—the number of women relative to the number of men in the eligible mating pool. In countries that contain a surplus of women relative to men, such as Croatia, Estonia, Latvia, Lithuania, and Poland, women are far more likely to engage in mate poaching, both for short-term and long-term mating. In cultures that contain a surplus of men relative to women, such as mainland China, Taiwan, Korea, and Japan, women are far less likely to mate-poach. One especially interesting finding from these studies is that, whereas a relative surplus of women increases women's levels of poaching, analogous results were not found for men. In cultures with a relative surplus of men, men report lower levels of mate poaching and lower success rates when they do attempt to poach. I think the explanation for this is that, in cultures with a relative scarcity of women, the men who are fortunate enough to attract mates guard them ferociously and work hard to embody their partner's desires, which makes poaching a less effective strategy.

TACTICS USED BY MATE POACHERS

Mate poachers use an arsenal of shrewd tactics to lure others away from their regular partners.[5] They flirt, provide financial resources, enhance their physical appearance, ply their targets with alcohol, display humor, flatter, show warmth, offer special favors, and exhibit generosity. Male poachers sometimes attempt to dominate a rival in athletic events, will try to subordinate him socially, and will occasionally challenge him to a physical fight. Sometimes mate poachers make it clear that they are offering easy sexual access, or present themselves as "costless sex." Particularly overt methods such as showing up naked in a potential mate's room, or making other frank sexual overtures are far more effective for women than for men: men are generally more receptive to the idea that an affair would be primarily about sex.

One clever tactic is to go out with a targeted mate on a friendly premise, and then turn the opportunity into a romantic encounter, the tried and true *bait-and-switch method*. Poachers insinuate themselves into a couple's life as trusted friends, become emotionally close, and then switch to poaching mode when the opportunity presents itself. Indeed, friends often end up being mating rivals. The principle that's called assortative friendship explains why. We tend to pick friends because they share interests and values, and often share many of the same desirable qualities that we possess. So people have an above-average probability of being attracted to the friends of their mate.

Another common tactic used by poachers is trying to get a couple to break up by driving a wedge into their relationship. One common way of doing this is to imply, or try to prove, that the current mate is cheating. Some poachers take the different tack of derogating the target's current mate, pointing out flaws in the partner or in their relationship, telling a woman, for example, "He doesn't treat you well," or "You're too good for him." Poachers will also sometimes ridicule a rival's physical appearance, or point out that the rival isn't giving the targeted mate what he or she really deserves. Conversely, some try to boost the person's ego in an attempt to increase his or her self-perceptions of desirability, and by implication suggest that shopping around for a better mate might not be such a bad idea. One effective way of convincing a potential mate to switch horses is by more closely embodying the model partner the mate wants, such as by revealing an emotional side that the current mate is lacking.

An especially insidious tactic is to try to set a rival up with someone else for a brief "hookup," thereby demonstrating to the targeted mate that his or her current partner can't be trusted. A clever stealth tactic is merely to wait in the wings for a fissure to open up in the existing relationship, and then make a move when the opportunity arises. The waiting-in-the-wings tactic need not be solely passive. A poacher may change his schedule around to have more time with his target, or will drop by unexpectedly, or call the target about potential "business." Occasionally people hang around in the wings long enough to witness the eventual breakup of the couple. The poacher is right there with a shoulder to cry on.

These tactics, when discovered, give victims of the poachers a motive for murder.

DIFFERENT MOTIVES
FOR MATE POACHING

We explored the reasons that people give for wanting to poach someone else's mate, and the answers conform to the differences between what men and women are looking for in mates, which we've addressed before. Men reported that mate poaching allowed them to "mate with a very good-looking woman" and said they wanted the opportunity of "being with a young and healthy sexual partner." Women, by contrast, were more likely to report that mate poaching was "a good way to obtain a rich relationship partner" and "a powerful and high-status man." One unique benefit of mate poaching that came out of our interviews, which was shared by both women and men, is that of enjoying a pre-approved partner. People infer that someone who has already passed the relationship test must be a "good catch"—hence the often commented-on irony that when you're already in a relationship you seem to be more attractive to people. Evolutionary biologists call this phenomenon "mate copying."

The evolutionary theory of mate selection is also backed up by a study we conducted that looked into which rivals people find most threatening. My colleagues and I conducted a cross-cultural study in which we asked Dutch, Korean, and American people to rank eleven qualities of potential rivals according to which would be most upsetting. The rival characteristics ranged from "having a better sense of humor than you" to "being a more skilled sexual partner than you." Men in all three cultures, more than women, reported that they would experience greater distress when a rival surpassed them on the dimensions of *financial prospects, job prospects,* and *physical strength*. Women in all three cultures, more than men, reported greater distress when a rival had *a more attractive face* or *a more desirable body*.

THE DANGERS OF MATE POACHING

Though mate poaching can be a highly effective means of luring a desired partner, all potential poachers should be aware that this strategy is a risky business. In our study, we found that poachers report quite a long list of "downsides" to having stolen someone away. These ranged from the admonishment of friends and family members, to the person's own feeling of guilt, to damage done to the person's social reputation. Though plenty of people engage in poaching, they don't hesitate to frown on the behavior when others do it. Two of the costs of poaching are especially interesting, in that they are examples of "revenge effects," ironic, unintended consequences.

The first is increased anxiety about how faithful the poached mate will be. After all, if you've succeeded in luring someone away from a committed relationship, that person has proved to be susceptible to advances. Who knows better than a successful poacher what a threat poaching is to a relationship?

The second of these revenge effects is where murder comes in. Sometimes the partner whose mate has been poached becomes violent, a danger dreaded more by men than by women. In our study, many men worried that the woman's ex might "go psycho," and many expressed the distinct fear that the jilted mate might try to kill them. One vivid example comes from a story reported by a man I'll call Martin,* who, after a few months of escalating flirtation, managed successfully to talk a woman I'll call Nicole* into leaving her husband. She moved out of the marriage home and into a duplex apartment by herself.

After a few days, Martin called Nicole, and she invited him over for dinner. After dessert, they wound up in bed, having passionate sex. He stayed the night. At six o'clock in the morning, they were awakened by the roar of a motorcycle pulling up outside. It was her husband. Martin realized with horror that his car, which he knew the husband would recognize, was parked just outside. A switch flipped in Martin's brain, and he went into an overwhelming panic about being killed. He frantically headed to the back of the apartment to try to make an escape, but there was no exit. The front door was the only way in and out of the duplex.

The husband began banging the door furiously. Nicole slipped out the door, locking it behind her—and of course also locking Martin in—and managed to calm her husband down and convince him to leave. That was Martin's last sexual encounter with Nicole, and he was deeply impressed by the intense fear of death he had experienced. That fear, as we found in our studies of murder, was well founded.

An interesting question provoked by the fact that poaching is such a prevalent and successful strategy for finding a mate is why, then, it is so frowned on socially, and why it provokes such violent reactions. If your mate has been lured away, why would you still want to be with that person anyway? The answer can be traced back to the unsentimental nature of evolved mating strategies.

Reproductive costs can be astonishingly steep for those who fail to retain a mate.[6] For men, a single failure at mate guarding can result in genetic cuckoldry—when a man's wife becomes successfully inseminated by a rival man's sperm. As we discussed earlier, in addition to the direct loss of opportunity for reproduction, the husband risks investing years or decades of his own effort in a rival's child in the mistaken belief that the child is his own. To compound these reproductive losses, his wife's maternal efforts now benefit his rival's child rather than his own. If the lapse becomes public, the cuckolded man risks damage to his social reputation, which could decrease his mate value, cause his status to plummet, and increase his future vulnerability to other mate poachers. Finally, the cuckolded man suffers opportunity costs—matings that he could have pursued as alternatives had he not engaged in this particular mateship.

Failure to defend against mate poachers can also result in the permanent defection of a man's partner. If a man's partner leaves him for a rival male, he loses access entirely to her future reproductive value. He loses whatever maternal efforts she would have invested in his future children. He risks losing access to social alliances that she brought to the mateship. And she carries with her personal information about his habits, strengths, weaknesses, and vulnerabilities—information that could be exploited to advantage by a competitor with whom she shares the information.[7]

Women too suffer reproductive costs if they fail to fend off poachers. A single lapse may be less costly to women than to men, since women do not risk genetic cuckoldry, as men do. As we've seen, internal fertilization guarantees the woman that she is the mother of her children, regardless of her partner's sexual infidelities. Nonetheless, we know that men channel resources to women with whom they have sex, so women who fail to fend off poachers risk the loss of those resources. Like men, women suffer an increased risk of contracting a sexually transmitted disease from their husbands' mistresses. If a woman's partner leaves the relationship, she risks a total loss of his resources, all of which can get redirected away from her and her children and toward his new mate and her children. Although the damage to her reputation may not be as heavy as the corresponding damage to a cuckolded man's reputation, it can be damaged nonetheless. People naturally conclude that the deserted partner probably has some hidden defect or is lower in desirability than surface appearances seem. As we will see, reputations destroyed and mate value damaged furnish powerful motives for murder.

So, although it may sometimes be rational to let a mate who has strayed simply go with good riddance, evolution has furnished us with powerful mate-guarding mechanisms that function to try to make a mate stay, or at the least to prevent anyone else from being with the one we love.

MATE POACHERS BEWARE

These substantial evolutionary costs explain the strategies we've developed for mate guarding. Like grasshoppers, crickets, katydids, elephant seals, and chimpanzees, humans have evolved many methods for fending off mate poachers. In my first research study to identify these defenses, I discovered nineteen different tactics of mate guarding, a strategy used to fend off poachers and prevent a mate from straying, that ranged from vigilance to violence.[8] Examples of *vigilance* include calling her at unexpected times to see who she was with, having her friends check up on him, dropping by unexpectedly to see what she was doing, not letting him out of her sight at a party. Examples of *violence* include: hitting the guy who made a pass at her, slapping the woman who made a pass at her partner, threatening his partner, and getting his friends to beat up the guy who was interested in her.

Other tactics of mate guarding include the *concealment of a mate* (e.g., not taking her to the party when other males will be present), *monopolization of a mate's time* (e.g., spending all his free time with her so that she cannot meet anyone else), *verbal threats* (e.g., threatening to break up with him if he ever cheats on her), *derogation of competitors* (e.g., pointing out to her the other guy's flaws), *resource display* (e.g., buying her an expensive gift), *appearance enhancement* (e.g., making himself "extra attractive" for her), *sexual inducement* (e.g., performing sexual favors to keep him around), *physical signals of possession* (e.g., holding her hand when other guys are around), and *possessive ornamentation* (e.g., asking him to wear a ring signifying that he is taken).

Men and women differ in how frequently they perform these mate-guarding tactics.[9] Men are more likely than women to attempt to conceal their mates, use possessive markings (e.g., asking her to wear his jacket), display resources, threaten rivals, and use physical violence toward rivals as tactics of mate guarding. Women are more likely than men to enhance their physical appearance and flirt with other men as tactics of mate guarding.

Another critical issue centers on predicting the intensity of effort a person allocates to guarding a mate and fending off poachers. It is the intensity of effort that can lead to a murderous end. Mate guarding should theoretically increase in intensity to the degree that one is mated to a valuable partner, to avoid a large reproductive loss. It should also increase when interested rivals appear on the scene. One of the troubling ironies of the mating market is that, other things being equal, the higher the mate value of one's partner, the more rivals will attempt to poach.

Our study of 107 newlywed married couples explored predictors of the intensity of effort a person allocated to mate guarding.[10] Men married to young and physically attractive women, those high in reproductive value, mate-guarded them most intensely. These men were more likely than other men to conceal their mates, display emotional outbursts at the slightest signals of infidelity, and threaten other men with violence. Examples of the specific actions these men performed include:

- Refusing to take her to the party where other men were present
- Insisting that she spend all her free time with him
- Yelling at her for talking to another man
- Telling her that he would die if she ever left him
- Derogating the other man's intelligence
- Staring coldly at the other guy who was looking at her

Just as women's youth and physical attractiveness figure heavily in men's initial mate preferences, they also determine the intensity of effort men devote to holding on to her.

Women's mate guarding, in contrast, was not at all influenced by their husbands' physical appearance or age. It was affected by the husband's income and how determined he was to climb the status hierarchy. Women married to men with abundant resources and men higher on initiative and status striving were more likely than other women to display increased levels of vigilance, express emotional distress at the slightest hint of a partner's wandering eye, put extra effort into enhancing their appearance, and show more submissiveness in the service of holding on to a partner. Specific acts by these mate-guarding women include:

- Staying close by his side when they were at the party
- Threatening to break up if he ever cheated on her
- Making herself "extra attractive" to maintain his interest
- Telling him that she would change to please him
- Asking him to wear a ring to signify that he was taken

Just as women's desire for men who have status and resources influences initial mate selection, these same qualities continue to influence the effort women devote to keeping the men they have attracted and fending off rivals.

The most extreme form of mate-guarding behavior is, of course, murdering a rival, and our study of Michigan murders revealed this as a remarkably pervasive theme. One involved a man of Indian origin named Deepak,* age forty-five, his wife, Indira,* age thirty-nine, and an interloper named Bhadrak* of unknown age. Deepak had been letting Bhadrak stay at his house temporarily, while Bhadrak looked for a place of his own. As weeks stretched into months, Deepak began to grow suspicious of Bhadrak, and eventually came to believe that Bhadrak was trying to take his wife from him. He purchased a shotgun at a local gun store, along with a box of shotgun shells. He later claimed that he made these purchases because he was afraid of Bhadrak. Three weeks later, Deepak brought things to a head by confronting his wife and Bhadrak about their relationship. Bhadrak announced that, indeed, he was in love with Deepak's wife and was going to take her away with him. Bhadrak took Indira by the arm and strode to the car to leave. At that point, Deepak got his shotgun, which he had already loaded three weeks earlier.

He pointed the gun at Bhadrak as he was about to enter the car. Deepak later claimed that he only wanted to scare him. While the gun was pointed at him, however, Bhadrak reached out and knocked the gun to the side. Unfortunately, the gun discharged, injuring Indira. Then Deepak regained control of the gun and took dead aim at his rival. He fired; Bhadrak fell to the ground; but the fight wasn't over. While on the ground, Bhadrak reached up and tried to seize the gun. Deepak fired again, this time delivering the fatal blow. When questioned by the police, Deepak confessed to killing his rival, but claimed that he never meant to shoot his wife. He loved and worshipped her. When asked why he killed his rival, he repeated over and over that Bhadrak was trying to ruin his life by taking his wife.

Another case involved Bobby,* a male, age thirty-seven, who had been married for eight years and had two children. The trouble started when his wife became romantically involved with Randy.* Although he and his wife had been "drifting apart," Bobby did not want a divorce. His wife insisted, citing "irreconcilable differences." According to Bobby, aside from his wife's complaint about his marijuana use, "everything else was fine and then all of a sudden she wanted a divorce." After the divorce, his wife married Randy. Over the next several years, conflicts continued between Bobby and Randy. Randy taunted Bobby when he came to visit his children, threatening to "kick [Bobby's] ass"—a real threat, since Randy had been trained in the martial arts. The final straw came when his kids told him that Randy had been abusing them—slapping them, spanking them so hard they couldn't sit down, ridiculing them, and forcing his stepdaughter to wear tiny tight-fitting dresses that embarrassed her. Attempts to deal with the matter through the courts yielded no positive results.

One day when he dropped his kids off, Randy began to taunt him again: "You might as well give me the [child support] money right now because you're never going to see your kids again." Bobby then thought to himself, "It's either me or him." Some time later, Bobby drove to his rival's house. When Randy opened the door, Bobby said, "I have something for you." Bobby unloaded five rounds of .22-caliber bullets into his body. He told police later: "That guy thinks he can slap my kids around and get away with it. I made police reports and the court wouldn't do anything, so I took care of it myself. I took care of that son-of-a-bitch. He'll never slap my kids around again."

In this case as in so many others, we see the stark logic of evolutionary psychology operating—sexual rivalry and mate poaching, with the final straw being the mate poacher's abuse of his children, the precious carriers of his genetic cargo. Killing was not Bobby's first solution to these adaptive problems. But it proved to be his final solution.

Although their numbers are smaller, women are not exempt from the powerful urge to kill mate poachers. In the early-morning hours of a July day, the burned body of Geneva S.* was found in a field by a jogger. She had been killed quite some time earlier: the body was already in an advanced state of decomposition. Geneva had been reported missing five days earlier by Michael B.* At the time, he told the police that he was worried because his wife, Angelina,* had made threats against Geneva, who was his girlfriend. He told police that he and his wife had argued the previous day about his having a girlfriend on the side. Angelina had even witnessed them having sex once, and had confronted Geneva about it. She later told police that Geneva had flaunted their affair: "Bitch, if you'd take care of your husband you wouldn't have to worry about me doing your husband." The final blow came when Angelina discovered a love letter from Geneva to her husband. Michael B., however, refused to promise that he would break things off with Geneva: he wanted to keep both his wife and his mistress. At the end of the argument, Angelina walked out, saying, "That's OK because I'm gonna get your bitch." He saw her carrying a gun around, and believes that she was stalking his girlfriend. He stated that he believed that his wife had tricked Geneva into getting into her car, and had kidnapped her.

Angelina never confessed to the murder. She acknowledged having *thoughts* of killing Geneva, but insisted that this did not lead her to do so. A witness, however, eventually came forward and confessed that he had helped Angelina dispose of the body. Angelina was found guilty of premeditated murder. Although she put an end to the mate poacher's life, she would have to spend many years behind bars.

In our study of homicidal fantasies, we also recorded many cases of murderous thoughts prompted by the stealing of a mate by a rival, which were often quite violent in nature. Here are several excerpts:

CASE #217, *male. I thought about killing my ex-friend. . . . He had sex with my ex girlfriend and then lied to my face . . . etc. We fought and knives were drawn. . . . He slept with my girlfriend at the time while I was on a trip with the school band in London. Then when I came back, they both lied and then proceeded to date while trying to keep me from finding out. . . . I almost really killed him. . . . A girl ran in front of me and my friends tackled me and took the knife away. . . . I was over the edge. . . . At first I was just gonna talk to him and then he kept provoking me to do something. I said I was done talking and he kept asking me to do what I wanted to. Plus I saw he had put his knife in his hand when he thought I wasn't looking.*

CASE #434, *male. I found out* [about the trespass] *after I realized that I wanted to try to work things out with my girlfriend again, and I found out that this guy had been with my girlfriend, and that he* *was <u>rubbing her ass at a party</u>, and he knew that she had a boy-friend, but he did not care. So when I heard this, I wanted to kill him . . . not with a gun or knife, just beat him to death . . . just punching, kicking . . . throwing, breaking bones.*

CASE #272, *male*. *He hits on my girlfriend and I don't like it. He wouldn't stop when I asked him to. It drove me crazy. I haven't done anything yet. <u>First he hit on her</u>, then he started to talk dirty about her to me. <u>Then one time he grabbed her ass while I was around.</u> Then I thought about killing him.* [How did you think about killing him?] *First I attacked his head with my fist. Then I dropped kicked him in the balls. Then I proceeded to destroy his manhood with my teeth. He then bled to death. . . .* [What prevented you from killing him?] *I'm a civilized person. It is against my morals and religion.*

Although men are clearly the more violent sex when it comes to physical aggression, this does not stop women from having extremely violent fantasies about destroying their rivals, as the following cases show.

CASE #69, *female*. *She stole my boyfriend, was mean to me and my friends. Treated my younger brother badly. . . . I would have buried her up to her neck then run over her head with a lawn mower.*

CASE #119, *female*. *She was calling my boyfriend and asking him to go to her house. When he did, he cheated on me with her. . . . I thought about running her over with my car.*

These fantasies reveal marked sex differences in the sources of rage and motivations to kill. Men tend to focus on the poacher's sexual advances, which are an indicator of the threat of genetic cuckoldry. Women's anger tends to focus on a potential rival's attractiveness and the threat that it poses to the partner's commitment and devotion. To a woman, a rival's *emotional* involvement with her partner is the more galling factor. Whereas men focus almost exclusively on the partner's *sexual* involvement with a rival, women are more profoundly upset by signs of psychological intimacy, which signal the long-term loss of a mate.

The rage women can express about a rival's attractiveness is vividly demonstrated in the one homicidal fantasy we recorded that involved an imaginary rival, the model Kate Moss.

> **CASE #19,** *female. My boyfriend is always telling me how gorgeous he thinks Kate Moss is. Really, she is just a skinny bitch. The method: I thought about taking a wire coat hanger and putting it through her eye to make her brain dead. Then I would hang her skinny body up in my closet and show my boyfriend that she isn't so gorgeous after all.*

How could someone develop such a specific and virulent hatred for someone her boyfriend has never even met? A plausible explanation is that, in ancient, ancestral environments, any person one's mate developed a crush on would have been a real potential threat, because our societal groups were so intimate in size. In our modern world, though, we become acquainted, in a manner of speaking, with people we never meet, the celebrities we watch so avidly in movies and on TV, or in advertising campaigns. This is another example of how our psychological mechanisms governing mating were not designed to deal with the modern context. Consider also the fact that men get sexually aroused merely by pictures of naked women—nothing more than dots on a flat page, or pixels on a computer monitor. These are adaptations of attraction played out in a modern world that contains novel stimuli never encountered in our evolutionary past.

In this light, feeling threatened by Kate Moss has a perfectly rational basis. For this woman, the boyfriend's attraction to Moss represents his desire for a svelte body form that she might not be capable of emulating. Although the rage directed at Kate Moss may seem disproportionate, it may well function to make her more vigilant about a real threat when it comes along in the form of a slender rival.

As we found in the women's fantasies of killing rivals, the woman fantasizing about killing Kate Moss is most enraged by her boyfriend's obsession with Moss's physical attractiveness. She even denigrates Moss's appearance by calling her "a skinny bitch." By contrast, only one man in our study of five thousand homicidal fantasies focused on a rival's physical appearance.

What's more, in women's fantasies about killing rivals, the methods they fantasize about using to kill often include destruction of their rivals' beauty, as the following cases illustrate.

CASE #P2075, *female, age 19.* [Who do you think about killing?] *Wendy.** [What was person's relationship to you?] *Cousin.* [Cause?] *Well, she tried to take things from me, she tried to steal my boyfriends and for some reason she thinks her ho-bag mother is just so cool even though she's a prostitute that lives off of the money of men from affairs she has.* [How would you kill?] *Uhh . . . smashing her face into a wall repeatedly.* [What prevented you from killing?] *Hmm . . . consequences, I don't want to ruin my life to end her pathetic existence.* [What would have pushed you over the edge?] *Adrenaline. I've got a bad temper.*

CASE #2479, *female, age 18.* *She slept with too many guys who had girlfriends that were either me or my friends. She blamed everything on me, she's such a liar, even though nobody believed her dumb ass.* [How would you kill?] *I never had a complete plan, but first I was going to make her as ugly on the outside as she is inside.* [What prevented you from killing her?] *I am way too stable of a person to actually do it. But had she tried to fight me I would have beat her ass until she died.*

The following cases demonstrate the other major feature of women's anger about rivals—that it focuses on their mates' emotional connection with the rivals:

CASE #310, *female.* *A girl that my boyfriend is friends with. I found out they fooled around and that <u>she still has feelings for him</u>—*

all while knowing about he and I. I imagined shooting and stabbing them. I saw the blood coming out of her chest as her head jerked back. I wanted her to see that it was me doing it. [What prevented you from killing?] *A sense of morals and knowing that I never would actually go through with that.* [What would push you over the edge to kill?] *If she keeps showing her feelings for him.*

CASE #15, *female.* *Well, I have been dating this guy a little over 5.5 years, and he's the most faithful honest person I know. Two weeks ago he said he was going home to study & the next day I found out that he hadn't been home for more than 30 minutes. He left & went to talk to this girl (a friend of his) who lives alone & he slept over. I went to her house. I've never met this girl, just heard of her because she bought my boyfriend's old car and they've been friends since the 9th grade. I found him at her house the next morning, but he says he didn't do anything. I believe him; he just needed to talk. But she's been calling every day, but I don't think he's been calling her back. I hate her and killing her was a thought anyone has when they find their love at [a rival's] house. She won't leave us alone & I'm starting to think the fat bitch wants my boyfriend! . . .*

Note that in this case the woman seems to believe that her boyfriend has not slept with her rival. But the psychological connection, revealed by her boyfriend's choosing the rival when he "needed to talk," combined with the persistent threat of a long-term successful poach, looms ominously as the most threatening component of the connection between her boyfriend and her rival.

SANCTIONED MURDER OF MATE POACHERS

Killing is certainly not the most frequent solution to the problem of mate poachers. But it's a solution that is seriously entertained by plenty of people facing the pain of this dilemma. In fact, killing a rival who has sexually trespassed is so common across cultures that it is often recognized as a legitimate means of dealing with mate poachers.

The Gisu are a Bantu tribe inhabiting the eastern border of Uganda. They earn their living from agriculture, and seeking work often requires that the husband leave home for weeks or even months at a time. Although this opens the window of opportunity for mate poachers, a man's family and friends have a duty to keep an eye on his wife. There are sometimes lapses, and mate poachers can come in the guise of Trojan Horses, as revealed in the following case:

> *"Bulugwa Wamini, a youngish man from a remote part of Bugisu, went, as many Gisu do, to Buganda to find work on the cotton farms there. He left his wife behind to look after his property. Three months later he returned and when he reached the hut he heard voices inside—his wife's and that of a close relative, Yowani Mudama. Mudama could be there for no innocent purpose. No Gisu man goes into another's hut when the wife is alone; such an action is considered adulterous and treated as such. Bulugwa, furiously angry, hammered on the door and his wife opened it. He pushed past her and seized hold of Yowani, who had tried to escape. There was a struggle, during which Bulugwa hit the other man on the head several times with a stick. When he saw that he had killed him he went and reported himself to the nearest police station. In his statement he admitted everything and obviously considered that he had had ample justification."* [11]

An elder in the village who had deep knowledge of traditional law and mores of the Gisu remarked: "What! The man was actually in his brother's hut? With the door closed? Then serve him right!" [12] He explained that the offense was even more heinous because the mate poacher was the close kin of Bulugwa's. The Gisu view killing a man who is caught *in flagrante delicto* with another man's wife as entirely justified.

Among the Walbiri, when a man is caught committing adultery, he must present himself to the cuckolded husband. [13] The husband then proceeds to thrust a spear into the thigh or leg of the poacher. This salves the cuckold's honor, and his reputation is restored. If the offender tries to flee and escape this punishment, the Walbiri sanction lethal violence.

Among the Tiwi tribe, located on the two small islands of Melville and Bathurst, off the coast of North Australia, a man found having sex with another man's wife shares a similar fate.[14] He must stand in the village center while the offended husband throws spears at him, the event being witnessed by the entire tribe. If he dodges the spears for too long, the other husbands, especially the elders in the tribe, will pick up spears and hurl them at the offender. The only way to restore the honor and reputation of the cuckold is for the young man to take a spear in the leg, so that the wound produces copious bleeding.

The Dsimakani, of Papua New Guinea, use analogous methods of dealing with mate poachers. The men fashion special arrows containing many small hooks. These hooks break off as the arrow enters the victim's body. The wounds are painful, and recovery is prolonged. Like the Walbiri and Tiwi, however, some men try to flee in order to escape punishment. If they do so, a Dsimakani mate poacher encounters a more brutal fate—he is shot in the back, often fatally.

In East Africa, the Nuer tribespeople know that "a man caught in adultery runs a risk of serious injury or even death at the hands of the woman's husband."[15] In northern Sumatra, "the injured husband had the right to kill the man caught in adultery as he would kill a pig in a rice-field."[16] Among the Yapese, when a man catches his wife fornicating with another man, he "had the right to kill her and the adulterer or to burn them in the house."[17] Among the Tiv of central Nigeria, a man who premeditates murdering a wife's lover for four or more months and then proceeds to kill him receives the penalty of death. If he kills the interloper when he discovers the lovers *in flagrante delicto,* however, the penalty is merely eighteen months of hard labor.[18]

In Western cultures, of course, men don't use spears to cope with mate poachers. Nor is killing the most favored strategy. But those in Western cultures do sometimes consider poaching an offense that justifies murder.

The French offer a special discount for murder committed while in the throes of the dangerous passion of jealousy. Similar laws have been on the books in Italy, Belgium, Romania, Spain, Poland, Bulgaria, Denmark, Greenland, Uruguay, Switzerland, Yugoslavia, and Brazil. The logic of the law was anchored in the premise that men committing such crimes were under the influence of uncontrollable passions so irresistible that the circumstances render it excusable. Judges and juries alike levy light penalties for this specialized circumstance of killing.

In Texas, until 1974, it was perfectly legal to kill a man found in bed with one's wife, with absolutely no penalty, "when committed by the husband upon the person of anyone taken in the act of adultery with the wife, provided the killing takes place before the parties to the act of adultery have separated."[19] If the husband discovered the infidels in bed, walked away, thought about it, and then came back and killed, it was murder. If done when the couple was caught *in flagrante delicto*, it fulfilled the "reasonable man" legal standard—that a reasonable man would become unhinged to the point of homicide by the discovery of another man naked with his wife. The law in Texas, at least up to 1974, intuitively recognized that homicidal circuits are part of human nature. This intuition is not limited to Texans.

> At common law, a man who killed his wife and her lover after seeing them *in flagrante delicto*—committing adultery—could reduce the degree of his crime to manslaughter by claiming he acted in the heat of passion. Such mitigation acknowledged the killer's passionate response to provocative behavior holding him blameworthy while professing some sympathy with the motive of the slayer. In four states proof that the defendant saw his wife *in flagrante delicto* was grounds for acquittal. In Georgia, for example, acquitting such a defendant was analogized to self-defense. Wives, the courts opined, embodied delicacy and chastity and husbands were their protectors. The doctrine came into existence in the mid-1800s and was not repealed until the late twentieth century.[20]

Remarkably, in every culture that has written laws, they invariably include restrictions on who can have sex with whom.[21] And after incest, which societies also universally prohibit, a man having sex with another man's wife is singled out as the most forbidden behavior.[22] Many societies have even tried to implement officially sanctioned deterrents to poaching. The Walbiri, the Dsimakani, and the Tiwi all arrived at a publicly approved solution that usually stops short of killing—inflicting substantial bodily injury on the mate poacher. Publicly inflicting a bloody injury on the mate poacher serves several critical functions. It deters the offender from future attempts to mate-poach. It sends a signal to other potential mate poachers to back off. And it restores, at least in some measure, the reputation of the man who was cuckolded. Of course, sanctioned murder is not the preferred solution in most societies today. An innovative alternative method tried in one case of poaching was to issue a fine. In a court ruling, a judge ordered that an interloper had to pay the offended man, a dentist, two hundred thousand dollars for "alienation of affection" when the man's affair with the dentist's wife was discovered.[23] Although this sort of punishment is rare, it reflects the widespread human intuition that a man commits a deep transgression by having sexual intercourse with another man's wife.

What is probably the most effective deterrent, though, is our deep knowledge that mate poaching can be deadly. Given the high degree of danger involved in mate poaching, we would expect that evolution has created special defenses to pick up on this threat, and our studies have shown we do indeed have an array of such defenses. Consider the case below:

CASE #32, *male, 17. We went to the same high school and dated the same girl. This person had been in trouble with the law quite a few times with assault and drug charges. I was dating a girl in high school and her ex-boyfriend (the guy in question) was really jealous and did not like her talking to me and did not like me talking to her. He would call me and tell me to stop talking to her or I would regret it. I thought he might catch me off guard and just try to physically hurt me when I was alone or that he might hurt my family. He pushed me and threatened to find me and beat me up. When I would see this person, he would clench his fists and his face would become very stiff and he would start talking very loudly. There were times that I thought this person would shoot me with a gun. I tried to talk things over with the person. And when that didn't work, I did what he asked and cut off my friendship with his ex-girlfriend. I figured that this person could be appeased with words because he had misunderstood the situation and I thought that if I could clear things up, his passion for hating me would decline and he would see that there was no reason to hate me. [What would have pushed him over the edge?] If I had attempted to push this guy and tried to fight him, he would have killed me.*

In our studies to explore our evolved defenses against being killed, we found an acute awareness of the danger of being killed for mate poaching. This fear was dramatically revealed in research that asked people to imagine themselves confronting various scenarios: Pretend for the moment that you are a participant in one of our studies. Imagine two situations. In the first, you come home early from work and find your romantic partner naked in the act of passionate sexual intercourse with someone else. What is the likelihood that you would try to kill the interloper? Now imagine the reverse scenario—you are discovered in a naked embrace with someone else's romantic partner. What is the likelihood that the enraged mate would try to kill you? We discovered an astonishing finding: most people *overestimate* the likelihood that their lives are in danger; they give higher estimates for the second situation than for the first, despite their parallel structure. In essence, people overestimate the likelihood of extremely costly consequences, as part of an evolved strategy for avoiding those consequences. In the present case, men break out in a cold sweat when they imaging an enraged husband catching them in bed with his wife. It's a reflection of men's evolved sensitivity to evolutionarily recurrent contexts in which their lives were truly in danger.

The following excerpts from interviews, some crude in depiction, reveal the psychology of antihomicide defenses concerning the risks of poaching.

CASE #147, *male. I had sex with his girlfriend . . . and when he found out he told several people that he would like to kill me, and this person is very emotional and irrational, so I thought an attempt wouldn't be totally unreasonable.* [What did you do to prevent being killed?] *Well, not being around him and not stuffing his woman seemed like the best possible course of action at the time.* [What prevented him from trying to kill you?] *Time to think about it . . .* [What would have pushed him over the edge?] *If I would have kept giving his girlfriend the hot beef injection.*

As this case illustrates, a man having sex with someone else's woman can sometimes prompt death threats. Here the threat was highly effective: the interloper stopped having sex with the woman, because he took the threat seriously, which he was smart to do.

Female mate poachers are also aware of the dangers of their mating strategy.

CASE #419, *female. I stole her boyfriend, and I guess from guilty feelings I was over-reacting. She stopped talking to me. I thought she would pull a plug from my car engine or cut my brakes. I was scared to drive, for like a week.* [How did you avoid being killed?] *I made up with her. I know she really didn't want to kill me though, and I was just making everything up in my mind. You can't be too safe though, you know?*

Notable in these cases is that, though each person takes the threat seriously, each also expects the fear might be exaggerated, that the "rational" thought would be that it's unlikely a murder attempt would really be made. Because the costs of being killed are so severe, our evolved emotions cause us to overestimate the likelihood of death whenever the odds of being killed actually are nonzero. Our minds have evolved an acute awareness that just one such threat, if carried out, will be fatal.

This fear does motivate people to cease and desist from mate poaching, as the following cases illustrate.

CASE #647, *female, 25.* [Who did you think might kill you?] *My boyfriend's ex-girlfriend. She was crazy! She was obsessed with her ex-boyfriend, who was mine currently at the time. Once she tried to run me off the road. Another time she chased me at extreme speeds down the highway with a gun in her car. She intentionally tried to run into me with her car.* [How did you avoid being killed?] *I filed police reports and tried to avoid her as much as possible.* [What prevented her from killing you?] *Possibly the fact that she had a child.* [What would have pushed her over the edge?] *If I would have stayed involved w/ my ex-boyfriend. After these incidents, I got out of the relationship! She scared the hell out of me.*

CASE #S494, *female, age 23. Miranda* was my ex-boyfriend's girlfriend. She was jealous of me; afraid her boyfriend may be interested in getting back with me. Jealous of me when my ex-boyfriend and me were together.* [What caused you to think she might try to kill you?] *I started keeping in touch with him through snail mail and he entertained it; keeping the fact that he had a girlfriend (Miranda) away from me throughout, and keeping the fact that I was mailing him away from her (Miranda). Through the exchange of mail, it was clear he was interested in contacting me by phone and going out with me. He left his pager number and I paged leaving him voice mail. Having his access code, she realized it was me and called me and said she would get me if I didn't leave him alone. This happened several times and she threatened to meet me at my school gate.* [Describe how you thought this person might kill you.] *She would come down to my school after my lessons ended. She is the gangster sort. I thought she would drag me somewhere with the help of her friends and beat me into a pulp and leave me to die.* [How did you avoid being killed by this person?] *I stopped contacting him!! Realized he was a jerk after all. Nothing lost.*

These cases demonstrate a profound dictum of the principle of coevolution. Stealing other people's lovers has evolved as a fundamental mating strategy in the human arsenal, and as the statistics cited in this chapter demonstrate, a highly effective one. So, of course, the "victims" of mate poachers have evolved defenses to prevent encroachment on their partners. Although many of these defenses are nonlethal, the threat of murdering is one of them.

When it comes to mate poaching, perhaps all is fair in love and war. Risking murder is one of the hazards we take when luring another's mate. But homicide also occurs where we least expect it—in the sanctuary of our homes by our own flesh and blood, a topic to which we now turn.

Seven

BLOOD AND WATER

—•—

"Having children of one's own and raising them have always been the primary routes by which women and men attain genetic posterity."

—MARTIN DALY and MARGO WILSON[1]

DIANE DOWNS, a twenty-seven-year-old divorced postal worker in Springfield, Oregon, had finally found the love of her life in co-worker Lew Lewiston. The problem was, he was a married man.[2] Their passionate affair had started as just a fling, but days spilled into weeks and then into months. Lewiston, however, refused to see Diane whenever she had her kids. Despite her pleas, he wanted nothing to do with her kids. As the affair continued, Diane urged Lewiston to leave his wife, Nora, but instead Lewiston decided to break off the affair. Diane Downs was incredulous. In a letter found by the police, she wrote: "What happened? I'm so confused. What could she [his wife] have said or done to make you act this way? I spoke to you this morning for the last time. It broke my heart to hear you say 'don't call or write.' . . . I still think of you as my best friend and my only lover, and you keep telling me to go away and find somebody else. You have got to be kidding. . . ."[3]

On a cool evening, May 19, 1983, less than a month after Diane wrote the letter, she packed her three kids in her car and went for a ride. In the back seat were Christie Downs, age eight; Cheryl Downs, age seven; and Danny Downs, age three. At around 9:45 P.M., she stopped the car, pulled out a .22-caliber handgun, and shot each of her children. She then shot herself in her left wrist, and slowly drove to the hospital. The emergency-room staff heard her arrive with horn blaring. She told them that they had been ambushed by a stranger on the dark country road, a white man with a head of bushy hair. When she refused to hand over the keys to her car, he shot each of her kids, and then aimed at her, according to Diane's account. The police arrived and immediately became suspicious. Wouldn't an attacker have shot the most formidable person in the car first, rather than three helpless children? And why did Diane suffer merely a wound to her left wrist?

Miraculously, only Cheryl, the middle child, died from the gunshot. Three-year-old Danny lived, although he remains in a wheelchair to this day. Eight-year-old Christie also survived her wounds and provided riveting testimony during the trial of her mother. When asked whether there had been any stranger present the night she was shot, she said no. When asked who had shot her, she said, "My mom." Diane Downs was convicted of premeditated murder and received a life sentence. Her appeals of the verdict and sentence have failed.

WHY PARENTS MURDER THEIR CHILDREN

The killing of a child by a parent is one of the most unfathomable and horrifying kinds of murder. To kill one's own child seems to run counter to everything we know about human nature. Since behavioral biologists almost never study humans, the scientific research on the causes of parents' killing their children has been left mostly to sociologists and criminologists. They focus on social circumstances, such as socioeconomic status, poverty, income inequality, and exposure to media violence, as causes of such killings.

I think an evolutionary-psychological theory of murder does a better job. Certainly, on first glance, such murders seem to refute an evolutionary theory of murder. After all, our children are the vehicles by which we pass on our genes. For a mother to kill her own child seems especially contradictory to evolutionary theory, because, whereas a father may find out that a child is not really his own, a mother always knows that her children are her true progeny. Indeed, so strong is the mother-child bond that even the mothers of serial killers, despite overwhelming evidence of their sons' guilt, usually stand by their sons to their dying days, stubbornly refusing to believe the grisly crimes of which their sons are accused.

Do child killings, then, result from pathology, from some form of insanity that causes a complete malfunction of the evolved parental machinery? Or is there a deeper explanation for this behavior, one that doesn't invoke insanity?

One key lies in the fact that humans have very few children compared with most other species. Moreover, we typically spend years and sometimes two decades or more feeding them, teaching them skills, keeping them out of harm's way, and socializing them to become participating members of our society. Ironically, it is precisely because our investment in children is so great that we must be extraordinarily choosy about the very few on whom we lavish our finite resources. Evolution will favor parents who withhold their investment from children who are losing propositions. In the extreme case, evolution has favored adaptations that motivate us to kill children who severely interfere with our prospects for reproductive success.

If there is an evolutionary explanation for murdering one's own children, then we should find evidence of such killings across human cultures in highly predictable circumstances, and in fact we do. Infanticide occurs in all cultures for which there exist good data.[4] From the kid killing among the !Kung San of Botswana, Africa, to the killing of infant girls plaguing China today, some parents in every culture end up killing their own flesh and blood. Furthermore, infanticide by a genetic parent is one of the few types of murder that women commit more than men. In one Canadian sample of 141 infants killed by a natural parent, for example, 62 percent of them were killed by their genetic mothers.[5]

Here is a description from an anthropologist who studied the Ayoreo, an indigenous group residing in Bolivia and Paraguay, of the common practice of child killing:

> We lived with the Ayoreo for 6 months before we began interviewing women. . . . Like mothers everywhere they anguish when their babies are sick and beam with joy when told their babies are beautiful.
>
> Some of the women in the sample became our good friends. Soon after we moved into her village, Eho welcomed us with a gift of a chicken. She often visited us and more than once lamented that we had no children and told us when we did they would surely be beautiful. We were somewhat incredulous when we first heard of Eho's infanticides. . . . It is difficult to believe that someone one knows as a charming friend, devoted wife, and doting mother could do something that one's own culture deems repugnant.[6]

Horrifying as it is, there are at least three primary circumstances in which evolutionary pressures may favor adaptations to kill kids.[7]

The first is when a child has a serious birth defect, illness, or deformity. In this event, in our ancestral past, the child would not be expected to survive and thrive no matter what efforts were made by the parents. Killing the child would free the parents to invest instead in having another child—a healthy one. The facts back up this prediction of the theory, as physical deformity turns out to be a universal predictor of infanticide. In the cross-cultural record, parents, mostly mothers, kill their infants for observable deformities more than for any other single cause of infant killing.[8] Among the Ayoreo, researchers found that the "women inspect the newborn for signs of deformity. If the infant is unwanted, it is pushed into the hole with a stick and buried, never touched by human hands."[9]

The second circumstance in which parents would be motivated to kill their children is when a mother already has children and investing in a new infant would put too great a burden on her resources for raising the others. Again we find a great deal of evidence, cross-culturally, that this prediction is correct. Among the Arunta, an Australian Aboriginal tribe, anthropologists have noted, "The Arunta native does not hesitate to kill a child—always direct it is born—if there be an older one still in need of nourishment from the mother."[10] The same ruthless forces seem to be at play when, in some traditional cultures, a woman who has twins typically kills one of them.[11]

In his book *Kinship and Marriage in Early Arabia,* published in 1885, William Smith speaks to this survival dilemma that our ancestors undoubtedly faced: "The pressure of famine had far more to do with the origin of infanticide than family pride. . . . The nomads of Arabia suffer constantly from hunger during a great part of the year. The only persons who have enough to eat are great men. . . . To the poorer sort a daughter was a burden, and infanticide was as natural to them as to other savage people in the hard struggle for life."[12]

Evolutionary anthropologist Napoleon Chagnon, who studied the Yanomamö over several decades, described one such agonizing case of a woman who killed her child: "Bahimi was pregnant when I began my fieldwork, but she destroyed the infant when it was born—a boy in this case—explaining tearfully than she had no choice. The new baby would have competed with Ariwari, her youngest child, who was still nursing. Rather than expose Ariwari to the dangers and uncertainty of early weaning, she chose to terminate the newborn instead."[13]

The third circumstance in which a parent may be motivated to kill a child, which is closely related to the second, is when a woman has children but is neither married nor in a committed relationship with a man willing support the children. In this circumstance, there are two underlying evolutionary motivations that come into play.

One is that the woman fears she doesn't have the resources to raise the children successfully. Investing in them would be a fruitless endeavor. A sad case that demonstrates the kind of desperation some women feel in this situation is that of Maria Del Carmen Rodriguez Gonzales. She was charged with abandoning her baby in Austin, Texas, in August 2001.[14] Police found the baby in a cardboard box. Maria, who was twenty-five, told police that she got pregnant after she was raped by a "coyote," the term given to men who smuggle illegal immigrants across the Mexican border into the United

States. Once in the United States, she struggled to find food for herself. By the time she gave birth, she had still not found a man to marry. Unable to take care of the infant, she first asked neighbors if any of them wanted a child. None did. She put the baby in the box and abandoned it. Unfortunately, had she known, Maria could have avoided legal trouble entirely by taking advantage of the Baby Moses Law in Texas, which allows women to leave infants less than a month old at fire stations and emergency stations, no questions asked—a perfect example of the ways in which the environmental factors that shape our evolution have changed over time.

The other motivation, which is the most provocative and seems in our contemporary context almost unfathomable, comes from the obstacle the woman's children may pose to her finding a long-term mate. Having children from a prior relationship lowers a woman's ability to attract a good long-term mate who will protect and provide for her. A man generally views kids sired by another man as a cost, not a benefit, of entering into a mateship with a woman.[15] Plenty of men are, of course, perfectly happy to become stepfathers. As we will see later, however, tensions all too often characterize stepparent relationships. In fact, for a single mother, a man's willingness to invest in her children is a key component of successfully attracting her. Many single mothers are even willing to settle for men lower in desirability if they show a willingness to invest in the woman's children.

This is, of course, a deeply disturbing argument. It suggests a degree of self-interested callousness toward children that is horrifying. Fortunately, the adaptations for killing are counteracted by many opposing forces— antihomicide defenses in potential victims, the interests of other parties involved, such as the husband and woman's kin, the fear of reputational damage, and, in modern environments, a fear of spending years behind bars. But sometimes none of these forces are enough. It was exactly this problem in which Diane Downs found herself, and her children became unwilling victims in her quest to unite with her lover.

The famous case of Susan Smith also falls into this category. On the cloudy afternoon of October 25, 1995, Smith pounded on the door of a house near the highway. She spilled her story to the police, who arrived minutes later. Wracked with frantic sobbing, she said that a young black assailant had hijacked her at gunpoint at a traffic light. He forced her to drive several miles, and ejected her from the car. Despite her pleas, the man stole her car and drove off with her two children—three-year-old Michael and one-year-old Alex—seated in the back.

For nine days, Smith, a twenty-three-year-old secretary, fooled Union County, South Carolina, and the whole country. Then her fabricated story about a black assailant fell through. She confessed that she had seat-belted her two young children into her car, perched it on a boat ramp on John D. Long Lake, got out, and then let the car slide into the water. When the police fished the car from the lake bottom, the children were found in the back seat, still secured by safety belts.

Susan Smith eventually confessed that her new boyfriend, Tom Findlay, was getting cold feet about commitment. He did not like the idea of being saddled with her two children, who were fathered by a previous partner. In a letter breaking off the relationship, Finlay wrote, "You will, without a doubt, make some lucky man a great wife. But unfortunately, it won't be me. . . . Susan, I could really fall for you. You have some endearing qualities about you and I think that you are a terrific person. But like I told you before, there are some things about you that aren't suited for me, and yes, I am speaking about your children. . . ."[16]

Susan was frantic about the loss of her new lover, and saw getting rid of her kids as the only way to win him back. She had practically her whole mating life ahead of her, and her mate value was being dragged down by two young children. With the prospect of gaining the most desirable mate who had ever shown interest in her—Tom Findlay was the son and heir apparent of the largest employer in Union County—she found the only impediment to be her children.

The data about killings of children by their parents from all around the world also demonstrate this pattern. Far more genetic children are killed by their mothers than by their fathers, especially at very young ages, because it is the mothers who face the problem of burdensome children to the greatest extent. In Canada, for example, single women produce only 12 percent of the children born, yet commit more than 50 percent of all infanticides.[17] Among the Ache of Paraguay, children who lack an investing father have survival rates more than 10 percent lower than children with an investing father.[18] Eho, the Ayoreo woman described earlier, killed her first three children because they had all been produced by transient boyfriends. Later she found true love and married, and ended up nurturing four fine daughters to adulthood.

If homicide adaptation theory is a valid explanation of the motives behind these killings, then we would expect that more such killings would be committed by relatively young women: a young woman who kills an infant suffers far fewer reproductive costs than does an older woman, because the younger woman has more time left to produce additional children. Once again the findings across cultures bear this out. In fact, teenage women kill their infants at a rate thirty times higher than do women who are a decade older.

Most women who murder their children do so when their children are young, before they reach two or three, which makes sound reproductive sense. If kids cause a woman's mate value to plummet, why should she invest in them for several years, only to kill them later? The evidence supports this line of reasoning. Mothers who kill children usually do so at birth or shortly thereafter, sharply curtailing the costs and preserving their investment for more advantageous conditions. Infanticide within the first few years outnumbers kid killing at all other ages combined.[19]

One such case was particularly poignant, and it also speaks to a remarkable ugly side of human nature.[20] Melody H.* was a twenty-four-year-old woman, divorced and financially struggling, with a four-year-old daughter named Tiffany* and a two-year-old son named Jonathan.* She became involved with Mark G.*, whom she met while trying to find work. They quickly fell in love, and they dated for several months, moving swiftly from eating out at restaurants to sexual liaisons at Melody's tiny apartment. Mark had a solid income and a spacious abode, and eventually he invited her to move in with him. It seemed to her like a gift from the gods. Melody jumped at the opportunity to live with someone she loved, who would also eliminate her financial worries. What Mark hadn't told her, remarkably, was that he was married and living with his wife and three kids in the same house that he had invited her to move into, near Waco, Texas.

To carry out this unusual arrangement, Mark had told his wife that Melody was a live-in housekeeper, who would also look after their children, in exchange for room and board. Mark's wife apparently had no idea that Mark and Melody were lovers. Melody later told police that when she first arrived, and discovered that her lover already had a wife and children, she wanted to leave. But Mark had threatened her, saying that if she left he would come after her and kill her and her children. Melody's motives for staying were apparently mixed. When the police later asked her why she stayed with Mark, she said simply, "Because I loved him."

The worst was Mark G.'s unhappiness about the arrival of Melody's children. He even encouraged his own children to abuse hers, especially her older, four-year-old Tiffany. One witness observed Mark's boys hitting her with fists, slamming her head into the ground, and kicking her in the back.

Mark G. was explicit in telling Melody H. that her children were a burden, and at one point Melody overheard him and his wife agreeing that Melody's children were causing problems and had to go.

Mark G. meanwhile displayed all the signs of a jealous man. He guarded his new lover closely, refusing to let her leave the house. He forbade her to call anyone on the phone unless he was present to listen to the conversation. Melody later said she felt she was living in a prison.

Although two years past toilet training, because of the stress she was under Tiffany began to wet her pants, which angered her mother. One witness overheard Melody's rage after one pants-wetting episode: "I ought to kill you," she reportedly said. "You are gone. That's it. You are gone." At another time, she reportedly told her daughter, "You're history. . . . I'm going to get rid of you somehow." The beginning of the end came when Tiffany's bladder lost control and she left a dark wet spot on one of the nice living-room couches. This time, her mother hauled off and slammed Tiffany furiously in the side of her head with a fist. The merged family then assembled peacefully and went off to Sunday church services.

When they returned, Melody's anger was rekindled at the sight of the wet spot on the sofa. The coroner concluded that someone had sent a flurry of blows to Tiffany's head with a blunt object, which has never been recovered.

The helpless four-year-old girl crumpled to the floor, gasping for breath. Her mother tried to make light of the punishment she had inflicted, saying that she had merely "smacked" her daughter with an open hand and "gave her a tap on the head" in an attempt to teach her to stop urinating in her pants. But the autopsy revealed a large hematoma on the forehead and a cut across the bridge of her nose. The pathologist found a purple discoloration around her eyes, so-called raccoon eyes, which occurs from blunt-force trauma to the back of the head, causing the brain to crash into the front of the inner skull and break blood capillaries around the eyes. Autopsy also revealed bruising to her neck, and bruising all over the front and back of her young body. Some bruises were fresh. Others were older.

As Tiffany lay on the floor dying, her mother went into the kitchen to begin preparing dinner. Mark noticed that Tiffany was breathing irregularly, alerted his wife and mistress, and tried to administer CPR. After several hours of futile revival attempts, during which Tiffany's life might have been saved, someone in the house finally called 911.

In further questioning, Melody told police, "Tiffany was hit in the head with an object and I believe Mark G. did it," despite her previous admission that she too had hit her daughter that fatal day. She told police that, although she had "smacked" her daughter in the back of her head, she did not believe it had been hard enough to kill her. All evidence suggested that it was.

There was nothing in Melody's past that would have predicted she would become a murderer. She grew up in a middle-class home, got good grades, and enjoyed two years on the cheerleading squad of her high school. Her parents provided a stable upbringing, did not abuse her, and are still married to this day. She could be your next-door neighbor, or mine.

This tragic story points to the deep tensions that often characterize relationships between mothers and children when surrogate parents are present. If evolutionary pressures have fashioned adaptations that might actually drive us to kill our own children sometimes, how much more fraught with danger must relationships between children and surrogate parents be—parents who have no genetic stake whatsoever in the children they are charged with tending?

THE SLINGS AND ARROWS
OF STEPPARENTS

According to an ancient French proverb, "The mother of babes who elects to rewed / Has taken their enemy into her bed" (*Quand la femme se remarie ayant enfants, / Elle leur fait un ennemi pour parent*).[21]

Among African lions, a female pregnancy lasts for roughly 110 days. After birth, the mother nurses her cubs for a year and a half. During the nursing period, she remains infertile, since lactation inhibits ovulation. Between pregnancy and lactation, nearly two years will pass before she is capable of breeding again. When African lions reproduce, and until the cubs reach reproductive maturity, the female offspring remain in the pride but the males must leave. The departing males attempt to team up with other males to form a coalition, or roving "Delta Force" squad. They have only one mission in life—to overthrow the adult males of a different pride and take over the females. If successful, they do not wait patiently until the females complete nursing and begin ovulation. Their mission includes killing the cubs to hasten the process of making females fecund again.

In the Serengeti Plain of Africa, an astonishing 25 percent of all lion cubs that are born end up being murdered by their stepfathers.[22] The mothers then recommence ovulation and show no qualms about mating with the killers of their cubs. Males who kill the cubs of the ousted males sire more cubs than those who don't kill. No animal biologist who has studied African lions doubts that the males have evolved adaptations to kill. Analogous adaptations to kill a deposed rival's offspring have been discovered in an astonishing variety of species, including gorillas, lions, tigers, cheetahs, and cougars. To a twenty-first-century evolutionary biologist, these results are not surprising. A mother's parental resources are extraordinarily valuable. Males in many species have evolved adaptations to ensure that those resources are expended on their own offspring rather than on the offspring of competing males. And male lions are too impatient to get on with mating to wait until females complete their period of lactation. Killing a rival's cubs hastens successful mating.

The pioneering evolutionary psychologists Martin Daly and Margo Wilson discovered that the single best predictor of children being killed by a parent was the presence of a surrogate parent in the home. In America, children living with one or more surrogate parents—stepparents by marriage, or equivalents who step into the role—are a staggering forty to a hundred times more likely to be killed in the home than are children living with both genetic parents.[23] Canada and other Western cultures show similar statistics. The majority of these killings occur at the hands of a stepfather, probably because upon divorce roughly 90 percent of the children end up living with their mothers.

In one Canadian study, using data tallied from 1974 through 1990, the beating-death rate by *genetic* fathers was merely 2.6 per million.[24] For *stepfathers* in registered marriages, the beating-death rate was twenty-seven times higher, mushrooming to 70.6 per million. For *live-in boyfriends,* the beating-death rate of stepchildren ballooned to 576.5 per million. It is noteworthy that the methods by which genetic and stepparents kill infants and young children typically differ dramatically. In one study of lethal assaults on small children, stepkids were beaten to death by their stepfather 82 percent of the time, but the analogous figure for genetic fathers was only 42 percent.[25] In contrast, 25 percent of genetic fathers, but only 1.5 percent of stepfathers in the study, shot a child. Genetic fathers are more likely to want to end the child's life quickly and relatively painlessly. Stepfathers are more likely to beat a child to death, whether over a prolonged period of repeated assaults or through one massive outburst of fury.

These alarming figures are undoubtedly underestimates. Some infant deaths are never discovered. Some are chalked up to "natural causes." And many cases formerly attributed to "sudden infant death syndrome" and accidental deaths are actually emerging as instances of premeditated murder.

In cases of abuse reported to the police in Canada—clearly a gross underestimate of the total amount of abuse, since so many cases go unreported—only one out of three thousand preschoolers living with both genetic parents are abused, compared with one out of seventy-five living with one genetic parent and one stepparent.[26]

Again, we see the same pattern around the globe. A case in point is the Ache hunter-gatherers of Paraguay. In one study, 19 percent of all children who grew up with two genetic parents died before they reached age fifteen. Disease, food shortages, and lack of modern medicine all undoubtedly contributed. But if that figure seems high, consider this one: a whopping 43 percent of children raised by a mother and a stepfather died before age fifteen.[27]

Although most stepchild murders occur when the kids are quite young, some occur at older ages. In one recent case from the United Kingdom, Michael Baldwin, age thirty-six, stands accused of killing his fifteen-year-old stepdaughter, Jenna Baldwin.[28] Baldwin claims that Jenna fell down the stairs during a family argument, accidentally killing herself. Baldwin's cellmate, Mark Dando, says that Baldwin revealed to him that Baldwin beat her to death during an argument in which Jenna revealed that she was pregnant. The father of her child was none other than her stepfather, Michael Baldwin. According to Dando, Baldwin said that he became furious about the pregnancy and hit her on one side of her neck. He heard "a crack," presumably indicating that he had broken her neck. According to Dando, Baldwin expressed no regret: "Mike said she got what she deserved and that she was a pain in the arse."[29] Michael Baldwin was convicted of murder.

CINDERELLA STORIES

Although the majority of cases of stepchild killing are perpetrated by surrogate fathers, our culture and others have tended, ironically, to place greater stress on the dangers of stepmothers. Webster's unabridged dictionary provides two definitions of "stepmother": (1) "the wife of one's father by a subsequent marriage," and (2) "one that fails to give proper care and attention." Cinderella stories of cruel stepmothers go well back in history and appear in many cultures. In the children's story of "The Juniper Tree," written in Germany by the Brothers Grimm, a stepmother kills her stepson, cuts off his head, and puts it in with a crate full of apples. She secures the head with a scarf, and then manipulates her daughter into "accidentally" beheading him.[30] The wicked stepmother then cooks the dead boy into a stew, and instructs her daughter to bury his bones beneath a juniper tree. The dead boy, so buried, turns into a bird and is given a millstone from the townsfolk for his singing. Eventually, he tricks the stepmother into coming outside and drops the millstone on her head, crushing her to death. The bird then miraculously turns back into a boy, and the children all live happily ever after with their genetic father.

In the Russian children's story, "Baba Yaga," a husband loses his wife and marries again: "But he had a daughter by the first marriage, a young girl, and she found no favor in the eyes of her evil stepmother, who used to beat her and consider how she could get her killed outright."[31] She encourages her stepdaughter to visit her sister, the girl's stepaunt, who is a cannibalistic witch, even more wicked than the stepmother. As in "The Juniper Tree," the story of "Baba Yaga" has a happy ending. The girl manages to escape with her life and lives happily ever after with her father, but only after he has shot his wife dead upon discovering her evil scheming.

Although the details are different, the underlying theme of the wicked stepmother remains the same. From India to Russia, from Japan to North America, children's stories of cruel stepmothers carry universal psychological resonance. We can only wonder why stories of dangerous stepfathers haven't been as common.

DO HUMANS HAVE ADAPTATIONS TO KILL STEPCHILDREN?

Stepkid killing horrifies us, as it should. Unfortunately, the scientific finding that stepchildren suffer a dramatically elevated risk of murder has also appalled many social scientists so much that some have gone to extraordinary lengths to deny that it exists.[32] The data, however, are quite clear, and I believe homicide adaptation theory provides the most powerful explanation of the patterns of stepchild murders.

Put bluntly, a stepparent has little reproductive incentive to care for a stepchild. In fact, a stepparent has strong incentives to want the stepchild out of the way. A stepfather who kills a stepchild prevents that child's mother from investing valuable resources in a rival's offspring. He simultaneously frees up the mother's resources for investing in his own offspring with her. And to top it all off, he frees up more of his own resources so that they can be redirected to his own genetic children. If the mother is relatively young, then the killing would also, theoretically, accelerate the pace at which she will be ready to reproduce again. Finally, in the next generation, the stepfather's own children will have less competition from his rival's children, since there will be fewer of them around. Iterated over evolutionary time, these benefits provide the selection pressures that easily could have fashioned psychological circuits to kill stepchildren in certain circumstances.

People may fear this evolutionary explanation because they worry that if it's "natural," people will use the argument as a justification for these murders, or indeed any murders committed where evolved motives come into play. There may also be a concern that stepparents will be unfairly stigmatized in an era where stepparental families are quickly becoming the norm. But I would argue that, if the human mind contains evolved psychological circuits that lead to child murder, and of course to many other kinds of murder, then we must understand and study how those mechanisms influence our behavior, regardless of how repulsed we may feel at the notion. Only by understanding the underlying psychology can we hope to intervene effectively to prevent murder.

STEPCHILDREN'S DEFENSES

Fortunately, because stepchild killing has been such a hazard throughout human history, selection has also forged adaptations in parents designed to protect children who might be in danger. First, mothers' antihomicide adaptations often succeed in preventing their kids from being killed. Single mothers usually exercise extreme care in selecting a mate, choosing one whom the child likes and who signals fondness for the child. They also usually exercise great vigilance over how the stepfather interacts with their children once he's in the home. Many mothers enlist kin to help with keeping an eye on the children. If a stepfather becomes abusive, many threaten separation or divorce, and then carry through on the threat and remove their children from harm's way.

Children have also developed antihomicide defenses of their own. One such, mentioned in chapter 1, is "stranger anxiety," which appears nearly universally in infants around six to nine months, precisely the time when they become capable of crawling away from caregivers.[33] Infants do not have to be taught to fear strangers. The seemingly irrational panic derives from what anthropologist Sarah Hrdy calls in her book *Mother Nature* "a built-in prejudice so deep it persists despite every reassurance the parent offers."[34] The intense fear of strangers exhibited so reliably by infants across cultures is an antihomicide device designed to evoke parental protection. According to all available evidence, it evolved in response to the strong likelihood that, as Sarah Hrdy aptly puts it, "infanticide may have been a chronic threat during hominid evolution."[35] The fact that infants fear strange men so much more often and intensely than they fear strange women reveals the precision of design of this antihomicide defense, since statistics show that strange men, far more than strange women, pose the gravest actual threats to unrelated infants.[36]

A second line of children's defenses is to influence the mother in her selection of a new mate.[37] Children assess the attitudes and intentions of their mothers' new potential mates, and try to get their mothers to reject those they sense are likely to be cruel. Kids more warmly accept those who seem willing to bestow benefits. And, consequently, men interested in mating with mothers often put on a display of affection for the children as a key tactic within their overall courtship strategy. Once a strange man is in the house, other defenses come into play for children. These include keeping a low profile, avoiding antagonizing the stepfather, enlisting the mother's protection, staying away from home, and leaving the family nest early. In fact, children living with a stepparent leave home two years earlier on average than children living with both genetic parents.

Children are well aware of the underlying risk a stepparent presents, a finding borne out both in our studies of homicidal fantasies and in our research about when people think they are in danger. A couple of examples highlight the terror in which some stepchildren live.

CASE #585, *female.* [Who did you think might try to kill you?] *My stepfather; he was my mother's husband. He ended up in jail for domestically abusing my mother. One day he began to beat up my mom in the living room while my sister and I were in our bedroom. I heard my mother screaming, and I thought that he was going to kill her. <u>Then I started thinking he might kill my sister and me. I thought he was going to hit me and strangle me.</u>* [How did you avoid getting killed?] *My sister and I remained extremely quiet in the closet. We were hiding from him. I remember shutting my sister's mouth, so she wouldn't make any noise, and she kept biting my hand.* [Why did you do this?] *I don't believe I had a choice. When you are a child, all you know how to protect yourself is to go into hiding. You think and know you are very weak.* [What prevented him from killing you?] *I don't know; he ended up leaving that night.* [What would have pushed him over the edge to kill you?] *If I would have interrupted him beating my mom or tried to stop him.* [What else did you think he might do, other than kill you?] *I thought he might sexually molest me.*

In this case, we see a critical antihomicide defense in operation—remaining quiet and out of the way, hiding, and preventing her sister from uttering sounds that would betray their location. Also apparent is the threat of sexual predation. Fortunately, this girl lived to grow up, escaping the slings and arrows of a potentially lethal stepfather. So did the following person, in this case a boy terrorized by a stepfather.

CASE #108, *male, age 23.* [Who did you think might try to kill you?] *My stepfather. . . . My mother and my step dad had just gotten married. As tensions mounted in the family, I became reclusive and introverted. My mother began to worry for my mental well being.*

Glenn began to focus his aggression on me. One evening, I came home and he was holding a baseball bat. He put it between my legs and pulled it upward. I whirled around, completely out of instinct, and it came out of his hand, hit the wall. That's when I became very afraid of his rage. I thought it would have been very easy for him to do, just get rid of me. From his perspective, with me out of the way, then everything would be less a problem.

[How did you think he might try to kill you?] *I figured he would snap during or after an argument. <u>I always thought he would beat me to death.</u> Literally, he often seemed to want to just hammer me with his fists and could have easily destroyed me. I definitely feared his rages. One time he slapped me across the face. Another time he pushed me into a wall. After that he would punch me into a wall. I finally spoke with my mother about it. She didn't even seem to notice the marks that I pointed out to her, or she at least ignored them. It was getting out of hand. I finally reported him to my teacher at school and talked with her and a police officer about the problem. We kept our distance from one another until I moved out of the house.* [What prevented him from killing you?] *I think it was fear of going to jail.* [What could have pushed him over the edge to actually kill you?] <u>*I honestly thought that it was only a matter of time before he killed me.*</u>

This case is fascinating for several reasons, and illuminates the sequence of antihomicide defenses of a boy defending his life against a potentially homicidal stepfather. As his last comment reveals, he truly believed that he was living with a killer, and that "it was only a matter of time" before the stepfather acted on his homicidal desires. His fears were not fleeting. They persisted and worsened as his stepfather's abuse escalated. Even though only a boy, he took extraordinary steps to stay alive.

Although the number of stepmothers who actually kill their stepchildren is small compared with the number of kids living with stepfathers, the roiling of tensions in this relationship as well was demonstrated starkly in our study, in which several homicidal fantasies were prompted by experiences of abuse by a stepmother.

CASE #P86, *female, age 18.* [Who do you think about killing?] *My step-mom. She was always saying rude things and then she began hitting me, and throwing me down the stairs. . . . One day, after throwing me down the flight of stairs into the basement, I told my dad. He didn't believe me and that was when I started thinking about killing her.* [How would you kill?] *I thought about slitting her throat with a kitchen knife.* [What prevented you from killing her?] *If I killed her, my life would suck and she'd still "win."* [What could have pushed you over the edge to actually kill her?] *If she would have harmed me again, I would have gone ballistic. But I left home instead, and moved in with my boyfriend.*

This case reveals the depth of the conflict, as well as the alternative solutions available for solving the problem of an abusive stepmother. Children living with stepmothers, like those living with stepfathers, often escape by leaving home early. In some cases they are driven out, which solves the stepmother's dilemma without her having to resort to homicide.

CASE #P2123, *female, age 19.* [Who did you think about killing?] *My stepmom, who is 43 years old. She was okay when she married my dad. But it turned out to be a front. She is the most petty adult I have ever met. Not getting her way in every small detail sends her into a fury. She tries at every turn to convince my father that I am a horrible person. She has been caught blatantly lying about me on numerous occasions. When I was a teenager, she went through my room and my car about once a week, certain she would find proof to her belief that I was a drug addict, which I'm not and was not. When I was 16, she went through my purse by my bed while I slept and found my birth control pills. The result of that scene was that they took away my car (which I bought with money from my own money from my job), made me quit my after-school job, forbade me to see my boyfriend or best friend, and grounded me.*

[How did you think about killing her?] *Thought about lots of ways: (1) hire a friend to be a sniper (he agreed to do it, but I was afraid of getting arrested); (2) mess with her car; (3) hit her with my car; (4) find a new social security number for me and my sister, shoot her in cold blood and leave with a new identity; and (5) I would've loved to strangle her with my bare hands.* [What prevented you from killing her?] *The only reason I didn't is because I didn't think I could get away with it.* [What could have pushed you over the edge to kill her?] *If she hit my sister.*

The following case highlights the central theme of conflict over resources.

CASE #P2076, *male, age 21.* [Who do you think about killing?] *My stepmother. She's 45 years old. I never was very thrilled about my father dating this stupid hussy. But the rudest shock was when I found out that she had actually married him over the course [of] one summer when I was out of town. Since then, I have had as little contact as possible with she or my father (aside from the making my monthly call for money). She makes a point of putting on a face of concern about me in front of my father. Then in private she shows her "true colors". She is an evil repugnant witch who only wants my father's money and she despises me because I seem to be the only one who realizes this.* [How did you think about killing her?] *I thought about knocking her out with chloroform. Then I would drive her out to an isolated site in the country—I hack her unconscious body to bits and then dig a hole, throw in the remains over them with several pouches of lye, and then add water to start the chemical reaction. Then I fill in the hole, covering her with dirt.* [What prevented you from killing her?] *The fact that I would actually have to do it and no matter how hard I tried the plan would always have some hole. I thought I would get caught. Oh, and the wrongness of it. Thinking about it isn't wrong, but doing is.*

The bitterness and hostility that stepchildren reveal in their thoughts of murder betray the evolved conflicts of interest at play. It's often in the best interests of a stepmother to sequester all of her new mate's resources for herself and her own children. It's in the best interests of the stepchild to strive for the resources that would have flowed freely but for the presence of the unwanted stepmother. If the conflicts over resources and roots of abuse from stepmothers are revealed by the homicidal fantasies of stepchildren, they also emerge floridly in the antihomicidal fears of stepchildren. The following case is emblematic.

CASE #219, *male, age 25.* [Who did you think would kill you?] *My stepmother. She was jealous of my presence and effect I had on my dad against her favor. She always wanted to get her way. She was always looking for things wrong with me and trying to fix me to fit her standards and when that didn't happen she told my dad and I was punished sometimes by paddling. When I saw what kind of control she had over my father to beat his child to make his wife happy it made me wonder what else could happen. She would glare at me when he wasn't looking, but she was so nice to me in front of family. It was different when we were alone. I don't know how she would kill me or if she really would but I just thought it was distinctly possible. I didn't like to spend the night over there and always locked my door just in case. I was a little child and my father wouldn't believe me anyways.* [What could have pushed her over the edge to actually kill you?] *If I stood up to her and started a problem within the family.*

Why the evil-stepmother motif is so much more prevalent in children's stories than that of a cruel stepfather poses an intriguing puzzle. The prevalence of the stories of evil stepmothers may have two plausible explanations. One explanation may be that living with a stepmother was far more prevalent over human history than it is today. In the past, many mothers died while giving birth, leaving children behind with men who remarried. Martin Daly provides a second explanation: "My take on cruel stepmother stories is that the people who tell them are genetic mothers; they tell children how awful stepmothers are, and the secondary message is: The worst thing that could possibly happen to you is for me to disappear and your father [to] replace me."[38]

WHEN KIDS KILL THEIR PARENTS

In Sophocles's famous play *Oedipus Rex,* a son slays his father, not knowing that the man he killed is his father, and becomes king. Then he ends up marrying his mother, not knowing that she is his mother. When he discovers the tragedy of what he has done, he blinds himself by plunging daggers into his eyes and then goes into exile. Though the gripping tale may have fueled Freud's theory of the Oedipus complex, which asserts that boys harbor deep-seated desires to kill their fathers, in real life children rarely kill their parents, and when they do, the reasons are usually quite clear.

During the course of a single year in Detroit, in which police typically log between four and five hundred homicides, there were only four recorded cases of parricides, the killing of parents by their children. All four perpetrators were teenagers. Three of the four were male. Detroit is fairly representative of America and Europe in this respect. Most children who kill their parents are male teenagers. The ratio of male to female teenagers who kill their parents is roughly fifteen to one.[39] Fathers fall victim twice as often as mothers. And the best estimates suggest that parricides account for roughly 1 to 2 percent of all homicides.[40]

In many of these cases, the father was abusive to the mother, and the child acted to defend her, as in the case below:

> On Sunday afternoon, January 2nd, the victim (male, age 46) was killed in his home by a single gunshot blast at close range. The killer (male, 15) was the victim's son, and the circumstance was familiar to the investigating police.
>
> The victim, employed as a sandblaster, had a criminal record that included two convictions for assault. The home was a scene of recur-

ring violence, in which the victim had assaulted his wife and sons, had threatened them with the same weapon he eventually died by, and had even shot at his wife in the past. On the fatal Sunday, the victim was drunk, berating his wife as a "bitch" and a "whore," and beating her, when their son acted to terminate the long history of abuse.[41]

The other three cases in the Detroit sample bore striking similarities. In all killings, the father had been thrashing his wife before the murder occurred. All contained a long history of such beatings, so that the precipitating trigger was not merely the single beating that occurred that day. And in each example, the teenager secured the family gun and unsuccessfully begged the father to stop.

In our study of homicidal fantasies, we found similar themes. Consider the following two examples.

CASE #P233, *male, age 22.* [Who did you think about killing?] *My Dad. He constantly beat my mother, my older brother and occasionally when he got tired of them, he beat me. He was an alcoholic, drug addict, adulterer, gambler, liar, thief, etc. Every time he hurt us, I wanted to kill him.* [What method did you use?] *I wanted to take the knife he used to threaten us with and stab him to death.* [What prevented you from killing him?] *I could never actually bring myself to inflict physical pain on him because I was so scared of him and of what would happen.* [What could have pushed you over the edge to actually kill him?] *It got to the point where he'd leave after he'd finished the beatings and I could never do anything because he wasn't around long enough afterwards but if he hadn't started leaving, I don't know.*

CASE #S629, *male, age 20.* [Who do you think about killing?] *My father, who was 43 at the time. A few years ago, when I was in college, I started to lose interests in studies. My grades began to deteriorate. My father, naturally was unhappy. He did not understand me* *but rather started scolding me. Once I remember he even took the belt and beat me up. Frankly speaking, he verbally abused me till the point I felt useless and my "manhood" was insulted terribly. He even cursed and <u>swore that he would kill me to save his pride.</u> This really drove me mad and <u>I really wanted to kill him first instead.</u>* [How did you think about killing him?] *I thought about using a gun and shooting him right in the brain.* [What prevented you from killing him?] *He is after all my father. His relationship towards me improved when I did well in school.*

Physical abuse from the father, directed either toward the child who thought of killing him or toward other close kin, exceeded all other triggers of patricidal fantasies. We also discovered two key triggers that don't involve self-defense or defense of kin against a physical threat, and that conform to the logic of evolutionary competition. One was the circumstance of the father cheating on the mother:

CASE #E17, *male*, 21. *I thought about killing my father, who was 49 at the time. He cheated on my mother, having an affair. He met a young girl, had an affair, got caught, and then divorced my mother leaving us stranded and in poverty.* [How did you think about killing him?] *I thought about hitting him in the head with a baseball bat. These thoughts lasted just about every day for about 150 days for about 10 minutes each.* [What did you actually do?] *I slashed his tires and keyed his car.*

Another son described a more vivid homicidal fantasy triggered by a father's abandonment, which inflicted severe costs on him and his mother:

CASE #148, *male*, 18. [Who did you think about killing?] *My genetic father who abandoned me and my mom. He was a total asshole to my mom. My genetic father has another family and I saw them. He toyed with my mom's emotions and then left her with children to raise alone. We were in a deep financial crisis. I would see my* *mom cry all the time. She never mentioned his name or what he did, but I knew. How do you leave a single mother like that? I wanted new shoes; mine were already tearing and falling apart. My mother said "sorry honey, well see what we can do, just keep praying—He (GOD) will supply all our needs."*

I learned how to deal with it. I became a rebel, but never against my mom. I built up anger, lots and lots of it. I would throw rocks from my back yard. My grandmother got me a punching bag. I demolished it. She enrolled me in karate classes. I was the best for my age, won tournaments, and got my black-belt. Then at age eleven I was pulled out of my kick boxing class—to play football. I was beat up by all the 8th graders, because I protected my fellow sixth graders. I became the leader and nobody messed with me. I would always get in fights and win them. Then one day I came home and I saw my mom and how tired she was and how much she had worked. I was sad and angered and took it out on everyone at football practice. Then I started to think that I should really take it out on my genetic father.

[How did you think about killing him?] I wanted to smash his face in with my knee, then leave him in a cage full of starving animals. I also thought about chopping off his testicles and penis and throwing them into a blender and making him drink it. I also wanted to knee him in the face and beat him with a baseball bat until he was unconscious, and then feed him to starving animals. [What did you actually do?] I prayed and asked God to not let me think that way and give me strength and to forgive me and to let me be forgiving like Him. [What could have pushed you over the edge to actually kill him?] If he were to try to touch or hurt my mom in any way.

Sometimes the costs inflicted by a parent on a child and the child's kin go beyond abuse and abandonment. Two in our sample wanted to kill a father because of an unimaginable cost he inflicted. Here is one example:

CASE #HA69, *female, age 20.* [Who do you think about killing?] *My birth father. He's in his forties now. He killed my birth mom*

*when I was 5 years old! Every now and then I think about the possi-
bilities of him getting out of jail. I want him dead, not free. [How
would you kill him?] I've had only one thought about how I would
do this—stab him to death with butcher knife. It was the way he
killed my mom.*

Parental abuse, abandonment, and other extreme costs inflicted on kin
pervade the thoughts of children who contemplate killing their parents.
Although our study found that men and women were equally likely to have
thoughts of killing their genetic parent, men act on these thoughts more
often than women, and actually commit most parental murders. In one
study of 155 parricides committed in Canada between the years 1974 and
1983, 88 percent were committed by the sons and only 12 percent by the
daughters.[42]

A handful of women in our study expressed vivid fantasies about killing
their mothers. Physical and psychological abuse by the mother triggered *all*
of the murderous thoughts, without exception. The following case illustrates the psychological torture that some mothers inflict on their daughters, but with a fascinating twist.

CASE #S494, *female, age 23.* [Who do you think about killing?]
*My mother, who is 39 years old. She would say mean things espe-
cially to hurt my feelings; mean, harsh, crude things that at such a
young age, I shouldn't have heard her say. When I was younger, she
said things like <u>no one really cares for me</u> and that <u>dad didn't love me</u>
and that <u>I was a burden to her because she would have remarried and
found a life for herself.</u> She nagged all the time, and constantly com-
plained. She condemned and insulted me to embarrass me in front of
others. Beat me in front of others. When I was growing up, she called
me a "slut" and "bitch" and said I would end up a loose and good for
nothing girl. I may not be a saint, but it doesn't mean I do the things
she claims I do.*

*[How did you think about killing her?] (1) Tying her up in tele-
phone wire, (2) scream at her all the same things she's ever shouted at*

me, (3) watch how helpless she is, (4) enjoy it, and finally (5) blud-
geon her to death with a hammer or chop her to bits. [What prevented
you from killing her?] *After thinking about it a lot, I realized I wasn't*
going to get away with it. I was afraid that I wouldn't be able to pull
it off and she would kill me instead, I would only do it in a fit of
rage. I realized how much I love her, yet hate her just as much. [What
would have pushed you over the edge to actually kill her?] *I think I'm*
rational enough. I have been pushed to the very edge, but mum is still
alive. I have really wanted to kill her, but even if I had a knife near
me, I wouldn't pick it up. Yet, sometimes, I wonder if that was THE
edge I experienced. I believe the worse is yet to come, so I will never
know what I'm capable of.

One cannot help feeling great sorrow for a girl who grows up with a
mother whose psychological slashes leave her feeling unloved, unwanted,
undermined, and unjustly accused. This case echoes a theme we found earlier in the cases of Diane Downs and Susan Smith—unmated mothers
whose children become burdens in their search for a fresh romance in the
mating market. For every mother who kills a child to clear the path for a
new romance, there are thousands who inflict sublethal abuse. And although
it is statistically unlikely that the girl quoted above, now a twenty-three-
year-old woman, will go after her mother with a knife or hammer, she
expects things to worsen and does not rule out the possibility that her murderous thoughts will one day push her over the edge.

CAIN AND ABEL

It is related that when our mother Eve bare Cain and Abel, she bare a
daughter along with each. God Most High commanded the Messen-
ger Adam, saying "For the sake of their offspring, give to Cain the
girl born with Abel, and give to Abel the girl born with Cain." The
Messenger Adam did so. Now the girl born with Cain was exceed-
ingly fair; and Cain said, "O father, let the girl born with him be his,

and let the girl born with me be mine." Adam answered, "God Most
High commanded otherwise." But Cain loved that girl exceedingly;
so he went and slew Abel. Thus because of a woman was blood first
shed upon the ground.[43]

Siblicides are statistically rare, and when they occur, they almost invariably involve brothers killing brothers. One sample of 508 killings in one
year in Detroit found that brother-brother murder constituted only 1.4 percent of the total, or seven cases.[44]

But through the ages of human history, these killings have been a theme.
In agricultural societies, in which one son typically inherits the family farm
while the others are shut out entirely, fratricide is more frequent. Among
the Bison-Horn Maria, brother-on-brother killings accounted for 7.5 percent of a sample of 107 homicides. Comparable statistics reveal 6 percent
among the Bhil of India, and 10 percent among the Munda and Oraon of
India.[45] In these societies, of course, land proves to be a critical resource
both for survival and for attracting women, establishing again an intimate
link between mating and motives for murder.

A typical case of fratricide occurred among three Munda brothers,
Bahadur Singh Munda, Suman Singh Munda, and Madan Singh Munda.[46]
Bahadur was the oldest. They all lived together. After their father died,
Bahadur immediately seized half of the property, leaving the remaining
half to be divided between his two younger brothers. This greatly upset
Suman and Madan, who believed their brother was cheating them out of
their fair share. Land and the resources it brings are critical both in attracting wives and in attracting *Nachani,* or dancing girls. Well-off Munda and
Oraon men typically keep one or more *Nachani,* who entertain them with
dancing and sexual services. Suman and Madan feared their older brother:
Bahadur had a history of violence and dominated his younger brothers. So,
for a time, Suman and Madan suffered the inequitable land distribution in
silence. Eventually, Suman mustered his courage and demanded an equal
share of the family property. He took the bold step of bringing his case to
the village elders and gained their support. Suman threatened Bahadur by
saying that he would call a meeting of the village to adjudicate the property

dispute. Bahadur was upset at this turn of affairs, and outraged by the impudence of his younger brother in trying to defy him. Without warning, he shot Suman in the chest with an arrow. Suman died on the spot.

From an evolutionary perspective, siblicides should be rare, since full siblings share half of their genes. Evolution has produced a powerful psychology of brotherly and sisterly love.[47] But siblings also do *not* share half of their genes, producing an area of potential conflict. Parents often have limited resources, and in some cases siblings compete with one another for them. Tales of intense sibling conflict go back throughout human recorded history. In the book of Genesis from the King James Bible: "Israel loved Joseph more than all his children, because he was the son of his old age: and he made him a coat of many colours. And when his brethren saw that their father loved him more than all his brethren, they hated him, and could not speak peaceably unto him."

Motives for murdering brothers in these stories almost invariably revolve around the parental and nonparental resources that are ultimately critical in attracting women. The Biblical accounts of Cain and Abel provide an X-ray into the psychology of sibling conflict. Cain slayed his brother Abel over land and a woman. Dardanus, the son of the Greek god Zeus and mortal mother Electra, killed his older brother to seize the kingdom, and then parlayed his new resources into founding the Trojan line. Siblicides to ascend to a throne, thereby killing a key resource competitor, are integral parts of European history.

Distant as this history may seem, we found these same themes emerging in our study of fears of being killed. Here is one account by a man who was brutally honest in admitting that he had cheated his brother out of an inheritance:

CASE #S489, *male, age 47*. [Who do you think might want to kill you?] *My brother, who is 34 years old. When my parents died, I sold the farmhouse. My brother asked for his share and I refused to give it to him. He swore he would one day kill me.* [Describe how you thought this person might kill you.] *He probably will visit me one day in my home and kill me then.* [How did you avoid being killed by this person?] *Nothing.* [Why did you adopt this course of action?] *Because I am in the wrong.*

Most people offer rationalizations for cheating or stealing. This man honestly confesses his misdeed, and expects to be killed by his brother for it. Many modern fratricides, of course, occur over sums considerably less vast than kingdoms, plots of land, or inheritances. One man in Kansas City killed his brother during an argument over who would get the cash for a gold tooth they had found. A man in Ghana shot his brother for failing to arrange a marriage for him. In Bangalore, India, a sixteen-year-old killed his twenty-three-year-old brother after an argument over a mere hundred rupees, worth roughly two American dollars. In all of these cases, of course, it's likely that there was a long history of sibling conflict over resources, and the ostensible cause, such as a dispute over a trivial sum of money, merely served as the spark that ignited the cumulative buildup of tensions.

In our study of people's fears of being killed, the suffering of extreme physical abuse at the hands of an older sibling came up repeatedly. One reported that his brother had tried to suffocate him with a pillow until he kicked him violently to enable his release. Another man reported that his brother had held his head under water to the point where he "thought he was going to die." Another revealed a similar frightening experience:

CASE #132, *male, age 19.* [Who did you think might try to kill you?] *My brother, who is a total jerk. I had no idea what was going to be done until moments before it happened. I saw the crazy gleam in his eyes that I had seen many times before, and I knew to get the heck away from him. I was on a beach. My brother and I were surfing, and we had just come in to talk with my father, who was on the shore. We were talking, and everyone was in a pleasant mood. Eventually, the topic of conversation turned to me and my brother's rivalry; I am a bit of a nerd, and he is an athlete. Eventually, it turned to who would win in a fight between me and him. I shrugged it off, knowing that I would lose.*

We then got back into the water. When we were about up to our knees in the water, he caught me, put me in a headlock, and dunked me under water repeatedly. Up until that point, I had been dry from the torso up, and the first time you get any part of your body wet in cold water, it leaves you gasping for breath. I had empty lungs, and my brother was holding me under water longer and longer for each successive dunk. My dad thought that it was merely playing, but after a bit he realized that my brother would not stop unless he intervened, which he did. If it had been just my brother and I on that beach, I have no doubt that he would have kept me underwater until I stopped moving. I saw this weird expression he gets when he gets really angry, a blank expression on his face combined with a murderous look in his eyes. That combined with a look of single-minded determination. [How did you avoid being killed?] I did nothing, he was much stronger than I was, and he had me at a severe disadvantage. I couldn't fight back, due to the weakness in my limbs caused by the shock of the cold water and my general lack of any upper arm strength. My father pulled him off of me.

As the case above indicates, not all siblicidal ideation is explicitly over women, land, or tangible resources. Another common theme was *envy*, which may have been at play in the case above. Envy is particularly strong among sisters. Three women in our sample recounted having thoughts about killing a sister—one for getting her into serious trouble with her parents; one for being superior to her in grades and sports, and for becoming the homecoming queen of their high school; and one over feelings of jealousy from age eleven, when her parents gave birth to another girl and devoted all of their attention to the newborn. In this last case, she recounted thoughts of wanting to burn her baby sister with scalding-hot water when her mother insisted that she give the infant a bath. One woman feared being killed by her sister "because I am prettier and smarter than she is." She thought her sister would attempt to throw acid on her face.

There is also the gruesome tradition of "honor killings" in some cultures, when brothers kill their sisters to salvage the "family honor." These cases almost always involve a women's infidelity or promiscuity. In Amman, Jordan, a man stabbed his older sister to death for disgracing the family by her multiple marriages and sexual promiscuity. Another Jordanian man killed his sister, stabbing her twenty-five times, for marrying an Egyptian man against the wishes of her family; she was eight months pregnant at the time. And a forty-five-year-old Indian man, Mumtaj Ali, stabbed his thirty-two-year-old brother, Ashiq Ali, to death when he when he discovered that Ashiq had been carrying on a love affair with Mumtaj's wife.[48] When an entire family or clan will suffer great disgrace, jeopardizing their future status, reputation, and reproductive opportunities, they believe that killing serves the greater good of the kin.

Clearly not all cases of homicide within families follow from the theory of evolved homicide adaptations. Some cases, such as that of Andrea Yates, who drowned each of her five children, or cases we've all heard in the news of a man who suddenly murders his entire family and then kills himself, seem to be the products of pathology. They show all the signs of a malfunction in the psychological circuits. Like all bodily organs and all psychological mechanisms, homicidal circuits can sometimes malfunction.

These sorts of pathology-caused killings damage the reproductive success of killers, and would have done so whenever they occurred over human evolutionary history. But the overall patterns of killings within families conform quite closely to the theory. Acknowledging that these underlying sources of tension exist within our families can only help to ward off more such murders.

In this chapter, I've focused not on the murderers next door, but on the murderers literally lurking within our own doors—fathers, mothers, stepfathers, stepmothers, and occasionally sisters and brothers. In the next chapter, we move back out into the broader arena of human social hierarchies, and also consider the special cases of serial killers and mass murderers.

Eight

STATUS AND REPUTATION

— —

"Suffering an affront to one's honour without hitting back is tanta-
mount to admitting to a lack of virility."

—J. Guillais, *Crimes of Passion*[1]

"So that in the nature of man, we find three principal causes of quarrel. First, competition; secondly, diffidence; thirdly, glory. The first
maketh men invade for gain; the second, for safety; and the third, for
reputation. The first use violence, to make themselves masters of
other men's persons, wives, children, and cattle; the second, to defend them; the third, for trifles, as a word, a smile, a different opin-
ion, and any other sign of undervalue, either direct in their persons
or by reflection in their kindred, their friends, their nation, their profession, or their name." —Thomas Hobbes, *Leviathan*[2]

AUSTIN, TEXAS, where I live and work, enjoys a reputation as a laid-
back, fun-loving city. Bumper stickers and tee shirts proclaim "Keep
Austin Weird." It's a tolerant town where aging hippies still smoke dope
openly and sport graying pony tails. The crime rate is relatively low, and
income levels and quality of life are high compared with most cities of this
size. But we have our share of murderers next door in Austin too.

Violence erupted on the night of Friday, October 6, 2000, in the Voodoo
Room, a club in a trendy section of the thriving downtown. Mike Adelman,
relaxing after a hard week of work, with a group of his friends and several
beers, reached out and playfully touched the buttocks of Kimberly Haley

while she was dancing. Haley became incensed. She used the speed-dial button on her cell phone to call her boyfriend, Kristofer Marsh, telling him angrily about the inappropriate butt touch. Marsh then jumped into his car, sped to the Voodoo Room, and confronted Adelman, demanding a public apology. Adelman merely laughed at him, embarrassing Marsh in front of his girlfriend and a jury of their peers. That appeared to be the end of the conflict. According to one report, Kristofer Marsh and Kimberly Haley left, and Mike Adelman continued to enjoy his evening. Around 2:30 A.M., Adelman decided to go home.

Driving along in the warm glow of the autumn Austin night, Adelman cruised toward home, unaware that the humiliated Kristofer Marsh was following him with Kimberly by his side. As Marsh kept a discreet distance behind, he seethed with anger. A metal baseball bat rested on the floor of his back seat. Marsh followed Adelman all the way home to his apartment, and while Adelman busied himself with parking his car, Marsh scurried ahead and hid behind a Dumpster, lying in wait.

As Adelman passed the Dumpster, Marsh emerged from hiding and blindsided him with the metal baseball bat. Adelman had no chance to put up a defense. The bat found its mark nine or ten times. According to one witness, Marsh continued to strike blows after Adelman lay unconscious on the ground. His rage still unabated, Marsh then shattered Adelman's truck window, adding insult to injury, and departed. Adelman never regained consciousness. He died five days later, his skull crushed, his brain dead. When caught, Marsh insisted that all he wanted was a public apology from Adelman for groping his girlfriend.

The conditions under which Kristofer Marsh murdered Mike Adelman are far from unique. We've all heard of such outbreaks of rage, almost always between men, that lead to uncontrolled violence. Public affronts to a man's status—in this case exacerbated by additional humiliation in front of peers—are very risky. To understand why a man would be driven to kill over something as seemingly trivial as a public humiliation, we must explore the underlying evolutionary psychology of status, reputation, and the importance of a man's honor.

THE EVOLUTIONARY LOGIC
OF STATUS COMPETITION

The basic truth is that men who lack status become losers in the game of mating. Other men abuse them with impunity, take their metaphorical lunch money, and poach their partners. The intricate links between status and mate competition, which men are all too well aware of, are revealed in the following case from our study of fantasies and fears of murder, in which a man believed that his life was in danger but nonetheless refused to back down.

> **CASE #116, *male, Ralph*.** [Who did you think might try to kill you?] *Well, I was walking in the mall with my friend. I was walking one way, and coming toward me, was the huge black guy walking with some friends. At the time, there was no one in the near vicinity, so there was plenty of room to pass. My friend was walking closest to the wall, and I was as far to the side as I could be, while still walking next to her. Anyways, the guy was kinda at the fringe of the group, which consisted of about 4 or 5 big black guys. We're on a collision course, but there's plenty of room to their left, so I figure that we wouldn't hit. Well, I keep walking, and they get closer and closer, but <u>being the macho idiot that I was, I didn't want to give ground because I was walking with a girl.</u> So I didn't, and as we passed, I bumped shoulders pretty roughly with that guy. I have to stress at this point that it wasn't entirely my fault; the guy had plenty of space to move, he just chose not to.*
>
> *At any rate, he turned and made an inflammatory remark, and things kind of escalated from there. . . . Well, for one, he shouted, "I'm gonna kill you, you mother-fucker." Actually, at first, he just made a remark like, "watch it chink," or something like that, to which I responded. Since I said something rather unflattering, to say the least, his friends got all riled up and started goading him.*

I embarrassed him in front of his friends, so he couldn't let it go. He started with "what did you just say, you fucking chink?", and ended with "I'm gonna kill you, you mother fucker." There was a lot in between, but most of it just posturing and swearing. Oh yeah, and I'm not Chinese. . . . I thought he was going to take out a gun or knife and shoot or stab me. [How did you avoid getting killed?] _As he was reaching in his pocket for what I thought was a knife or a gun, a mall security officer came running up and broke it up._ [What could have pushed him over the edge to actually kill you?] _Uh, pretty much anything. For all I know, he was already over the edge._

Despite utopian visions and wishful thinking about egalitarian values, all human societies are subject to strict, and sometimes frustrating, rules regarding status. All societies, throughout the eons of evolution, have had status hierarchies. For men, one of the great benefits of status has been its appeal to women. The collapse of communes in the peace-and-love era of the 1960s and 1970s, which were founded on the ideal of equality, occurred largely as a consequence of the deeply entrenched nature of this rule. Although the explicit values stressed free love for all, the male leaders of the communes tended to have sex with a disproportionate share of women. The attraction was mutual, since the women more avidly sought out sex with the leaders. Bitter resentments developed among the men who were left out, as well as intense rivalries among women competing for the attentions of the same man. People started hoarding personal property, blatantly violating the ideals they had professed to support, which included sharing everything equally. The utopian visions of true equality, free love, and the elimination of hierarchies collapsed under the weight of the forces of human nature.[3]

Obtaining and defending status tends to be more important to men than to women—though the quest for reputation is an important force in women's lives as well. In our evolutionary past, elevated status granted both men and women more food, better territory, and superior social support, but it granted men an extra bonus—more numerous and more desirable mates.

The mating benefits that men accrued from high status, iterated generation after generation over many thousands of years, created evolutionary pressure that strongly favored a powerful motivation in men to strive for status, as well as the vigilant guarding of any potential peril to their position. Selection favors men who have a drive to get ahead, who learn the best methods of doing so—such as giving preferential attention to those at the top—and who watch out carefully for those who threaten to usurp them.

HIERARCHY NEGOTIATION: KILLING THE COMPETITION

Complex and arduous are the maneuverings required if one is to rise through the ranks. Barriers seem to block us at every turn. First there are those in the positions of power, who usually cling to their stations, impeding others from getting ahead. Then there are those in our peer group with whom we must jockey in competition for a limited number of slots up the ladder. As if that weren't enough, we also have to worry about those younger ones who are rising up from below. Given the close link between a person's status in the social hierarchy and access to the resources needed for reproduction, it would be astonishing if humans had not evolved an array of solutions to overcome the many obstacles to status ascension.

One of the favored tactics is to derogate a rival verbally. Harvard psychologist Steven Pinker notes that these tactics are common among professors, whose status is so closely linked to the perceived value of their ideas. Outside observers might think that the ideas stand or fall simply on their own merits, that they are either compelling or not, the theories either supported by evidence or not. But the way in which academics evaluate one another's contributions is more complicated than that. As Pinker writes about academic ideas: "Their champions are not always averse to helping the ideas along with tactics of verbal dominance, among them intimidation ('Clearly . . . '), threat ('It would be unscientific to . . . '), authority ('As Popper showed . . . '), insult ('This work lacks the necessary rigor for . . . '), and belittling ('Few people today seriously believe that . . . ')."[4] And there is always "the stinging question, the devastating reposte, the moralistic outrage, the withering invective, the indignant rebuttal. . . ."[5] As these cases illustrate so well, words have become weapons in the battle for status.

At the other end of the tactical continuum, there is the extreme strategy of murder. Even in the academic world, so often characterized as the ivory tower, removed from the rumble-tumble of "real" life, murder has been not only considered but perpetrated, as one solution to removing the human obstacles who interfere with status ascension. Murder is surely the least often used solution, but the following cases of killings within the ivory tower reveal the legitimacy of the danger lurking.

In 1978, graduate student Theodore Streleski snuck up behind his math professor Dr. Karel deLeeuw and smashed him in the head with a small sledgehammer. Twelve hours later, he decided that life on the lam was not what he wanted, and turned himself in to the police. His motive for murder? He claimed that the professor had unfairly delayed his graduate studies. At the trial, he maintained that murdering his professor was "logically and morally correct."[6] Streleski was convicted of second-degree murder and served seven years in prison.

In 1991, Gang Lu, a twenty-seven-year-old graduate student of physics at the University of Iowa, could contain his anger no longer.[7] He had high hopes that his doctoral dissertation on plasma physics would be nominated for a prestigious academic honor that carried with it a thousand-dollar prize. His professors failed to put him forward for the award. Instead, Linhua Shan, Lu's fellow graduate student and someone he perceived as his chief rival, received the nomination. Two physics professors, Dr. Christopher Goertz and Dr. Robert Smith, cast the critical votes nominating Linhua Shan for the prize. Lu filed a complaint with Iowa's associate vice president of academic affairs, T. Anne Cleary. She concluded that there was no merit to Lu's complaint.

When Lu's protests went unheeded, he took matters into his own hands. On November 1, he entered the Friday-afternoon physics-and-astronomy gathering in the third-floor conference room as usual. This time he had something other than academic conversation on his mind. Rather than papers and pens, he harbored a .38-caliber revolver. When he found Goertz and Smith, he shot them at point-blank range. Professor Goertz died on the spot; Smith was merely injured. Then Lu turned the gun directly on Linhua Shan and shot her in the face. Proceeding to the second floor of the building, Lu tracked down department chairman Dwight Nicholson and pulled the trigger. Lu then backtracked to the third-floor conference room and blasted more bullets into the bodies of Smith, Goertz, and Shan. Smith died from this second round of shots.

Still not sated, Lu left the building and walked three blocks to Jessup Hall, which housed the Office of Academic Affairs. He calmly asked the receptionist if he could speak to Anne Cleary. Lu was admitted to her office, and after a brief exchange of words, he shot her in the face. She took her last breath the next day.

Friends of Lu turned over to police an undated letter revealing three key causes of his anger—the academic prize awarded to his rival, the failure of a professor to write him a letter of recommendation, and his lack of a job. Lu murdered the people whom he perceived as having blocked his rise in the academic status hierarchy.

In the modern world, killing is clearly not a successful strategy for getting ahead. But for most of our evolutionary history, there were no police forces, judicial systems, or jails. Our psychology was forged in the evolutionary furnace of small-group living, and in that context, murder under some circumstances would have been a successful way of gaining and maintaining position in status hierarchies.

The power of this psychological circuitry is attested to by the prevalence of homicidal fantasies in our study that were prompted by threats to status. Consider the following case of a man vexed by a rival who bested him twice in a sporting competition.

CASE #110, *male, age 25. I lost to him twice in the qualifying round of a Tournament of Athletes qualifying tournament. That means I went through two days of long distance travel, round after round of preliminary debating, and extreme discomfort in those ridiculous outfits called suits for nothing. It should also be noted that he already had eight bids for this tournament, and you only need two to qualify. He was just doing this to satisfy his own ego. . . . I actually killed him several times in my mind, usually while doing an exercise workout or after experiencing a graphic violent form of entertainment. I also thought about crushing his skull with with a baseball bat as I continued to try for the Tournament of Athletes bids. . . . Beating, asphyxiation, exposure to killer bees, surgical application of a scalpel, stomping on his head . . .* [What would have pushed you over the edge to actually kill him?] *Overhearing him planning to block me again followed by an opportunity for the perfect murder.*

The following case is typical of many in our studies in which men confront problems of infighting for position and blocking by bosses. It also dramatically highlights the psychological toll such situations take on the status losers.

CASE #A146, *male, 41.* [Who did you think of killing?] *A fellow worker who was occupationally my boss. He was an extreme opportunist and manipulator. This person gave me the impression that I was a real loser. He would mock me in front other people's presence. It was very embarrassing and hurting. I hated him and wished that he was dead. In fact, occupationally, I was very successful until he began to exaggerate tiny mistakes I've made. I felt humiliated. He became quarrelsome, made malicious comments about me, made me look like a fool. He deprived me from my future and my career development. He never appreciated what I had done, but when I made a mistake, he would never let me and everyone else forget it. He talked about my future and career upgrading, but in fact he was the main obstacle.* [By what method did you contemplate killing him?] *I thought about tampering with his car's brakes, which I know how to do. He then would have had a braking failure on the motorway. I also thought of planting explosives in his car, so the moment he starts the engine it would detonate the bomb. During this period, I began to doubt my own competence. I became very depressed, and* *developed an alcohol problem.* [What prevented you from killing him?] *Fear of being caught. And I feared being executed for murdering him.* [What could have pushed you over the edge?] *If there would have been no chance of punishment and if no other persons would have been injured or involved.* [What did you actually do?] *I destroyed him occupationally. I searched for allies at workplace and we ganged up on him. After some time, he wasn't our boss anymore. This was a great satisfaction for me.*

There are many adaptive solutions to the problem of rivals and bosses who impede our attempts to ascend through the ranks. Fortunately, in this case as in most, the worker resorted to other means, and he managed to oust his boss. But it's worth pausing to consider that for every carried-out kill, for every man who actually "goes postal," there are hundreds or thousands who ruminate and revel in vivid fantasies about doing precisely the same thing.

Just as people fantasize about murdering those who obstruct their ascent in the hierarchy, people who do the blocking sometimes worry that they will be victims. And these emerged from our studies of antihomicidal fantasies. The following case vividly illustrates this theme.

CASE #297, *male, age 23. We were acquaintances in an organization, fellow officers in that organization. He would do anything in order to not fall behind. We both were running for political office and he knew that he would not win against me. He began to tell people untrue, negative things about me in order to defame my character. He became very frustrated with me and was obviously less qualified than I. He was so hopeless on a level playing field that the thought of eliminating me was attractive to him. He never would have killed me, but the thought <u>definitely</u> crossed his mind. He became fidgety when he was around me and he was not able to handle my presence very well. He resorted to lying on several occasions in order to "handle" various situations. It never really got that far, but I'm sure he thought he would have done it when no one else* *was around.* [What could have pushed him over the edge to actually killing you?] *If I would have repeatedly embarrassed him and constantly pointed out his weaknesses, that might have put him over the edge. He would have been more likely to kill me if I exposed him as fraudulent.*

Although men constituted the vast majority of those who expressed homicidal thoughts motivated by interference with status ascension, a few women also experienced such fantasies.

CASE #130, *female, age 19.* [Who did you think about killing?] *I met this girl when I was a freshman in high school through a Unitarian youth group. She was never really friendly or outgoing to begin with, but I tried to give her a chance. As time went on we were never close. She was always stepping on other people to get what she wanted, which she did in fact always get. She talked down to not only myself but to my friends. So as time went on, our Junior year in high school came rolling by. Now in this youth group, there is a thing called Sweetheart and Beau. This is basically the honorable position of being elected "homecoming queen and king" in the youth group. Well it just so happened that she, I, and two other girls were nominees for the position.*

I had never truly liked her, but I felt this was the time for the guys in the youth group to truly see how nice and outgoing I am. I never put anyone down and I thought the guys would for sure see that and vote for me. As it ended up, I did all the work, programming, and spent tons of money. While all this girl did was give sexual pleasure to the teenage boys! She ended up winning sweetheart and throwing it all in my face. And once she had won, she was rude to all the guys and could really care less about the title. The guys to this day still tell me I should have won. Maybe I should have. I am over it now, but to this day this girl still has the guts to be rude to my face! [What prevented you from killing her?] Well of course, let's be realistic. This was high school, and I would most likely end up in JAIL! If not that,

given the death sentence. I would like to get a degree and start a fam-
ily someday, and with this on my record none of that would ever
happen. [By what method did you think of killing her?] *I didn't*
really think about the procedure. I would never really EVER go
through with it.

Not only are women's homicidal fantasies less common in the category of hierarchical interference, but when they occur they are less vivid and less likely to contain details about method. Our studies contained only one exception to these generalizations. This was of a woman, age nineteen, who wanted to kill her father's former boss: "The man fired my dad from a stable job for profit reasons. My family has been screwed up since then. I wanted to torture him with poverty, make him starve to death, or make him live in a third world country." Notice that this case did not involve interference with her own status or position, but with that of her father, with costs cascading to her entire family.

A man's status is determined by a complex mix of things in contemporary life, including career success and its attendant wealth. But obviously many other factors come into play as well, such as the prestige of his profession, his social sophistication, his looks, and his perceived masculinity. Social hierarchies carry with them an intricate maze of adaptive problems, and those who don't want to slip down any rungs must carefully monitor that elusive but powerful commodity, their social reputation.

REPUTATION, HONOR, AND MACHO MALE MURDER

A common children's saying, undoubtedly fostered by parents encouraging kids to get along, is, "Sticks and stones can break my bones, but words can never hurt me." One has to search far and wide to find an aphorism as false as that one. Much truer to reality is a statement from the Apocrypha, Ecclesiasticus: "The stroke of the whip maketh marks in the flesh: but the stroke of the tongue breaketh bones."[8] In the currency of evolutionary fitness, as we will see, social reputation carries more dramatic consequences than a broken bone, a welt, or a wound.

According to Martin Daly and Margo Wilson:

> Men are known by their fellows as "the sort who can be pushed around" or "the sort who won't take any shit," as people whose word means action and people who are full of hot air, as guys whose girlfriends you can chat up with impunity or guys you don't want to mess with. . . . In most social milieus, a man's reputation depends in part upon the maintenance of a credible threat of violence. . . . One's interests are likely to be violated by competitors unless those competitors are *deterred*. Effective deterrence is a matter of convincing our rivals that any attempt to advance their interests at our expense will lead to such severe penalties that the competitive gambit will end up a net loss which should never have been undertaken.[9]

This brings us to the explanation of why public challenges to a man's status—insults to his reputation—are so potentially dangerous. Police often bemoan the fact that many male-on-male homicides result from what they call "trivial altercations" such as the one that occurred between Mike Adelman and Kristofer Marsh at the Voodoo Room. As one Dallas homicide detective observed, "Murders result from little ol' arguments over nothing at all."[10] When the insults haven't been directed at us, we can easily find them simply silly. In the battleground of reputation, however, what appear as inconsequential insults are far from trivial, and men's mental mechanisms predispose them to be aggressive in response. As men are all too aware, people—both men and women—perceive public insults as challenges to a man's masculinity, his strength, his virility, his worth as an ally, and his ability to protect his woman from sexual trespass. If the man who is insulted fails to respond or attempts to shrug off the challenge, he loses face. In the apt idiom of the inner city, he's been "dissed." And in the long ages of our evolutionary past—and today as well—the loss of face, and the attendant plunge in status, carries disastrous consequences for men in the mating game.

Though we may like to believe that societies today respect a man more for walking away from an insult or threat than for confronting it, such insults have powerful consequences, because of the deeply ingrained messages they send, messages our brains have evolved to read. An insult taken without retaliation sends a signal first to the one who hurled the words that he can get away with dominating the one he's offended. In our distant past—and even today, in truth—it tells the challenger that he can tread on his victim's turf if he wants to, he can take over his territory, and he can come on to his wife or girlfriend if he chooses. It tells him that his victim lacks the personal courage, the physical prowess, or the strength of allies to back him up. A challenge left unmet unfortunately also sends these messages to the crowd watching, however subliminally it may be for some of them. Witnesses to the challenge may view the insulted person as exploitable, encouraging further infringements on his interests.

Affronts to reputation spread through a social group like wildfire, and rarely can a reputation lost be regained. This is the underlying set of reasons why men sometimes become so disproportionately violent in response.

Insults to honor are such powerful triggers for killing that some states historically attempted to create laws to prevent activating this psychological circuit. West Virginia, for example, passed a law making it illegal to taunt someone for refusing to participate in a duel: "If any person post another, or in writing or in print use any reproachful or contemptuous language to or concerning another, for not fighting in a duel, or for not sending or accepting a challenge, he shall be guilty of a misdemeanor, and, upon conviction, shall be confined to jail not more than six months, or fined not exceeding one hundred dollars."[11]

In our studies, being humiliated by a same-sex rival in front of others proved to be one of the most common triggers of homicidal thoughts, occurring in 28 percent of men's homicidal fantasies. Consider the following case:

CASE #278, *male, age 23.* [What caused you to think about killing someone?] *There were so many things. I was young, and had a background in martial arts, and so was defiant. I was a dork, a big one, and everyone knew it but me. There were always big kids around my locker, popular ones, and I was an easy target. I hated them, and they hated me. One of the times, the guy "accidentally" dropped his books on my head, and all his friends got a good laugh. When I stood up to confront him, they closed my locker, and ripped my backpack from my hands. They scattered its contents, and started pushing me and making insulting comments about me and my mom. They asked me what I was going to do, and I said nothing.*

[What method did you think about using to kill this person?] *Wow, OK. Which one should I tell you about? The most sadistic? The quickest? I have a very vivid imagination, and these fantasies were my only escape from the hell that was my life. One of the more frequent ones was where I broke both his legs so he couldn't run, and then beat him until his insides were a bloody pulp. Then I tied him to a table and dripped acid onto his forehead, Chinese water-torture style, so that it would run into his eyes. Eventually, the dripping acid would bore a hole into his head and melt his brain, but not until he had been driven crazy with pain.* [What prevented you from killing?] *God mostly, and morals, laws, the actual disgustingness of the way I killed him in my thought. Perhaps it was my lack of capability.* [What could have pushed you over the edge to actually kill?] *I don't know, it's been so long ago. Maybe if I were to have had a gun with me at the time, and he did something extra-horrible, like stab a girl. Probably nothing short of physically harming a girl in front of me, or trying to kill me first.*

Public humiliation in front of others tends to lead to especially violent fantasies about killing the tormentor, as the above illustrates. But this case is far from unique. The vividness and exquisitely elaborated details of such homicidal fantasies highlight the magnitude of the social cost and psychological agony experienced by those whose reputations are damaged.

This fierceness of response to status insults is a cross-cultural universal. Oscar Lewis, a leading anthropological scholar of Mexican culture, interviewed Mexican men about what it means to be "macho" and the rules of

status competition. He provides this account from one man about the rules
of the game:

> I have learned to hide my fear and to show only courage because
> from what I have observed, a person is treated according to the
> impression he makes. That's why when I am really very afraid inside,
> outwardly I am calm. . . . In my neighborhood, you are either a
> *picudo,* a tough guy, or a *pendejo,* a fool.
>
>   Mexicans, and I think everyone in the world, admire the person
> "with balls," as we say. . . . The one who has guts enough to stand up
> against an older, stronger guy, is more respected. . . . If any so-and-
> so comes to me and says, "Fuck your mother," I answer "Fuck your
> mother a thousand times." And if he goes one step forward and I
> take one step back, I lose prestige. But if I go forward too, and pile
> on and make a fool out of him, then the others will treat me with
> respect. I would never give up or say, "Enough," even though the
> other was killing me. I would try to go to my death, smiling. That is
> what we mean by being "<u>macho</u>," by being manly.[12]

The link between being tough in defending one's status, and the importance of being willing to kill to do so, is also made explicit in this quote
from sociologist Pino Arlacchi's study of Mafia culture in southern Italy:

> What does it mean to "behave in the manner of the mafia"? It means
> "to make oneself respected," "to be a man of honour" capable of
> revenging by his own force any sort of offence done to his own per-
> sonality and capable of equally dealing out offence to an enemy. . . .
> Taking a life, especially killing a fearful enemy, was honorific in the
> highest degree. "X is an exceptional man; he 'has' five killings." . . .
> Among the mafiosi of the Plain of Gioia Tauro the act of homi-
> cide . . . indicated courage and the capacity to impose oneself as a
> man. It brought an automatic opening line of credit for the killer.
> The more awesome and potent the victim, the more worthy and mer-
> itorious the killer.[13]

Plenty of such expressions are found in the anthropological studies of tribal peoples as well. In the Dani tribe of highland New Guinea, "a man without valor is *kepu*—a worthless man, a man-who-has-not-killed."[14] A thousand miles away, the Yanomamö of Venezuela make a social distinction between *unokai,* men who have killed, and non-*unokai,* those who have not killed.[15]

The Dani killers and the Yanomanö *unokai* also demonstrate the link between such maintenance of status and access to mates. In each of these societies, men who kill command a larger share of goods and acquire more wives. Among the Dani, for example, "few *kepu* men have more than a single wife, and many have none."[16] And if *kepu* men are fortunate enough to acquire a wife, "unless they have strong friends or family, any wives or pigs they may obtain will be taken from them by other men, in the confidence that they will not resist."[17]

Interestingly, there seem to be cultural differences in the frequency with which actual violence is provoked by insults to status. Mediterranean cultures such as Italy and Greece, for example, tend to take verbal insults more seriously than do Northern European cultures such as Sweden or Norway.[18] An interesting argument that's been proposed to explain these differences is called the "culture of honor" theory, put forward by psychologists Richard Nisbett and Dov Cohen. Their theory was developed specifically to explain the homicide-rate differences between Southern and Northern states within America, which are pronounced. Although there are exceptions, the farther south the state, the higher the homicide rate.[19] Alabama, Georgia, and Mississippi, for example, have homicide rates of 15.9, 14.8, and 14.3 per hundred thousand. Texas tops the list at 17.1. The corresponding rates in Maine, Ohio, and Pennsylvania are 3.2, 7.6, and 7.0. This theory may not hold up as a worldwide explanation, but it's intriguing to consider.[20]

According to "culture of honor" theory, the stress on a man's public reputation for toughness and physical courage originated in the world's herding economies. In these economies, herdsmen over the eons confronted the threat of losing their entire wealth if their animals were stolen, as often happened in raiding parties. When you've got all your resources stored in the bodies of your herd, you risk catastrophic destitution by raids. A man's public reputation was literally the key to his economic survival. A public stance of aggressiveness and the courage to defend against such raids became critical to deterring bands of marauding rustlers. Over time, men growing up in herding economies were therefore socialized to act tough, to respond with violence to public insults, and to preserve at all costs their social reputation. According to Nisbett and Cohen, the Southern states in the U.S. were settled primarily by emigrants from such herding cultures, primarily Ireland, Scotland, and Wales, so that this culture of honor took root in the South.

The Northern states, by contrast, were settled primarily by farmers, such as Puritans, Quakers, Germans, and Dutch. Because the economic resources of farmers are tied to the land, they cannot be stolen in one fell swoop, and through the ages, farmers therefore had less of a mandate to cultivate defensive toughness.

So Nisbett and Cohen argue that the higher rates of homicide among white males living in the South are due to the culture of honor that became more prevalent in the South. They explain the fact that homicide rates among black males do not differ from North to South by the relatively recent migration of Southern blacks to Northern states.

Although this theory may sound implausible, Nisbett and Cohen have amassed a large body of scientific evidence that the South-North cultural differences are real, profound, and likely to explain the homicide-rate differences. The culture-of-honor differences show up in studies of attitudes, behavior, and even experiments in which participants are publicly insulted. Southerners, for example, are roughly 13 percent more likely than Northerners to "agree a great deal" with the statements "A man has the right to kill another man in self-defense" and "A man has the right to kill a person to defend his family." Southerners are twice as likely to agree with the statement "A man has the right to defend his house."[21] In another study, respondents were asked how justified a man named Fred would be in shooting a person who committed actions such as telling others behind Fred's back that he was a liar and a cheat, "sexually assault[ing] Fred's 16-year-old daughter," or "steal[ing] Fred's wife."[22] Significantly more Southern respondents than Northerners said that Fred was quite justified in killing his antagonist.

The most dramatic cultural difference measured was in response to the event of sexual assault on Fred's daughter, with 47 percent of Southerners, but only 26 percent of Northerners, saying that Fred was justified in shooting the offender. Southerners were also far more likely than Northerners to say that Fred was "not much of a man" unless he responded violently to the various affronts to his character and family honor.

In a clever series of experiments, Nisbett and Cohen set up a situation in which an experimenter intentionally bumped into a male research participant while walking down a narrow hallway, and then called him an "asshole." This procedure was repeated over many trials with different participants. Independent observers who saw the confrontations and had no knowledge of the geographical origins of the research participants judged the participants' reactions in terms of how angry on the one hand, or amused on the other, they appeared. Southern men were judged to be more angry and less amused than Northern men after being called an asshole. In another experiment with the same setup, after the insult the experimenters measured cortisol levels, a physiological indicator of psychological stress, and testosterone levels. In response to the public insult, the Southern men's cortisol levels rose dramatically more than that of the Northerners. Their testosterone levels also rose more sharply. Testosterone has been shown to rise in response to the anticipation of combat or competition. So the physiological data support the psychological data, showing that a psychology of honor appears more easily activated in Southern than in Northern men.

In yet another experiment, Nisbett and Cohen sent a made-up "fact sheet" to college newspaper reporters, who were asked to write it up for pay for their local newspapers. Here is a summary of the pertinent details of the fact sheet:

Victor Jensen (a 28-year-old Caucasian) stabbed Martin Shell (a 27-year-old Caucasian) at a party.

According to witnesses: Shell spilled a glass of beer on Jensen's pants.

The two began arguing and had to be separated.

Shell shouted that Jensen's sister, Ann, was "a slut."

Several men were heard to make comments about what they would do if someone said that about their sister.

Jensen left the party. As he left, Shell and his friends laughed at Jensen. Shell then shouted that both Jensen's sister and mother were "sluts."

Jensen returned to the party ten minutes later. He demanded that Shell take back his comments "or else." Shell laughed at Jensen and said, "Or else what, Rambo?"

Jensen then pulled a four-inch knife out of his jacket and stabbed Shell twice. Shell was unarmed at the time of the stabbing.[23]

Raters then judged the subsequent story write-ups on the degree to which Jensen was provoked into committing the homicide, how blameworthy he was, and how sympathetically the writers treated Jensen. Writers from college newspapers in the South, more than those from the North, felt that Jensen was provoked by his victim and was less to blame for the killing, and they treated the killer more sympathetically.

Taken together, the studies clearly demonstrate a cultural difference that may well account for the higher rates of homicide by males in the South. So does that mean that the phenomenon of murdering in response to a public insult is in fact entirely a cultural thing? Not at all. Cultural values appear likely to set different thresholds for activating the homicidal circuits we all possess. The underlying motives for murders are identical in Southern and Northern men. Residing in cultures of honor, such as those of the American South, seems to lower the threshold for acting on these universal male motives, but the motives remain the same.

As I considered Nisbett and Cohen's theory, I realized that another factor would come into play in making herding cultures more prone to the violent defense of status. In human evolutionary competition, the greater the variability among men in access to resources and to women, the riskier the men's competitive strategies will become. In other words, the more a man might gain—in terms of both goods and mates—by being dominant, the more he will be willing to risk to attain dominance. This theory says that men are more likely to attempt to kill—exposing themselves to the risk of being killed by their adversaries—when they have the prospect of gaining a great bounty, of really winning big. They are much more willing to follow a "winner take all" strategy of violence, whereby they may well end up with nothing at all. Early herding cultures would have presented such opportunities, and, sure enough, raids of others' herds were common. This logic of winner-take-all violence may also go a long way toward explaining one of the present day's most violent subcultures—that of inner-city drug gangs.

Drug dealing is an enterprise in which the dominant players can obtain vast sums of money in a culture where there is a great deal of poverty. The bounty of cash to be gained by violent gang warfare may well explain why so many gang members are willing to risk their lives in turf battles, and may also explain why status has become such a vigorously defended personal commodity in the gang culture.

Killing evolved as one solution, albeit a dangerous one, to the adaptive problem of reputation management, and since status is so much more important to men's mating success, men do more of this kind of killing. In our study of Michigan murders, for example, seventy-one men, but only eleven women, named status or reputation as one of the core motives for murder. That is not to say, however, that reputation is not highly prized by women, because of course it is. One of the fascinating aspects of our study of homicidal fantasies is that it revealed that for women the type of threat to reputation that tends to trigger homicidal thoughts is that prized social commodity a woman possesses—her sexual reputation.

SEXUAL REPUTATION

In our study, the triggers for women's homicidal thoughts did not concern being physically dominated by other women, or insults to physical prowess or virility. They did not concern accusations of cowardice, the embarrassment about failure to fight, or backing down from a public challenge. The most frequent trigger, by far, was an insult to a woman's sexual reputation, which is perceived as damage to her desirability in the mating market. Here's a case in point:

CASE #P24, *female, age 19.* [Who did you think about killing?] *Girl I went to Jr. High with. She had been a good friend. She was my best friend. I made out with a guy summer before 8th grade. I confided in her, as good friends do. She took it upon herself to tell everyone what I told her and she even made up more to the story. She told everyone I was a slut and so, because it was junior high, everyone agreed with her. It ruined my reputation. I had no friends. I spiraled down into a deep depression which I didn't fully come out of until 2 years later.* [By what method did you think about killing her?] *I didn't ever plan how to kill her. I just wanted her out of my life because of all the damage she did. It seemed like if she was dead, she'd be permanently out of the way.* [What might have pushed you over the edge to actually kill?] *Perhaps, if I was on serious drugs or in a deeper depression.*

Because men place such a premium on sexual fidelity, women who acquire reputations as promiscuous, easy, loose, wanton, or slutty are well aware that they have suffered a serious blow to their desirability as a long-term mate. The fact is that rumors impugning a woman's sexual honor, even if untrue, are sometimes believed, and render her less attractive to men looking for committed relationships.

In the case above, the damage to the girl's sexual reputation in junior high school sent her into a two-year depression. The damage came at the hands of a female friend who had turned into a sexual rival. Sometimes the damage comes from men who sexually use a woman for short-term sexual access and then boast about it, as illustrated by the following examples.

CASE #P242, *female, age 22.* [Who did you think about killing?] *A fellow student, a man who was 17 years old at the time. I had been intimate with this individual (who was at that point what I considered a friend)—but did not have sex with him. The following weekday he proceeded to tell the vast majority of his friends that we had sex together. I walked by him and his group of friends and he was laughing with his friends. (At this time I was aware that he thought*

*they knew something). I told him to go fuck himself—he called me a
bitch and I thought of killing him.* [How would you kill?] *Basically,
in my thoughts I killed him with my hands, strangling and punching
him to death.* [What prevented you from killing him?] *I did punch
him, that enabled me [to] "get my anger out", so there was no need
to "kill" him. He'd been punched by a girl in front of his friends.*

CASE #133, *female, age 29.* *He lied to me about caring about me,
he embarrassed me and I still kept giving him chances. <u>I wound up
having intercourse with him. When I found out that I was pregnant, I
couldn't find him.</u> He just disappeared. I miscarried in my home.
Months later after I told him he called me a liar, and told all of his
friends that I was a liar. I wish I would die so that I wouldn't be hurting over the situation anymore. Before this happened, I loved my life.
I felt ruined and thought that nobody would ever love me. I wanted
to kill him, but felt despair because I think he has hurt me as much as
he possibly can. There's nothing more he has left to do unless he
hurts someone in my family.*

So important is a woman's sexual reputation, in fact, that it even
emerged in one case in our study of antihomicidal thoughts, in a man who
feared being killed by a woman he had slept with. Although this sort of
case is unusual, the fact that this man was aware of the potential threat of a
women whose reputation he had damaged is noteworthy.

CASE #115, *male.* [Who did you think might try to kill you?] *My
girlfriend. She was rather moody, prone to changes in temper rather
quickly. <u>After we had slept together for the first time</u>, she was joking
that she'd have to <u>kill me to "protect her honor."</u> She put her hands
around my neck and pretended to choke me, but <u>soon started to
actually cut off my air.</u> Even when I began to try to gasp she kept her
hands around my neck, only letting up when I began to see spots.
While she kept her hands there, I was convinced she was actually trying to end my life. . . . She became very quiet and withdrawn (which*

was strange, as she was usually quite exuberant), extremely intent on the way my face looked as she cut off my air.

[How did you avoid being killed?] *I flailed a bit with my arms, trying to break her grip, though this didn't accomplish anything. I only avoided being killed because she decided to stop choking me. I was totally unprepared for a situation like this, so I reacted instinctively. She didn't seem to feel much remorse for what she had done afterward, though perhaps she realized the craziness of what she was doing in the midst of it. I really don't know what her reasoning was.* [What could have pushed her to the edge of actually killing you?] *This is difficult to say. Perhaps she could just have easily choked me to death.*

A powerful indication of just how vital a woman's sexual reputation is perceived to be is that sometimes such damage can prompt a woman's friends, family, or boyfriend also to experience homicidal thoughts toward the perpetrator of the offense. In the following case, a woman's boyfriend has homicidal thoughts when her sexual reputation is publicly denigrated by a longtime rival of his. This case highlights simultaneously the importance of a man's ability to defend a woman's sexual reputation in establishing his own reputation.

CASE #P64, *male, age 21.* [Who do you think about killing?] *A classmate, age 18. Ever since I moved to a small town in the 3rd grade, I had problems with him. Throughout elementary school it was just being bullied around by him. He left our school in Jr. High and came back my junior year of high school. At first, I thought he was over the antics. And by this time, words said against myself really didn't bother me. Then he started saying crude comments to my girlfriend. Once in front of the entire cafeteria, he called her a slut and said he was going to rape her. This pissed me off severely.*

[How would you envision killing him?] *I had two thoughts about killing him. First, I was going to ignore most of what he said and become "friends" with him. Then one day pick him up, shoot him and bury his body in pre-arranged location. Second, I would run him over repeatedly with my car, then drag him up to his house and display the mangled body to his family. This is what I really wanted to do, but knew I couldn't get away with it.* [What prevented you from killing him?] *I don't really know. Just this sense that if I did kill him and got away with it, I would probably have to kill him fast and clean. I wanted him to die very slowly and I knew I couldn't find a way of doing this.* [What could have pushed you over the edge?] *If I would have been all alone and had run across him all alone with no witnesses.*

Another trigger for women's homicidal fantasies centers on reputational damage to their physical appearance. Men prize physical attractiveness more than women when looking for a mate, which is why this is one of the critical issues in competition among women, and also why one of the tactics women most frequently use to derogate their sexual rivals is public putdowns regarding a rival's appearance. We found in our study of fantasies that the costs women incur from being the victims of such derogation are sometimes psychologically painful enough to activate homicidal circuits:

CASE #7, *female, age 26. The girl was constantly making remarks about me and to me in front of other people, but they usually were so very subtle that I was the only person to <u>really</u> catch on to how much of a wretched bitch she really was. One day when I went to give blood, a teacher teased me about being too thin to meet the requirement (he was a dirty old man; I'm not extremely thin, I'm about average). Then I said "No, I'm sure I'll meet the weight requirement by more than 10 pounds or so, but I think I'm anemic." The evil girl, in front of my classmates, scoffed, "Umm . . . don't you have to be <u>thin</u> to be anemic?" This was the final straw. After six years of her crap, I wanted to hurt her. . . . I wanted to grab her by the hair and slam her forehead into the lab table <u>repeatedly</u> until she was unconscious. Then I would have kicked her in the face.* [What could have pushed you over the edge to actually kill her?] *If anyone* *in my class would have laughed at her comment, I would have lost it. I wouldn't have killed her, but she would definitely have gotten a good Louisiana-style ass-kicking. [What did you actually do in response?] I wrote on the bathroom wall that she was a stupid bitch.*

The last two cases also illustrate that homicidal thoughts are often not the result of a single incident, but are triggered by the culmination of a number of cost-inflicting events over a substantial period of time.

SERIAL KILLERS: A BLAZE OF GLORY

As I examined the ways in which status is involved in motives to kill, I also became convinced that the same underlying psychological circuit is at play in killings by two particularly ugly types of murderers—serial killers and mass murderers. I have not conducted extensive research as yet into these instances of murder, but the ways in which they can be explained by the status motivation are compelling enough that I want to include mention of them. We tend to attribute the murderous impulses of both these types of killers to pure evil, or to pathology. The Charles Mansons and Jeffrey Dahmers of the world surely seem to be insane, and some of these killers would undoubtedly be clinically diagnosed as having paranoid psychosis or antisocial-personality disorder. But I would argue that the underlying motivations that drive them to kill are the same as those behind the everyday killings over status and reputation. According to this theory, serial killers murder because they seek vengeance for status denied, and mass murderers kill to get to the top in a status hierarchy and stay there.

Murders by serial killers are in a sense statistically trivial: they represent only 1 to 2 percent of all homicides. Nonetheless, these killers fascinate us—and horrify us—with a special intensity. The ability to kill again and again, with the total lack of remorse that serial killers so often display after being caught, strikes us as inhuman, as simply out of the bounds of human nature. The question of what causes any given person versus any other given person to turn into such a coldhearted serial predator of other humans is a deep and mystifying one, and I do not profess to have the answer to that mystery. I have, however, been struck, in my extensive reading about serial killers, by the fact that so many of them were apparently motivated by social status.

I have been reading true-crime books about serial killers for more than two decades. Most of these books offer fascinating case studies rather than systematic scientific findings. One especially interesting book is by the eminent anthropologist Elliott Leyton, *Hunting Humans*. He provides fascinating backup for the argument that the status motive is key to these killings. Killers often seek both to wreak vengeance on those of higher status and to gain a form of status through notoriety. Leyton noted that the multiple murderer most often works "on the margins of the upper-working or lower-middle classes, he is usually a profoundly [politically] conservative figure who comes to feel excluded from the class he so devoutly wishes to join. In an extended campaign of vengeance, he murders people unknown to him, but who represent to him (in their behavior, their appearance, or their location) the class that has rejected him."[24]

Leyton observes that serial killers and mass murderers are among "the most class conscious people in America, obsessed with every nuance of status, class, and power . . . but find themselves unable to maintain their social position; the gap between their expectations and their realities is so wide that they can only vent their rage upon the hated group. . . ."[25] The Boston Strangler, Albert DeSalvo, who raped, molested, and then killed at least thirteen women in the 1960s, said that by killing he felt he was "putting things over on high class people."[26] Ed Kemper, serial killer of at least eight women during the 1970s, said he was making "a demonstration to authorities."[27]

Charles Starkweather made his first kill during a robbery. Shortly thereafter, he went on a killing spree that lasted a week, murdering ten more people, then continued to ply his killing trade in the 1950s. Starkweather grew up poor and felt acute anger about it: "I just got fed up with having nothing and being nobody. . . . Poverty gives you nothing." Whereas he lived in a shack, he felt enraged that "All these goddamn kids cared about was: 'What kind of a job does your old man have? What kind of house do you live in?' "[28] As a youth he often stood outside fine restaurants and watched the people inside eating the food he could not afford. He had heard of the saying that "a man makes his own world," but he said that he had observed that "people who say such things wear nice clothes, eat in fine restaurants and know what to say to the girls."[29]

The close connection between status and mating concerns also shows up explicitly in these cases. Starkweather, for example, said the following about his low-status job as a garbage collector: "A girl deserves better than a garbage hauler [and only] nincompoops . . . would do this dirty work. . . . A kid ain't no good without money."[30] In explaining the motivation behind his killings, he said that he realized that "dead people are all on the same level,"[31] and revealed that he had wanted to pull higher-status victims down with him. After he was caught and convicted, he not only expressed no remorse, but also articulated the serial killer's common desire to achieve a kind of status through notoriety: "Better to be left to rot on some high hill behind a rock [prison], *and be remembered,* than to be buried alive in some stinking place."[32] Murder, for Charles Starkweather, seemed to be a strategy for achieving fame in a world that he believed provided for him no other means of ascent.

Charles Manson, one of the most famous serial killers of the twentieth century, experienced deep resentment toward those in positions of power who he believed thwarted his efforts at fame and fortune. He had aspired to be a celebrity rock star, and even wrote a song, a version of which the Beach Boys recorded. Interestingly, the Beach Boys changed his lyric "cease to exist," which portended death, to the more sanitized "cease to resist," which infuriated Manson. After that, the Beach Boys distanced themselves from him.

When his rock-star aspirations failed, Manson devised his bizarre murderous scheme for getting ahead. His plan was to kill rich white people in Los Angeles, steal their wallets, and plant these in bathrooms of gas stations in black neighborhoods. He believed that African Americans would then find the wallets and use the credit cards, which would lead the police to conclude that they had perpetrated the murders. The goal of this twisted plan was to fuel racial tension, and thereby start a race war.

His delusional vision was that many would die in a bloodbath fueled by racial hatred, and the blacks would emerge victorious, but that ultimately they would turn to him to lead them. Manson was highly bigoted, and believed that blacks were intellectually inferior to whites, which was why they would need to turn to him.

Charles Manson is certainly one of the serial killers we can safely describe as psychologically disturbed. He professed to believe that there was a secret palace under the California desert that he and his "family" were meant to hide in during the racial war, and he and his followers actually spent many days searching in vain for the secret entrance. Manson also believed, or at least claimed to believe, that the rock group the Beatles was secretly communicating with him through their records, and that the song "Black Bird" was part of an instruction to him to start the race war. The words "helter skelter" and "piggies," written in the blood of Sharon Tate and other victims on the walls of their mansions, come from Beatles songs of the same names from the *White Album*. Despite his delusions and obvious paranoia, however, it is telling that his underlying motive for the murders he and his followers committed was to achieve a position of power.

Ted Bundy, one of the world's most prolific serial killers, with a death toll of at least thirty-six female victims, began his spree after his offer of marriage was spurned by a beautiful woman named Stephanie Brooks, a woman of higher social standing. She felt that he lacked real direction and clear future goals, the kind of upward social trajectory that she wanted in a man. Bundy grew up in a lower-middle-class environment that he loathed. He felt acute status anxiety during his childhood because of the paltry livelihood earned by his stepfather, who sold vegetables to market gardens in Seattle. After he was apprehended, Bundy revealed that he had felt intense humiliation when being seen in his stepfather's old and common car, a Rambler. He aspired to more. As an adolescent he began stealing luxury cars and other prestigious possessions to gain the status for which he yearned.

Though he wanted to become a lawyer, and he clearly possessed the intellectual capacity for this occupation, he lacked the industriousness to achieve this goal the old-fashioned way—he dropped out of the University of Washington law school, but continued to pretend that he was a law student. Marriage to a higher-status woman must have seemed to him a sure route of entry into the class to which he aspired, and when his uptown-girl fiancée spurned him, he began his killing rampage. In another indication of the deeply ingrained link between status and mating competition, Bundy explained his motivation for killing as "stealing the most valuable possessions of the established classes, their beautiful and talented young women."[33]

Serial killers and mass murderers, at least the "successful" ones, almost invariably achieve a certain sort of status—they often become legendary or infamous. The movie *Badlands*, starring Martin Sheen and Sissy Spacek, depicted the infamous killing spree of Charles Starkweather and his girlfriend who came along for the ride. Starkweather's name lives on. Charles Manson is the focus of dozens of books, and several movies about him have made indelible impressions on millions of viewers eager to see Manson and his family of followers. Notoriety came to Ted Bundy, the Night Stalker, and the Hillside Stranglers. Fame brings women, whether it comes from being famous or infamous. Killers from Ted Bundy to the Night Stalker received the attentions of dozens of admiring women. Many, in fact, married and had children after they were caught and convicted. Ironically, even modern-day serial killers manage to marry and reproduce. The children of Charles Manson and Ted Bundy are among us today.

KILLING TO GET TO THE TOP

The quest for high status also seems to be the primary motivation behind the astonishing brutality of so many mass murderers. These are men—and they are almost all men—who kill to achieve and maintain dominance in a culture or political system through a ruthless strategy of murder. They are men such as Joseph Stalin in Russia, Pol Pot in Cambodia, Saddam Hussein in Iraq, Big Daddy Amin in Uganda, drug lord Pablo Escobar in Colombia, and Mafia don John Gotti in the United States.

Though we all know that these men wielded murder as a weapon to maintain their power, often on a truly massive scale, it may be less well known that killing was also the primary means by which they rose through the ranks and consolidated their power.

John Gotti, also known as the Teflon Don for his repeated ability to avoid being convicted of criminal charges, ascended to power within the New York Mafia through his killing prowess. He started out as a low-level assassin, but quickly worked his way up the hierarchy, becoming captain of one of the crews run by the Gambino Family. His ascent appeared to be headed for a nosedive, however, when his gang was caught selling drugs, an activity that strictly contravened Gambino Family policy. The Gambino Family boss, Paul Castellano, ordered the Gotti crew to disband. Gotti then made a bold move that led to his ascension over Castellano: he orchestrated Castellano's murder. On December 16, 1985, after Paul Castellano finished a satisfying dinner at Sparks Steakhouse in Manhattan, Gotti's goons riddled his body with six bullets.

Halfway around the world, Saddam Hussein, born in 1937 in a small village near Tikrit, a town northwest of Baghdad, Iraq, began his killing career in 1958, at the age of twenty-one—assassinating a prominent communist in Tikrit at the behest of his uncle.[34] He served six months in prison, but was released for lack of evidence. A year later, he joined a Ba'ath team of assassins and tried unsuccessfully to kill the then prime minister of Iraq, General Abdel-Karim Kassem. In the wake of his failed attempt at murder, Saddam fled the country, was tried *in absentia* in 1960, and sentenced to death should he ever be caught. After the Ramadan Revolution in 1963, Saddam returned to Iraq, only to be jailed for opposing the reigning regime.

He escaped four years later, in 1967, and became a key player in a coup in which the Ba'athists overthrew the Iraqi regime. In 1968, Hussein became the head of internal security, began killing enemies of the Ba'athist regime, and rapidly ascended the ranks of the party, ultimately becoming president of Iraq in 1979. One of his first acts as president was to order the murders of a long list of his political opponents, and of course killing became his primary method of maintaining his power.

His position afforded Saddam the pleasures of many mistresses throughout his decades of domination. Status also flowed freely to his sons, Odai and Qusai. Not content with mere mistresses, Odai reportedly enjoyed raping any woman who took his fancy. "Raping is one of his, let me say, hobbies," said Janabi, Odai's former press secretary. "I am not exaggerating."[35] Janabi personally witnessed Odai committing many rapes of attractive women and girls as young as twelve. Odai attempted to seduce a visiting Russian ballerina in 1994, but she politely declined his advances. Odai then had his security men covertly film her while she was having sex with her trainer. He invited her to a party, surprised her by showing her the film, and then proceeded to rape her. The perks of power, foremost among them sexual access to women willing or not, cascade to one's kin.

In the drug underworld, killing is well known as the surest way to attain dominance. Pablo Escobar, born on January 12, 1949, began his life of crime while a teen as a thief on the streets of Medellin, Colombia.[36] In his twenties, he began building the drug empire that would become known as the Medellin Cartel. Dead bodies paved his ascent to power in the drug world. No one knows exactly how many died by either his own hand or as a result of orders he gave to subordinates, but experts estimate that he was responsible for more than a hundred murders.[37]

Idi Amin Dada Oumee was born around 1924 in the Kakwa tribe in Koboko, Uganda.[38] His father was an Islamic peasant farmer and his mother a member of the Lugbara tribe. Amin excelled in sports, becoming Uganda's heavyweight boxing champion for nine years, from 1951 until 1960. In 1960, while Uganda was under British rule, Idi Amin became a soldier and rose rapidly to the rank of commissioned lieutenant, one of only two native Ugandans to achieve this distinction. In 1962, Amin commanded his troops to massacre the tribesmen responsible for a rash of cattle stealing. When the British authorities investigated, they discovered that the victims had been beaten, tortured, and in some cases buried alive. They overlooked Amin's overly enthusiastic methods, however, given that Uganda's independence was only a few months away.

Idi Amin then threw his support in Uganda's first election after independence behind Milton Obote, who became prime minister in 1962, and later appointed himself president under a new constitution. Over the next few years, relations between Obote and Amin became strained. In 1969, assassins targeted Obote, but he escaped with his life. Idi Amin's sole rival within the army, Pierino Okoya, announced that he was closing in on those behind the assassination attempt, and said that their names would be revealed on January 26, 1970. The day before the meeting, Pierino Okoya and his wife were murdered in their home. Obote, suspecting that Amin was behind the assassination attempt on his own life, relieved Amin of his command role and put him out to pasture in an administrative position. Amin's strategy of murdering his way to the top might have seemed to be thwarted, but this was not the end of his story.

In 1971, Big Daddy Amin, as he later came to be called, learned through his contacts that Obote planned to arrest him and charge him with the misuse of millions of dollars' worth of government funds. On January 25, 1972, Amin staged a successful coup while Obote was out of the country. In taking over the country, he declared, "I am not an ambitious man, personally, I am just a soldier with a concern for my country and its people."[39] His next eight years of rule proved otherwise.

Within months of seizing power, he ordered the execution of all those he perceived to be loyal to Obote. Thirty-two army officers were murdered in their prison cells, and roughly six thousand army soldiers were killed. In 1972, the "Butcher of Africa," as Amin increasingly came to be known, declared Uganda a "black man's country," and ordered all Pakistanis and Indians to leave immediately.[40] Over the next few years, to solidify his power, he increased the size of his army dramatically, draining money that otherwise would have gone to aid residents of Uganda, and launched a ruthless crusade to vanquish all remaining Obote supporters and rival tribes. He killed judges, diplomats, ministers, academics, bankers, tribal leaders, journalists, and thousands of ordinary citizens suspected of opposing him. Estimates of Idi Amin's total number of victims range from one to five hundred thousand, with most putting the total tally around three hundred thousand.

Amin was eventually forced to flee the country, taking with him four wives, the most prized of his thirty mistresses, and twenty of his children.[41]

He lived to about the ripe age of eighty, dying as an exile in Saudi Arabia in the company of his wives, mistresses, and children.

The harsh truth is that, throughout human history, men have used murder, often mass murder, as a strategy to rise to power and to suppress potential rivals from rising up from the ranks to usurp that power. Pol Pot in Cambodia and Joseph Stalin in Russia murdered millions. François Duvalier (also known as "Papa Doc") and then his son Jean-Claude Duvalier ("Baby Doc") maintained power in Haiti for decades by killing an estimated twenty to sixty thousand Hatians.[42] Benito Mussolini in Italy, Ion Antonescu in Romania, Prince Yasuhiko Asaka in Japan, Mao Zedong in China, Kim Il Sung in North Korea, Ferdinand Marcos in the Philippines, Ante Pavelic in Croatia, Slobodan Miloševic in Serbia, Mohamed Suharto in Indonesia, José Efraín Ríos Montt in Guatemala, Ne Win in Burma, and thousands of other leaders from cultures the world over attained and maintained power through murder. The methodical strategy behind their murdering "madness" is starkly revealed in this quote of a young chieftain of the Dani culture of Oceania, who rose through the ranks of his tribe by becoming a multiple-murderer:

> I knew I was meant to be a kain [a leader]. My father told me. But everyone said I couldn't kill because I was too young. I began by stealing a pig. I succeeded and so I stole again and again. Each time I succeeded. The braveness in my heart grew bigger. I felt myself a brave man. Quietly, I tried to kill a man. I returned home with that victory. I wanted to go to war and fight with the others, but they still considered me to be a child. I felt so angry. I went, anyway. With bows and arrows in my hand, I killed the enemy one by one. I killed and killed until many enemy were dead. I have killed many, many people. In the end I was accepted by the people as overlord. I am not afraid of anybody.[43]

Murder often works better than other strategies for despots and others who rise to power by killing their adversaries. Merely inflicting nonlethal violence on opponents or exiling them are temporary solutions. Enemies who live have the potential to come back. A dead rival is gone forever. Murder sends a powerful signal to others in the group. It deters potential challengers by exploiting their evolved fears of being killed.

The sheer frequency throughout all of recorded human history of killing as a male strategy for attaining the status of dominant power speaks to the provocative conclusion that this behavior has been, over long time, adaptive in terms of evolutionary competition. The psychological circuitry behind killing the competition to get ahead and stay ahead became installed in the male brain over evolutionary time because it worked.

Nine

THE KILLERS AMONG US

—◆—

"We have met the enemy, and he is us."

—WALT KELLY, *Pogo*

IN THE COURSE of this book, we have looked at the murderers who are all around us, from the man whose honor was insulted to the woman who sees killing as the only way out. Murder affects the lives of all of us. Have you ever felt the hair stand up on the nape of your neck when a dangerous-looking man comes into your midst? Have you felt the eyes of a stranger watching your every move and forced yourself not to jerk your head up to assess his intent? Has anyone you know ever been murdered? Have *you* ever thought about killing someone? Killers are all around us. They are you and me. They may be in the next room, the next house, or the next neighborhood. It matters not where you live. There is no safe place on earth.

Nearly everyone has felt grave danger at some point, sensing that someone had a motive to murder. We will never know how many of us are alive today because a menace threatened and we acted to escape from it. But we do know, based on the reports of thousands of participants in our studies, that most of us have acted when we suspected a potential murderer in our midst—avoiding the dangerous stranger, fleeing a sexual predator, running from an angry rival, hiding from an ominous enemy, securing weapons of self-defense, seeking the protective haven of close kin, or clinging to our closest friends.

Over deep time, evolved defenses kept killing in check. But they have also had the unfortunate consequence of creating more subtle, refined, and sophisticated homicidal strategies designed to circumvent defensive armaments. The perpetual coevolutionary arms race continues today, with each new adaptation in the murdering mind creating corresponding counteradaptations to prevent people from ending up dead. At this moment in time, all of us are end products of the relentless coevolutionary process.

People have been murdering other people at appalling rates for thousands, probably millions, of years. Psychologists, psychiatrists, sociologists, criminologists, and anthropologists have devoted great effort in the last century to understanding why we kill. In the course of my research, I became convinced that the previous theories simply don't work. The social-learning theory of media violence advocated by leading aggression researchers Rowell Huesmann and Len Eron can't explain why killing is more common in cultures *lacking* television, movies, and violent video games. It cannot explain why the Yanomamö, Jivaro, Mae Enga, Dugum Dani, Gebusi, Maori, the supposedly peaceful Polynesians, and hundreds of other tribal peoples, using simple hand-fashioned weapons like wooden clubs and bows and arrows, have historically murdered at higher rates than their gun-toting, video-watching American peers. The child-abuse and pathology theories advocated by Richard Rhodes in *Why They Kill* and Jonathan Pincus in *Base Instincts* cannot explain why perfectly normal next-door neighbors with no apparent evidence of psychological abnormalities—people like Susan Smith, Clara Harris, Kristofer Marsh, Diane Zamora, Diane Downs, Jean Harris, Susan Wright, and thousands of other killers like them—commit murder.[1]

We must come to grips with the unpleasant reality that murder has been a remarkably effective solution to many of the challenges we've faced in the evolutionary trials of survival and reproductive competition: ascending social hierarchies, creating a reputation that deters encroachers, protecting and keeping our families, escaping from violently abusive relationships, gaining access to new lovers, and many others we've encountered along the way in this book. The vast majority of people experience *thoughts* of killing in precisely the circumstances in which homicide has been an effective means for solving these problems—an enormously improbable coincidence if the mind were not designed for murder. People believe their lives are most in danger from their fellow humans in exactly the same circumstances, again a statistical improbability if humans over eons had not confronted murderers in their midst in these conditions. Our moral abhorrence of homicide should not cause us to reject the compelling evidence that a deep psychology of killing has been and is an essential component of human nature.

Previous myths about harmonious peoples living in a pacified past have been shattered.[2] As we saw in the first chapter, the bioarcheological evidence of graves filled with skeletons embedded with arrow tips and damaged crania betrays a long history of killing. Modern humans have descended from ancestors who murdered. And they didn't just kill one at a time. In perhaps the most disturbing development in this history of the human species, we evolved adaptations to murder en masse.

NATURAL-BORN KILLERS

In anthropological accounts of tribal warfare we find powerful evidence that killing raids have historically been a strategic means of winning the merciless competition for survival and reproduction. The spoils that have traditionally flowed to the victors in warfare do not surprise us now—territory, food, water, weapons, and women.

Consider, for example, the case of the ancient Maori culture of New Zealand. On a recent research trip across the globe to study homicide among these original inhabitants of New Zealand, I acquired a Maori war club. These war clubs are called generically *patu,* with subvarieties such as the *mere,* which is the one I acquired. Although only two feet long, the mere is surprisingly heavy. Gripping it as the ancient Maori did imbues one with an eerie sense of power.

Maori warriors primarily targeted enemy men for death. They also killed some children and forced others into slavery, but young women were routinely taken as captives, awarded to victorious warriors. This pattern is seen in a chilling account written down in 1828 by a missionary in New Zealand, of a Maori warrior taunting the preserved head of an enemy chief, a practice they reserved for enemies who were particularly detested:

> You wanted to run away, did you? but my *meri* [war club] overtook you: and after you were cooked, you were made [into] food for my mouth. And where is your father? he is cooked:—and where is your brother? He is eaten:—*and where is your wife? there she sits, a wife for me:*—and where are your children? there they are, with loads on their backs, carrying food, as my slaves.[3]

Disturbing testimonials to the value of stealing away an enemy's young women emerge in accounts of tribal warfare all around the globe. Here is an excerpt from one such raid among the Yanomamö of the Brazilian rainforest:

> "Raiders!" The scream shook the body of every sleeping Indian. [Deemeoma] jumped from her hammock. The whole shabono [shelter] thundered. She heard a splat. . . . Her mother lay flat on the dirt floor. Blood ran from her mouth. Arrows flew in every direction. Her father was already on his feet shooting back at the enemy warriors. Enemies were everywhere, all around the shabono and still coming in the entrance. Women and children ran to find any place to hide. Most of the surprised warriors were trying to escape.
>
> The bravest, like Deemeoma's father, never ran. He stood by his hammock, shooting arrow after arrow. He hit an enemy, then another. An arrow struck him in the side but he didn't even stop to

pull it out. He shot until he had no arrows left. Now Deemeoma saw why men had sometimes called him Hard-to-Kill.

Deemeoma was still trying . . . to reach [her father] when the warriors grabbed her. They were just about to kill her when the old warrior shouted, "No! No! No! Don't kill her. Can't you see she is healthy? She will bear us many children." "Not for a long time," the young warriors objected. They were about to fight. But the old warrior was fierce and respected. "Only kill the boys and the babies and the wounded," he said. "We have to keep the healthy girls." He was right and they all knew it.[4]

Seventeen percent of all current Yanomamö wives have been obtained by men abducting them during raids.[5] Similar patterns emerge among the Tongan Islanders of the South Pacific, according to explorer George Vason, who lived among them for four years beginning in 1796. After the men were killed in battle, some of the women came forward and offered themselves up as prisoners to save their lives: "They became the property of the warrior who first took them. Such female prisoners were seen as an economic investment for their captors, inasmuch as they could be used in such occupations as beating out bark cloth and forming it into ngatu. It was also expected that they would submit to the sexual desires of their owners."[6]

Statistics bear this out. Among the Dani of New Guinea, for example, 29 percent of adult male deaths result from war. The comparable figure for females is only 2.4 percent.[7] There is only one reason why men get killed and women get spared in war. Obtaining or holding on to reproductively relevant resources has always been a major motive in war, just as it is a major motive of the murderers next door.

Triumph in battle historically offered the opportunity to enhance men's status and reputation, which, as we saw in the last chapter, is an extraordinarily powerful drive in men's lives. In Southeast Asia, dating back to 1000 B.C., according to archeologist Laura Lee Junker, "Raids against rival groups enhanced chiefly status and political sway by providing women for polygynous marriages, increasing agricultural and craft productivity through enslaved labor, and providing sacrificial victims for status-enhancing ritual feasts held by the chiefly elite."[8] "Warriors who had undertaken a great number of raids and returned with substantial booty and captives were rewarded with social rank and status insignia. . . ."[9]

The glory to be gained by risking one's life in war has perhaps never been so eloquently evoked as in these famous, stirring words from Shakespeare's *Henry V* (IV, iii):

> *We few, we happy few, we band of brothers;*
> *For he to-day that sheds his blood with me*
> *Shall be my brother; be he ne'er so vile*
> *This day shall gentle his condition:*
> *And gentlemen in England now abed*
> *Shall think themselves accurs'd they were not here,*
> *And hold their manhoods cheap whiles any speaks*
> *That fought with us upon Saint Crispin's day.*

Advances in DNA technology have provided strong genetic evidence that the coalitional killing that characterizes warfare actually works in reproductive competition. Recall the quote earlier by Mongol warrior Genghis Khan, expressing his great pleasure at vanquishing his enemies and sleeping with their wives and daughters. The Khan strategy had profound reproductive consequences. Oxford geneticist Chris Tyler-Smith and his colleagues collected, over a period of a decade, blood samples from sixteen populations from around the former Mongolian empire. In analyzing the DNA of the Y chromosome, they discovered that 8 percent of the men bore a chromosomal "signature" characteristic of the Mongol rulers.[10] This means that an astonishing sixteen million men in that region, roughly half a percent of the entire population of men on earth today, are likely descendants of Genghis Khan. The many sons of Genghis Khan ruled over large territories, and if they followed in the footsteps of their father, they had many wives and large harems. Genghis's oldest son, Tushi, is known to have sired at least forty sons. Over human evolutionary history, war was a means of driving rival male lineages extinct, with the victorious contributing disproportionately to the descendant population.

In the long history of warfare, we see many of the key motives of the murderer next door played out on a grander scale—competition for reproductively relevant resources; killing to prevent being killed; acquiring status, reputation, and honor; exacting revenge on competitors; vanquishing rival males; murdering the children of reproductive rivals; stealing the women of the conquered men; and exploiting new opportunities for reproduction.

MORAL DILEMMAS

Studies of other species provide an informative context for understanding the evolution of murder. We now know that killing members of one's own species, contrary to a myth disseminated by the famous ethologist Konrad Lorenz, is in fact widespread throughout the animal world. Among mammals, the tigers, lions, wolves, hyenas, cougars, and cheetahs slaughter their own. Among primates, langur monkeys, chacma baboons, red howler monkeys, savanna baboons, mountain gorillas, and blue monkeys all slay conspecifics. The chimpanzees of Gombe shocked Jane Goodall and those who followed in her footsteps with their horrific chimpicides. Animal researchers no longer doubt that these species possess adaptations to kill their own. This obviously does not prove that humans also have adaptations to murder; each species has its own unique constellation of adaptations. But it does illuminate mammalian and primate designs in which killing evolved, and suggests that there is no reason to be skeptical about the existence of analogous adaptations in humans.

The scientific studies conducted by my lab that I've referenced throughout this book have also furnished strong evidence of a mind designed for murder: the statistical analyses of the hundreds of case files of Michigan murders; the detailed homicidal fantasies of thousands of people from the United States to Austria to Singapore to Peru; the studies of death-prevention defenses that reveal a close correspondence between people's fears of being killed and the conditions under which people actually are killed; the scenario studies, which identified the precise conditions under which people say they would kill; the interviews with homicide detectives and police; the statistical analyses of the massive FBI database of nearly half a million murders; and the widespread cross-cultural evidence provided by biological and cultural anthropologists.

The accumulation of so much evidence coming from so many different data sources, seen in light of the impoverished previous theories that simply cannot explain *why* people kill in such diverse yet predictable circumstances, must surely give us pause. The burden of proof ought to shift now to those who still doubt that humans have minds designed for murder. We need a radical paradigm shift in how we think about homicide, and it's time to take off the blinders.

I anticipate that some scholars will react with moral indignation to the theory of the evolved murderous mind. Anyone who proposes that killing is part of human nature surely must be depraved. As an evolutionary psychologist, I've become accustomed to critics who confuse what *is* with what *ought to be*. When I published my research on men's evolved desire for a variety of sex partners, for example, some worried that I was condoning, or giving an excuse to, men who cheat on their wives. Similarly, people might mistakenly assume that the theory of adaptations for murder implies approval or acceptance of killing. It doesn't. I would suggest instead that those who create myths of a peaceful human past, who blame killing on the contemporary ills of modern culture, and who cling to single-variable theories that have long outlived their scientific warrant tread on dangerous moral ground. The problem of murder cannot be solved by wishing away those aspects of human nature that we desire not to exist.

Some might worry that, if we concede that humans have minds evolved for murder, defense lawyers will try to use this as a justification to get their clients off the hook. Yet this "naturalistic fallacy" in reasoning has been exposed as logically incorrect by philosophers decades ago, and I doubt that such arguments would carry much weight in our courts of law. Many things are "natural," such as diseases and parasites, but we decide that they ought not exist. Death from natural causes in old age is natural—our bodies, to our great misfortune, are built with an expiration date, designed for senescence. But we have decided that we want modern medicine to help us lead *unnaturally* long lives. That murder comes naturally to humans in circumscribed contexts does not in any way imply we should accept it or excuse it.

Yet another worry stems from the mistaken belief that adaptations for murder imply the inevitability of murder. As I have tried to show throughout this book, murder has evolved as only *one among a menu of contingent strategies* for solving very specific adaptive problems of survival and reproductive competition. These contingent strategies can, in principle, be activated or deactivated. We have callus-producing adaptations, but can prevent their activation by creating friction-free environments. We can prevent murder, in principle, through a deep understanding of its underlying psychological circuits and designing *environments* that prevent their activation. The deterrent effect of spending life in a cage, expressed by so many people as the critical factor that prevented them from acting out their homicidal fantasies, shows us that we have influenced the decisions of potential killers.

One of the great ironies of our modern lives is that we carry our killer psychology, so exquisitely adaptive in our evolutionary past, into a modern world where the conditions of our lives have changed so dramatically.

MURDEROUS MINDS
IN THE MODERN WORLD

As the many cases recounted in this book have made clear, modern humans have not escaped the challenges of sexual rivalry, mate poachers, abusive partners, or sexual predators. We still struggle to attain status and to save face, and we continue to confront mortal threats at the hands of kin, dangers from stepparents, and even sometimes attacks from gangs of marauding males. The underlying motivations to murder remain prevalent in our lives. Most of us no longer consider murder to be a socially or morally acceptable solution to these challenges, except in highly circumscribed contexts such as defending ourselves, our families, and our friends. And yet we must also contend with the psychological mechanisms that eons of evolution have installed in our brains. We have, as it were, one foot in our ancient past and one in our modern present.

The fact that our modern behavior is driven by ancient evolved mental mechanisms is intriguingly demonstrated by some of the errors in our contemporary assessments of when we are most in danger. One example is our great fear of being killed by a stranger, whereas in fact so many more murders are committed by people we know.

Our ancestors lived in small groups, ranging in size from roughly 50 to 150. As a consequence, every person knew everyone else in the group; there were no strangers among them. Indeed, when a stranger unexpectedly appeared, he was treated with great suspicion, and often killed.

Lacking modern means of transportation, ancestral peoples only ran into those who looked more or less like they did. People who looked different did so by altering their appearance with paint, dress, and body scars. And if they looked different, the odds were greater than chance that they had hostile intentions. Judging by the evidence from tribal cultures of raids and ambushes, attacks by conquering groups killed more than acquaintances within the group. Xenophobia made adaptive sense in the ancestral past.

Our lives in the modern world, with our tremendous geographical mobility and modern urban living, are of course filled with strangers, many of whom are from different ethnic and racial groups. But our psychological circuits have not caught up with this new reality. Our fears of murder are heavily populated with strangers, even though most mortal threats come from people we know. Our research of fears of being killed contain a disproportionate dread of other racial groups. The whites in our sample commonly worried about death at the hands of "this big black person," "one big black guy," or "a dark scary man." The African Americans in our sample, particularly the women, expressed fears of being killed by "white men who are openly racist." In fact, the overwhelming majority of actual murders occur *within* racial and ethnic groups. In the United States, 88 percent of white murder victims are killed by other whites, and 94 percent of African American murder victims are killed by other African Americans.[11] The expressions of xenophobia are anachronisms whereby a fear of strangers who appear different, so supremely adaptive in the evolutionary past, gets played out mistakenly in the modern world through the ugliness of racial fear and unwarranted hatred.

Another way in which our psychological circuitry lags behind the conditions of our times can be found in women's intensity of fear about being raped and murdered by a stranger. In fact, the majority of rapes are committed by men whom women know, and very few actually end in murder. Meanwhile, women tend to underestimate the danger they face from men who are familiar, because that danger has increased over time as our social patterns evolved and more and more women live far away from the protective shield of their families.

Women who do live close to their kin experience dramatically less violence at the hands of husbands than women whose families live hundreds or thousands of miles away.[12] It is likely that the rate at which women are murdered by their mates each year in the modern world is higher than it ever was in ancestral environments. The threat of blood revenge for a daughter or sister who was killed by a jealous mate would have raised the cost of wife killing in the past and deterred many murdering men. Many modern women lack that protective cushion.

The fact that our minds have not caught up with the new mandates of our modern conditions accounts for the disturbingly high number of murders that are still perpetrated every year, despite all of the modern deterrents we've developed. We have strong laws, ever more professional police, highly sophisticated forensic investigation methods, and formidable prisons. These deterrents do work, and quite well. Indeed, the most frequently cited reason in our research for not carrying through on a homicidal thought was the fear of getting caught and spending life behind bars. When we asked people to estimate the probability that they would carry out their homicidal fantasies if they could get away with them undiscovered, most men thought that the likelihood would quadruple. Many of us owe our lives to the fact that murder is so costly to commit in the modern world.

Although modern society, with its police and prisons, makes killing more costly than it would ever have been in the past, we still must face the troubling question: are all forms of murder truly maladaptive today in the evolutionary currency of reproductive fitness? I don't pretend to know all the answers, but they are not as clear as they may appear. Perhaps in some cases the answer seems obvious. The police know that when women are killed the odds are better than fifty-fifty that a jealous husband or jilted boyfriend did it, and the killer risks spending life in a cage. The police should know, if they don't already, that when a young stepchild suddenly dies the odds are high that a stepparent delivered the lethal blow.

In other cases, the answer is not as apparent, and may be quite disturbing. What about the seventeen-year-old single girl who abandons her infant, delaying reproduction to a more auspicious time? What about the inner-city youth who murders to join a gang, thereby raising his local status, attracting women, reaping money by selling drugs, and funneling resources to his close kin? What about the woman who suffers years of abuse at the hands of her husband, and sees killing as her only way to get herself and her children to safety? Although it's a disturbing thought, could these forms of murder still be evolutionarily advantageous today?

Furthermore, our deep psychology of homicide-prevention defenses may remain disturbingly functional in the modern world. Consider the man who threatens his wife: If you ever leave me, I will track you down to the farthest corner of the earth and kill you. How many women today stay in unwanted relationships because they fear for their lives? How many death threats, exploiting the evolved staying-alive strategies we all possess, still work in achieving their evolutionary ends?

It would be comforting if we could convince ourselves that all of the evolved mental mechanisms that motivate murder are no longer adaptive in the modern world. It's just not evident that they aren't.

MANAGING THE MURDERING MIND

Does the fact that our minds contain adaptations that motivate us to kill mean, in any way, that we should accept this as our nature and give up trying to combat murder? Clearly not. After all, although humans have adaptations for killing, we also have adaptations for cooperation, altruism, peacemaking, friendship, alliance building, and self-sacrifice.[13] When it comes to murder, human nature is the problem, but human nature also holds the keys to the solution.[14]

When I was invited to present my theory of homicide adaptations to the professors at the University of Virginia School of Law, it generated a spirited debate. Some worried that, if it is true that humans have evolved adaptations to kill, then this scientific information might be misused by defense lawyers: "My client couldn't help killing, Your Honor, his evolved murder mechanisms made him do it." I would be horrified if the science of murder were abused in this way. Attempts of this sort may be inevitable, but that doesn't mean they will be effective. Defense lawyers historically have attempted to justify their client's crimes by any means available—the abuse excuse, the Twinkie defense, television violence, poverty, racism, discrimination, father absence, self-defense, amnesia, drug hazes, hallucinations, and temporary insanity. Some lawyers may well attempt to add "evolved homicidal circuits" to this litany of justifications and excuses, but as I said before, the naturalistic fallacy they would be falling into has been soundly debunked, and our legal system should refute this line of argumentation powerfully.

Another set of law professors at the University of Virginia School of Law offered a legal perspective that I found fascinating, and that may show real promise in deterring murder. Since the goal of the criminal-justice system is to prevent murder, they argued, perhaps we should impose the heaviest sentences for precisely those circumstances in which murder comes most naturally. These evolutionarily novel costs might then help tip the scale in the cost-benefit calculations of would-be murderers, convincing more of them that the costs would be too high.

The theory and evidence presented in this book provides a roadmap of the circumstances—the particulars of the adaptive problems for which murder is one evolved solution—in which people are most likely to contemplate murder. By making murder more costly to carry out in these situations, perhaps the law would be able to increase the benefits of choosing and using *nonlethal* solutions to each of the relevant adaptive problems.

A deeper understanding of our motivations to kill, and how ingrained

they are in our minds, allows us to become better educated about the circumstances in which our lives really are in the gravest danger. Women
should be more aware that the most dramatic risk of being killed by a
romantic partner occurs when they have irrevocably dumped him, specifically within the first six months after the breakup. They should be highly
alert if an ex-mate begins stalking, because they may well be in great danger. Those who are forming stepfamilies should be more attentive to the
tensions that can develop in the relationships between stepparents and their
stepchildren. The better informed we are about the precise conditions in
which the murderous mind is likely to be engaged, the better equipped we
will be to avoid activating it and to defend ourselves.

I HAVE SPENT the past seven years of my life studying murder. I found that
this work changed me in profound and unexpected ways. You might think
that, after spending years poring over five thousand detailed descriptions of
homicidal fantasies and the grisly particulars of 375 murders in Michigan,
one would grow callous or desensitized to the brutality of murder. I found
precisely the opposite. I became increasingly disturbed by it. At one point,
while studying the details of a case in which a man murdered his girlfriend,
I turned the page and found three color photographs—the dead woman,
stripped naked, with bloody knife wounds all around her upper torso. It
nauseated me so much that I contemplated abandoning the entire project.
To this day I remain haunted by those images.

Another moment of crisis came when I was asked to testify as an expert
witness for the defense in a murder trial in Michigan. It was a case about
Anne P.,* a twenty-six-year-old woman, who had dated Peter K.* for three
months before breaking up with him. At first, Peter's persistence in trying
to win her back seemed harmless, but before long, he began to stalk her. He
followed her to work. He tracked where she went in her spare time. He had
his friends monitor her whereabouts. He watched her house. Then the
phone calls started.

His fury at being dumped had increased when he discovered that she
had been seeing someone else; Peter suspected that Anne had started dating

another man while they were still together. He began to threaten her, and she became frightened. As the intimidation escalated, Anne's anxiety drove her to tape-record their conversations, which she turned over to the police. I listened to an agonizing six hours of them.

The conversations revealed a complex web of emotions from both Peter and Anne. Peter berated Anne for seeing another man, telling her that she had betrayed his trust and that he felt thoroughly humiliated. He did not threaten her directly with physical harm, but implied threats many times by talking about his martial arts training, telling her that he could do anything he wanted to her, and saying that no one could stop him. He apologized to Anne when she expressed fear, but did nothing to allay her anxiety. He lapsed into fond reminiscences about the wonderful times they had together and how great the sex had been. But then he told her how much hate and bitterness he had inside.

Anne tried desperately to back him off. She insisted that she was not seeing another man. She told him of the terror she felt about going close to her windows. She swore that she did not mean to hurt him. She lashed out in anger at him for stalking her. She pleaded with him to leave her alone.

Abruptly, Peter's harassing phone calls and stalking stopped. Gradually, over the next few weeks, Anne started to feel safe, escaping the lonely psychological prison that had terrified her for the past four months. Then, a month after the phone calls stopped, Anne returned home from the grocery store with a male friend. As she got out of her car, Peter pulled up, took aim, and shot them both dead with a .22-caliber handgun. Anne had filed six harassment complaints with the police, but they did not save her life.

While I sat listening to the anguish and terror in Anne's voice over hours of recorded phone calls, I was at first primarily fascinated by the range of defensive tactics she employed. I sensed her franticness as she pled with Peter to let her go. She tried being nice, almost maternal in her maneuvers; she shifted to being abrupt and rude to back him off; she pretended that his threats were no big deal; she tapped her anger and made threats of her own; she sounded panicky and weak and begged him to stop; and, sadly, toward the end, she sounded exhausted and resigned. Then it struck me. I was listening to the pleading voice of a woman who was murdered in her prime. I was hearing the desperate last gasps of a woman who was now dead forever.

Again I almost closed down my research. But I could not bring myself to terminate a seven-year quest for the meaning behind murder. I did refuse to testify for the defense. Peter is now serving a life sentence without the possibility of parole for killing two innocent people in cold blood, and I'm glad he's no longer mingling among us.

Poring over the thousands of homicidal fantasies changed me in another unanticipated way. I found myself developing a deep empathy for all who have been fired from their jobs, beaten up by their rivals, humiliated by their peers, abused by their lovers, betrayed by their partners, encroached upon by interlopers, and dumped unceremoniously by the loves of their lives. I could feel their anguish and psychological torment more powerfully. And I found myself feeling a strange and unforeseen sympathy for why they contemplated murder as a means to stop their suffering.

MURDER GIVES US an X-ray of the inner core of human nature. It lays bare the things that matter most to humans everywhere—the necessities of survival, the attainment of status, the defense of honor, the acquisition of desirable partners, the loyalty of our lovers, the bonding of our allies, the vanquishing of our enemies, the protection of our children, and the successes of the carriers of our genetic cargo. These are the things that we humans and our astonishingly victorious ancestors have always been willing to kill and die for.

There are no simple panaceas for the problem of murder. Killing has been a marvelously effective solution to an astonishing array of human social conflicts. The circumstances that trip our homicidal circuits may present too many sprawling fronts to combat successfully. If there is, therefore, one last take-home message in this book, it is that you should listen to your life-preserving intuitions, the ancestral wisdom we all carry within us.

Be aware of just how real the threat of murder is, especially by those we know and those we love. Beware of the man whose uninvited sexual stare lingers a second too long. Exercise caution around a stepparent who just might prefer that you didn't exist. Take heed of the rival who sits silently seething at your success. Think twice about the stoic whom you have just humiliated in front of his peers. Watch out for the ex-mate of the lover you've just lured away. Be wary of the romantics who thought you were "the one" before you unexpectedly spurned them. Be vigilant of the mate turned stalker who just won't let go. Murderers are waiting, they are watching, they are all around us.

ACKNOWLEDGMENTS

THIS BOOK OWES a great debt to many people. First and foremost are the enormous contributions from my superlative friend and collaborator Joshua Duntley. Although the seeds of the ideas in this book were planted many years ago, it was not until Josh and I began our amazing collaboration that the theory and empirical research on homicide truly blossomed. The basic theory of murder presented in this book, and much of the empirical research, is a product of our collaboration, as reflected in our many co-authored scientific papers. Josh also provided many insightful suggestions on each chapter.

Special thanks also go to another friend and research collaborator, Dr. Todd Shackelford, who took the lead in analyzing and writing our co-authored publications on the massive FBI data set. Another wonderful friend, Dr. Carol Holden, Director of Evaluation Services at the Center for Forensic Psychiatry, enabled access to the rich cases of Michigan murders, and shared her insights into the psychology of killers. Special thanks also go to the Center for Forensic Psychiatry for their generosity in permitting access to these invaluable cases.

Collaborators Gary Brase (UK), Brian Farha (Singapore), Martin Voracek (Austria), and Jorge Yamamoto (Peru) contributed greatly by providing cross-cultural extensions of the research. Abdallah Badahdah generously provided insights and critical references to Arabic cultures.

Many friends and colleagues provided valuable comments on the theory: Rosalind Arden, Victoria Beckner, Anne Campbell, Sean Conlan, Leda Cosmides, Randy Diehl, Diana Fleischman, Sam Gosling, Martie Haselton, Sarah Hill, Joonghwan Jeon, Steve Pinker, Kern Reeve, James Roney, Todd Shackelford, Bill Swann, Don Symons, and John Tooby. Forensic psychiatrist Andy Thompson, special friend and thoughtful colleague, must be singled out for his unstinting generosity, encouragement, and insights provided over many years. I thank the professors of the University of Virginia School of Law (especially John Monahan) and the University of Texas Law School (especially John Robertson) for providing fascinating insights about the legal implications of this new theory of murder.

Thanks go to Dr. Dorothy McCoy, the Colleton County Sheriff's Office, the Clarkstone Sheriff's Office of South Carolina, and the Austin Police Department for providing access to experienced police and homicide detectives. And to the police and homicide detectives who generously shared their insights and expertise on murder.

I extend special thanks to the following research assistants, who contributed to our homicide studies over the past seven years: Tomas Alarcon, Alexandra Almasov, Laura Amoscoto, Jennifer Anderson, Nicole Berland, Benjamin Böcking, Jacline Denson, Erin Dies, Karen Eby, Jeff Fain, Jessica Findley, Mindy Fisher, Aaron Goetz, Kate Goodrich, Renee Graphia, Rachel Greenbaum, Robert Gresham, Chester Hanvey, Scott Hastings, Katie Hayes, Christina Hinojosa, Michelle Hodgin, Jonathan Hoyt, Sarah Hymes, Jennifer Izquierdo, Jenée James, Ewa Kacewicz, Joanna Lee, Amber Lingenfelder, Abbie Livingston, Kathryn Macapagal, Katie McCall, Erin McGowan, Deborah Medina, Mitch Mignano, Amber O'Bryant, Peter Renn, Kendra Robertson, Alexis Roosth, Regan Roth, Taylor Rusk, Elizabeth Spencer, Alisha Strand, Scott Streetman, Jessica Weiser, and Marissa Wimberly.

I owe a great professional debt to Martin Daly and Margo Wilson, pioneers in the study of homicide, whose work critically informed so much of my own.

Thanks go to my agents, Katinka Madsen and John Brockman, for insightful comments on the book proposal and for sage advice throughout the process. Finally, I was fortunate to be blessed with the intelligence, editorial magic, and unstinting dedication of Emily Loose, my editor at Penguin Press, who believed in this book from the beginning and contributed so much to bringing it to fruition.

NOTES

CHAPTER ONE: THE MURDERING MIND

1. H. Engle, *Crimes of Passion* (Buffalo, NY: Firefly Books, 2001).
2. Ann Rule, *Every Breath You Take: A True Story of Obsession, Revenge, and Murder* (New York: Free Press, 2001).
3. Ibid., p. 192.
4. Keeley, 1996, p. 91.
5. Larsen, 1997.
6. David and Gene Lester, 1975.
7. Mann, 1993, 1996.
8. Wilson, Daly, and Pound, 2002, p. 383.
9. Personal communication, December 20, 2004.

CHAPTER TWO: THE EVOLUTION OF KILLING

 1. Joseph Lopreato, *Human Nature and Biocultural Evolution* (Boston, MA: Allen and Unwin, 1984).

 2. http://www.fbi.gov/ucr/cius_03/xl/03tbl01.xls

 3. Harris, Thomas, Fisher, and Hirsch, 2002.

 4. Ellis and Walsh, 2000.

 5. Cain, 1982.

 6. Lester, 1991, p. 39.

 7. Ibid.

 8. MacDonald, 1986, p. 23.

 9. Lester, 1991.

10. Daly and Wilson, 1988.

11. Ellis and Walsh, 2000.

12. Daly and Wilson, 1988; MacDonald, 1986.

13. Lester, 1991.

14. Lester, 1991; Ellis and Walsh, 2000.

15. Berkowitz, 1993, p. 395. Emphasis added.

16. Ellis and Walsh, 2000.

17. Pincus, 2001, p. 27.

18. Ellis and Walsh, 2000.

19. Ibid.

20. Tooby and Cosmides, 1988; Wrangham, 1999.

21. Turvey, 2002.

22. Prentky et al., 1989.

23. Ibid.

24. Buss, 2004; Pinker, 2002.

25. Buss, 2000.

26. See Buss, 2004, for extended discussion of all these topics.

27. Wrangham and Peterson, 1996.

28. Chagnon, 1983, p. 182.

29. Chagnon, 1983, p. 183.

CHAPTER THREE: THE DANGEROUS GAME OF MATING

1. *Pericles*, I, i, cited in Meloy, 2000, p. 1.

2. *Texas* v. *Zamora and Graham,* Court TV Online (www.courttv.com/trials/ Zamora/chronology.html).

3. http://www.courttv.com/archive/trials/zamora/grahamconfession.html

4. Ibid.

5. http://www.offthekuff.com/mt/archives/002012.html

6. Ibid.

7. Buss, 1989a.

8. Symons, 1995.

9. Buss and Dedden, 1990; Schmitt and Buss, 1996.

10. Graziano, Jensen, Campbell, Shebilske, and Lundgren, 1993.

11. Buss, 2003.

12. Buss, 2000a.

13. Buss, 2003.

14. Holmberg, 1950, p. 58.

15. Townsend, 1998.

16. Wilson, Daly, and Gordon, 1998.

17. Eccles, 1987, p. 240.

18. Schmitt and Buss, 1996.

19. Buss, 2003; http://marriage.rutgers.edu/Publications/SOOU/ TEXTSOOU2004.htm#Marriage

20. Batemen, 1948; Williams, 1966; Trivers, 1972.

21. Wilson, Daly, and Pound, 2002.

22. William Shakespeare, *Hamlet,* II, ii.

23. Greenfield, 1998.

24. Daly and Wilson, 1988.

25. Daly and Wilson, 2001.

26. Daly and Wilson, 1988.

27. Genghis Khan, quoted in Royle, 1989.

28. Moses's instructions after the conquest of the Midianites, cited in E. O. Wilson, 1975, p. 573.

29. Gore Vidal, cited in Ghiglieri, 1999, p. 145.

30. http://www.findlaci2003.us/star-5-28-03.html

CHAPTER FOUR: WHEN LOVE KILLS

1. Michigan murder files.

2. *Austin American Statesman,* Jan. 24, 2003, p. 1.

3. *Austin American Statesman,* Feb. 8, 2003, p. A4.

4. N. Madigan, "Trial in Killing of Orthodontist Goes to Jury," *New York Times,* Feb. 13, 2003, p. A25.

5. Carlson, 1984, p. 9.

6. Campbell, 1992.

7. Greenfeld et al., 1998.

8. Easteal, 1993; Saran, 1974.

9. Guttmacher, 1955.

10. Daly and Wilson, 1988.

11. Campbell, 1992, pp. 106–107.

12. Daly, Wiseman, and Wilson, 1997.

13. Allen, 1990.

14. Wallace, 1986.

15. Shackelford, Buss, and Weekes-Shackelford, 2003.

16. *New York Times,* Feb. 15, 2000, p. D6.

17. Ibid.

18. Ibid., p. D1.

19. L. A. Fallers and M. C. Fallers, "Homicide and Suicide in Busoga," in P. Bohannan, ed., *African Homicide and Suicide* (Princeton: Princeton University Press, 1960), pp. 65–93.

20. Jankowiak and Fisher, 1992; Jankowiak, ed., 1995.

21. Shostak, 1981.

22. Sprecher, Aron, Hatfield, Cortese, Potapova, and Levitskaya, 1994.

23. Frank, 1988.

24. H. Fisher, *Why We Love* (New York: Henry Holt, 2004).

25. Haselton, Buss, Oubaid, and Angleitner, 2005.

26. Betzig, 1989.

27. Buss, 2000a.

28. Saran, 1974, p. 77.

29. Gangestad and Thornhill, 1997; Thornhill and Gangestad, 1999.

30. Greiling and Buss, 2000.

31. Gangestad, Simpson, Cousins, Garver, and Christensen, 2004; Pillsworth, Haselton, and Buss, 2004; Gangestad, Thornhill, and Carver, 2002.

32. Greiling and Buss, 2000.

33. Ibid.

34. Bleske and Buss, 2000, 2001.

35. Lundsgaarde, 1977, pp. 60–61.

36. Margo Wilson, personal communication, June 2, 1998.

37. Baker and Bellis, 1995.

38. Safilios-Rothschild, 1969, pp. 78–79.

39. H. Engel, 2001, p. 35.

40. Ibid.

41. Buss, 2000a.

42. Easteal, 1993.

43. Ellis and Walsh, 2000.

44. Ibid.

45. Thanks go to Andy Thompson for insights into the role of alcohol in murder.

46. www.aphru.ac.nz/hot/violence.htm

47. Easteal, 1993.

48. Ibid., 1993.

49. Ellis and Walsh, 2000.

50. Easteal, 1993.

51. Daly and Wilson, 1988.

52. Buss and Shackelford, 1997.

53. Lundsgaarde, 1977.

54. www.franksreelreviews.com/shortakes/stratton.htm

55. Wilson, Johnson, and Daly, 1995.

56. Wallace, 1986.

57. Easteal, 1993, p. 62.

58. *New York Times,* Feb. 15, 2000, p. D6.

59. Cerda-Flores et al., 1999.

60. Easteal, 1993; Daly and Wilson, 1988.

61. Easteal, 1993.

62. Brown, 1987.

63. Easteal, 1993, pp. 58–59.

CHAPTER FIVE: SEXUAL PREDATORS

1. Buss and Duntley, 2005.

2. Fox, 1996.

3. Easteal, 1993, pp. 69–70. Emphasis added.

4. Buss, 2004.

5. Russell, 1990.

6. Kirkpatrick and Ellis, 2001.

7. Edwards, 1954, p. 900.

8. http://www.cbsnews.com/stories/2004/23/48hours/printable613465.shtml, p. 2.

9. Ibid.

10. http://www.courttv.com/trials/paged/wright/verdict.html, p. 2.

11. http://www.cbsnews.com/stories/2004/23/48hours/printable613465. shtml, p. 2.

12. Duntley and Buss, 2005.

13. www.stalkinghelp.org

14. Duntley and Buss, 2005.

15. Haselton and Buss, 2000.

16. Mullen, Pathe, and Purcell, 2000.

17. Duntley and Buss, 2005.

18. Crowell and Burgess, 1996.

19. Essock-Vitale and McGuire, 1988.

20. Crime in the United States, Uniform Crime Reports, Sept. 28, 1997 (Washington, D.C.: U.S Department of Justice, 1996), pp. 23–25.

21. Ghiglieri, 1999, p. 83.

22. Brownmiller, 1975; Ressler, Burgess, and Douglas, 1992.

23. Brownmiller, 1975; Chang, 1997; Allen, 1996.

24. Haselton and Buss, 2000.

25. Buss, 2003.

26. Ghiglieri, 1999.

27. Buss, 2003.

28. http://abcnews.go.com/sections/GMA/GoodMorningAmerica/ GMA020819Self_defense_woman.html

29. Ibid.

30. http://www.conservativemonitor.com/news/2002005.shtml

31. Ibid.

32. http://www.prisonactivist.org/pipermail/prisonact-list/1995-December/000112.html

33. Ibid.

CHAPTER SIX: MATE POACHERS

1. Thornhill and Alcock, 1983.

2. Schmitt and Buss, 2001; Schmitt et al., 2004.

3. Schmitt et al., 2004.

4. Buss, 2003.

5. Schmitt and Buss, 2001.

6. Buss, 2002.

7. Thanks to Joshua Duntley for this insight.

8. Buss, 1988.

9. Ibid.; Buss and Shackelford, 1997.

10. Buss and Shackelford, 1997.

11. La Fontaine, 1960, pp. 101–2.

12. Ibid., p. 102.

13. Eibl-Eibesfeldt, 1989.

14. Hart and Pilling, 1960.

15. P. P. Howell, *A Manual of Nuer Law* (London: Oxford University Press, 1954), p. 156.

16. J. C. Vergouwen, *The Social Organization and Customary Law of the Toba-Batak of Northern Sumatra* (The Hague: Martinus Nijhoff, 1964), p. 266.

17. Muller, 1917, p. 229.

18. P. Bohannan, 1960.

19. Texas Penal Code, 1925, Article 1220.

20. Erica Dominitz, *In Flagrante Delicto*, 1995, http://www.law.georgetown.edu/glh/dominitz.htm

21. Daly and Wilson, 1988.

22. Ibid., p. 190.

23. Buss, 2003.

CHAPTER SEVEN: BLOOD AND WATER

1. Daly and Wilson, 1988, pp. 24–25.
2. Rule, 1988.
3. http://www.crimelibrary.com/notorious_murders/famous/downs/bars_2.html?sect=1
4. Daly and Wilson, 1988.
5. Ibid., p. 62.
6. Bugos and McCarthy, 1984, p. 512.
7. Daly and Wilson, 1988.
8. Ibid., p. 48.
9. Bugos and McCarthy, 1984, p. 508.
10. Spencer and Gillen, 1927, p. 221.
11. Daly and Wilson, 1988.
12. Smith, 1885, p. 294.
13. Chagnon, 1983, p. 27.
14. K. Scott, article in *Austin American Statesman,* Aug. 10, 2001, p. B1.
15. Daly and Wilson, 1988.
16. H. Engel, *Crimes of Passion: An Unblinking Look at Murderous Love* (Buffalo, NY: Firefly Books, 2001), p. 196.
17. Daly and Wilson, 1988.
18. Hill and Hurtado, 1996.
19. Daly and Wilson, 1988.
20. Some of the details of this case have been altered to protect the identities of the individuals involved.
21. Daly and Wilson, 1998, p. 4.
22. Packer et al., 1988.
23. Daly and Wilson, 1988.
24. Daly and Wilson, 2001.
25. Daly and Wilson, 1994.
26. Daly and Wilson, 2002.
27. Daly and Wilson, 1998.
28. http://news.bbc.co.uk/1/low/wales/3038668.stm
29. Ibid.

30. http://fabland.com/atasteofmoles/archives/000301.html

31. Daly and Wilson, 1998, p. 3.

32. Daly and Wilson, 1998.

33. Hrdy, 1999.

34. Ibid., p. 416.

35. Ibid.

36. Heerwagen and Orians, 2002.

37. Thanks to Josh Duntley for this hypothesis.

38. Quote from an interview at www.froes.ads.nl/DALYWILSON.htm.

39. Hillbrand, Alexandre, Young, and Spitz, 1998.

40. Ibid.

41. Daly and Wilson, 1988, p. 98.

42. Ibid., p. 100.

43. Sheykh-Zada, *The History of the Forty Vezirs; or, The Story of the Forty Morns and Eves,* trans. from Turkish by E.J.W. Gibb (London: George Redway, 1886), p. 395.

44. Daly and Wilson, 1988, p. 31.

45. Saran, 1974.

46. Ibid., p. 95.

47. Buss, 2004.

48. www.ahmedabad.com/index/printpage/article/14438/section/10

CHAPTER EIGHT: STATUS AND REPUTATION

1. Guillais, 1990, p. 27.

2. Hobbes, 1957 [1691], p. 185.

3. Pinker, 2002.

4. Pinker, 1997, p. 498.

5. Ibid.

6. K. Bartholomew, 2003; see also http://www.stanfordalumni.org/news/ magazine/2003/julaug/dept/century.html

7. http://www.angelfire.com/sc/Centner/Ralph1.html; see also *Chicago Tribune,* Nov. 4, 1991, p. 3.

8. Ecclesiasticus, 28: 17.

9. Mulvihill, Tumin, and Curis, 1969, p. 230.

10. "Ludicrous Laws," http://encarta.msn.com/grad_articleludicrouslaws/
    Ludicrous_laws.html

11. Lewis, 1961, p. 38.

12. Arlacchi, 1980, pp. 111–13.

13. Matthiessen, 1962, p. 15.

14. Chagnon, 1988.

15. Matthiessen, 1962, p. 15.

16. Ibid.

17. Nisbett and Cohen, 1996.

18. Lester, 1991.

19. Nisbett and Cohen, 1996.

20. Ibid., p. 27.

21. Ibid., p. 31.

22. Ibid., p. 76.

23. Leyton, 1986, p. 10.

24. Ibid., p. 17.

25. Ibid., p. 18.

26. Ibid.

27. Reinhardt, 1960, pp. 67, 75, 101.

28. Ibid., p. 42.

29. Ibid., pp. 13, 54, 56.

30. Ibid., p. 48.

31. Ibid., p. 51. Emphasis added.

32. Leyton, 1986, p. 18.

33. http://www.worldhistory.com/hussein.htm

34. http://abcnews.go.com/sections/2020/World/saddam_son_030214.html

35. Ibid.

36. http://www.wordiq.com/definition/Pablo_Escobar

37. Ibid.

38. http://www.moreorless.au.com/killers/amin.htm

39. http://www.moreorless.au.com/killers/amin.htm, pp. 3–4.

40. Ibid., p. 4.

41. Ibid., p. 7.

42. http://www.moreorless.au.com/killers/duvalier.htm

43. Sargent, 1974, p. 178.

CHAPTER NINE: THE KILLERS AMONG US

1. Rhodes, 1999; Pincus, 2001.

2. Keeley, 1996.

3. Yate, 1835, p. 130.

4. Richie, 1996, pp. 29–34.

5. Chagnon, 1983.

6. Ferdon, 1987, p. 267; Vason, 1810.

7. Ghiglieri, 1999.

8. Junker, 1999, p. 336.

9. Ibid., p. 347.

10. Zerjal et al., 2003.

11. Lester, 1991.

12. Figueredo et al., 2001.

13. Buss, 2004.

14. Pinker, 2002; Buss, 2000b.

BIBLIOGRAPHY

Allen, B. *Rape Warfare: The Hidden Genocide in Bosnia-Herzegovina and Croatia*. Minneapolis: University of Minnesota Press, 1996.

Allen, J. A. *Sex and Secrets: Crimes Involving Australian Women Since 1880*. Melbourne: Oxford University Press, 1990.

Arlacchi, P. *Mafia, Peasants and Great Estates. Society in Traditional Calabria*. Cambridge: Cambridge University Press, 1980.

Baker, R. R., and M. Bellis. *Human Sperm Competition*. London: Chapman Hall, 1995.

Bartholomew, K. "Century at Stanford." *Stanford Magazine,* July–Aug. 2003.

Bateman, A. J. "Intra-Sexual Selection in *Drosophila*." *Heredity,* vol. 2 (1948), pp. 349–68.

Berkowitz, L. *Aggression: Its Causes, Consequences, and Control*. New York: McGraw-Hill, 1993.

Betzig, L. "Causes of Conjugal Dissolution." *Current Anthropology,* vol. 30 (1989), pp. 654–76.

Bleske, A. L., and D. M. Buss. "Can Men and Women Just Be Friends?" *Personal Relationships,* vol. 7 (2000), pp. 131–51.

Bleske, A. L., and D. M. Buss. "Opposite Sex Friendship: Sex Differences and Similarities in Initiation, Selection, and Dissolution." *Personality and Social Psychology Bulletin,* vol. 27 (2001), pp. 1310–23.

Bohannan, P. "Homicide Among the Tiv of Central Nigeria," in P. Bohannan, ed., *African Homicide and Suicide.* (Princeton, N.J.: Princeton University Press, 1960), pp. 30–64.

Brown, A. *When Battered Women Kill.* New York: Free Press, 1987.

Brownmiller, S. *Against Our Will: Men, Women and Rape.* New York: Bantam Books, 1975.

Bugos, P. E., and L. M. McCarthy. "Ayoreo Infanticide: A Case Study." In G. Hausfater and S. B. Hrdy, eds., *Infanticide: Comparative and Evolutionary Perspectives* (New York: Aldine de Gruyter, 1984), pp. 503–20.

Buss, D. M. "From Vigilance to Violence: Tactics of Mate Retention in American Undergraduates." *Ethology and Sociobiology,* vol. 9 (1988), 291–317.

Buss, D. M. "Sex Differences in Human Mate Preferences: Evolutionary Hypotheses Testing in 37 Cultures." *Behavioral and Brain Sciences,* vol. 12 (1989a), pp. 1–49.

Buss, D. M. *The Dangerous Passion: Why Jealousy Is As Necessary As Love and Sex.* New York: Free Press, 2000a.

Buss, D. M. "The Evolution of Happiness." *American Psychologist,* vol. 55 (2000b), 15–23.

Buss, D. M. "Human Mate Guarding." *Neuroendocrinology Letters,* vol. 23 (2002), pp. 23–29.

Buss, D. M. *The Evolution of Desire: Strategies of Human Mating.* Rev. ed. New York: Free Press, 2003.

Buss, D. M. *Evolutionary Psychology: The New Science of the Mind.* 2nd ed. Boston: Allyn & Bacon, 2004.

Buss, D. M., and L. Dedden. "Derogation of competitors." *Journal of Social and Personal Relationships,* vol. 7 (1990), 395–422.

Buss, D. M., and J. D. Duntley. "Homicide Adaptation Theory." Submitted to *Behavioral and Brain Sciences,* 2005.

Buss, D. M., and T. K. Shackelford. "From Vigilance to Violence: Mate Retention Tactics in Married Couples." *Journal of Personality and Social Psychology,* vol. 72 (1997), pp. 346–61.

Cain, S. "Murder and the Media." In B. L. Danto, J. Bruhns, and A. H. Kutscher, eds., *The Human Side of Homicide* (New York: Columbia University Press, 1982).

Campbell, J. C. " 'If I Can't Have You, No One Can': Power and Control in Homicide of Female Partners." In J. Radford and D.E.H. Russell, eds., *Femicide: The Politics of Woman Killing* (New York: Twayne, 1992), pp. 99–113.

Carlson, C. A. "Intrafamilial Homicide: A Sociobiological Perspective." Unpublished bachelor's thesis, McMaster University, Hamilton, Ontario, Canada.

Cerda-Flores, R. M., S. A. Barton, L. F. Marty-Gonzalez, F. Rivas, and R. Chakraborty. "Estimation of Nonpaternity in the Mexican Population of Nueveo Leon: A Validation Study with Blood Group Markers." *American Journal of Physical Anthropology,* vol. 109 (1999), pp. 281–93.

Chagnon, N. *Yanomamö: The Fierce People.* 3rd ed. New York: Holt, Rinehart, & Winston, 1983.

Chagnon, N. "Life Histories, Blood Revenge, and Warfare in a Tribal Population." *Science,* vol. 239 (1988), pp. 985–92.

Chang, I. *The Rape of Nanking.* New York: Penguin, 1997.

Crowell, N. A., and A. W. Burgess, eds. *Understanding Violence Against Women.* Washington, D.C.: National Academy Press, 1996.

Daly, M., and M. Wilson. *Homicide.* Hawthorne, N.Y.: Aldine, 1988.

Daly, M., and M. Wilson. "Some Differential Attributes of Lethal Assaults on Small Children by Stepfathers Versus Genetic Fathers." *Ethology and Sociobiology,* vol. 15 (1994), pp. 207–17.

Daly, M., and M. Wilson. *The Truth About Cinderella: A Darwinian View of Parental Love.* London: Weidenfeld & Nicolson, 1998.

Daly, M., and M. Wilson. "An Assessment of Some Proposed Exceptions to the Phenomenon of Nepotistic Discrimination Against Stepchildren." *Ann. Zool. Fennici,* vol. 38 (2001), pp. 287–96.

Daly, M., and M. Wilson. "The Cinderella Effect: Parental Discrimination Against Stepchildren." *Samfundsøkonomen,* vol. 4 (2002), pp. 39–46.

Daly, M., K. A. Wiseman, and M. Wilson. "Women with Children Sired by Previous Partners Incur Excess Risk of Uxoricide." *Homicide Studies,* vol. 1 (1997), pp. 61–71.

Duntley, J. D., and D. M. Buss. 2005. "The Evolution of Stalking." Unpublished manuscript, Department of Psychology, University of Texas, Austin, Texas.

Easteal, P. W. *Killing the Beloved: Homicide Between Adult Sexual Intimates.* Canberra: Australian Institute of Criminology, 1993.

Eccles, J. S. "Gender Roles and Achievement Patterns: An Expectancy Value Perspective." In J. M. Reinisch et al., eds., *Masculinity/Femininity: Basic Perspectives* (New York: Oxford University Press, 1987), pp. 240–80.

Edwards, J.L.J. "Provocation and the Reasonable Man: Another View." *Criminal Law Review,* 1954, pp. 898–906.

Eibl-Eibesfeldt, I. *Human Ethology.* New York: Aldine de Gruyter, 1989.

Ellis, L., and A. Walsh. *Criminology: A Global Perspective.* Boston: Allyn & Bacon, 2000.

Engel, H. *Crimes of Passion: An Unblinking Look at Murderous Love.* Buffalo, NY: Firefly Books, 2001.

Essock-Vitale, S. M., and M. T. McGuire. "What 70 Million Years Hath Wrought: Sexual Histories and Reproductive Success of a Random Sample of American Women." In L. Betzig, M. Borgerhoff Mulder, and P. Turke, eds., *Human Reproductive Behavior: A Darwinian Perspective* (New York: Cambridge University Press, 1988), pp. 221–35.

Ferdon, E. N. *Early Tonga: As the Explorers Saw It 1616–1810.* Tucson, Ariz.: University of Arizona Press, 1987.

Figueredo, A. J., V. Corral-Vedugo, M. Frias-Armenta, K. J. Bachar, J. White, P. L. McNeill, B. R. Kirsner, and I. del P. Castell-Ruiz. "Blood, Solidarity, Status, and Honor: The Sexual Balance of Power and Spousal Abuse in Sonora, Mexico." *Evolution and Human Behavior,* vol. 22 (2001), pp. 295–328.

Fox, J. A. *Uniform Crime Reports [United States]: Supplementary Homicide Reports (1976–1994) [computer file].* ICPSR Version: Boston: Northeastern University, College of Criminal Justice [producer]. Ann Arbor, MI: Inter-University Consortium for Political and Social Research [distributor]. 1996.

Fox, J. A., and J. Levin. *The Will to Kill*. Boston: Allyn & Bacon, 2003.

Frank, R. *Passions Within Reason*. New York: Norton, 1988.

Gangestad, S. W., J. A. Simpson, A. J. Cousins, C. E. Garver, and N. Christensen. "Women's Preferences for Male Behavioral Displays Change Across the Menstrual Cycle." *Psychological Science*, vol. 15 (2004), pp. 203–207.

Gangestad, S. W., and R. Thornhill. "The Evolutionary Psychology of Extrapair Sex: The Role of Fluctuating Asymmetry." *Evolution and Human Behavior*, vol. 18 (1997), pp. 69–88.

Gangestad, S. W., R. Thornhill, and C. Garver. "Changes in Women's Sexual Interests and Their Partners' Mate Retention Tactics Across the Menstrual Cycle." *Proceedings of The Royal Society of London, Biological Science*, vol. 269 (2002), pp. 975–82.

Ghiglieri, M. P. *The Dark Side of Man: Tracing the Origins of Violence*. Reading, Mass.: Perseus, 1999.

Graziano, W. G., L. Jensen Cambell, L. Shebilske, and S. Lundgren. "Social Influence, Sex Differences, and Judgments of Beauty: Putting the 'Interpersonal' Back in Interpersonal Attraction." *Journal of Personality and Social Psychology*, vol. 65 (1993), pp. 522–31.

Greenfield, L. A. *Alcohol and Crime*. Washington, D.C.: U.S. Department of Justice, Bureau of Justice Statistics, 1998.

Greenfield, L. A., M. R. Rand, D. Craven, P. A. Klaus, C. A. Perkins, C. Ringel, G. Warchol, C. Maston, and J. A. Fox. *Violence by Intimates*. U.S. Department of Justice, NCJ-167237, 1998.

Greiling, H., and D. M. Buss. "Women's Sexual Strategies: The Hidden Dimension of Extra-Pair Mating." *Personality and Individual Differences*, vol. 28 (2000), pp. 929–63.

Guillais, J. *Crimes of Passion: Dramas of Private Life in Nineteenth Century France*. Cambridge: Polity Press, 1990.

Guttmacher, M. S. "Criminal Responsibility in Certain Homicide Cases Involving Family Members." In P. H. Hoch and J. Zubin, eds., *Psychiatry and the Law* (New York: Strauss & Cudahy, 1955), pp. 73–96.

Harris, A., S. H. Thomas, G. A. Fisher, and D. J. Hirsch. "Murder and Medicine: The Lethality of Criminal Assault 1960–1999." *Homicide Studies*, vol. 6 (2002), pp. 128–66.

Hart, C.W.M., and A. R. Pilling. *The Tiwi of North Australia.* New York: Holt, Rinehart, & Winston, 1960.

Haselton, M., D. M. Buss, V. Oubaid, and A. Angleitner. "Sex, Lies, and Strategic Interference: The Psychology of Deception Between the Sexes." *Personality and Social Psychology Bulletin,* vol. 31 (2005), pp. 3–23.

Haselton, M. G., and D. M. Buss. "Error Management Theory: A New Perspective on Biases in Cross-Sex Mind Reading." *Journal of Personality and Social Psychology,* vol. 78 (2000), pp. 81–91.

Heerwagen, J. H., and G. H. Orians. "The Ecological World of Children." In P. H. Kahn, Jr., and S. R. Kellert, eds. *Children and Nature: Psychological, Sociocultural, and Evolutionary Investigations* (Cambridge, Mass.: MIT Press, 2002), pp. 29–64.

Hill, K., and A. M. Hurtado. *Ache Life History.* New York: Aldine de Gruyter, 1996.

Hillbrand, M., J. W. Alexandre, J. L. Young, and R. T. Spitz. "Parricides: Characteristics of Offenders and Victims, Legal Factors, and Treatment Issues." *Aggression and Violent Behavior,* vol. 4 (1998), pp. 179–90.

Hobbes, T. *Leviathan.* New York: Oxford University Press, 1957 [1691].

Holmberg A. R. *Nomads of the Long Bow: The Siriono of Eastern Bolivia.* Washington, D.C.: United States Government Printing Office, 1950.

Hrdy, S. B. *Mother Nature: A History of Mothers, Infants, and Natural Selection.* New York: Pantheon, 1999.

James, W. *The Principles of Psychology.* New York: Dover, 1890, 1950.

Jankowiak, W. R., ed. *Romantic Passion: A Universal Experience?* New York: Columbia University Press, 1995.

Junker, L. L. *Raiding, Trading, and Feasting: The Political Economy of Philippine Chiefdoms.* Honolulu: University of Hawai'i Press, 1999.

Keeley, L. H. *War Before Civilization.* New York: Oxford University Press, 1996.

Kirkpatrick, L. A., and B. J. Ellis. "Evolutionary Perspectives on Self-Evaluation and Self-Esteem." In M. Clark and G. Fletcher, eds., *The Blackwell Handbook of Social Psychology,* vol. 2, *Interpersonal Processes* (Oxford: Blackwell, 2001).

La Fontaine, J. "Homicide and Suicide Among the Gisu." In P. Bohannan, ed., *African Homicide and Suicide* (Princeton, N.J.: Princeton University Press, 1960), pp. 94–129.

Larsen, C. L. *Bioarcheology: Interpreting Behavior from the Human Skeleton.* Cambridge: Cambridge University Press, 1997.

Lester, D. *Questions and Answers About Murder.* Philadelphia: Charles Press, 1991.

Lester, D., and G. Lester. *Crime of Passion: Murder and the Murderer.* Chicago: Nelson Hall, 1975.

Lewis, O. *The Children of Sanchez: Autobiography of a Mexican Family.* New York: Random House, 1961.

Leyton, E. *Hunting Humans.* New York: Pocket Books, 1986.

Lundsgaarde, H. P. *Murder in Space City: A Cultural Analysis of Houston Homicide Patterns.* New York: Oxford University Press, 1977.

MacDonald, S. *The Murderer and His Victim.* 2nd ed. Springfield, Ill.: Charles C. Thomas, 1986.

Mann, C. R. "Sister Against Sister: Female Intrasexual Homicides." In C. C. Culliver, ed., *Female Criminality: The State of the Art* (New York: Garland Publishing, Inc., 1993), pp. 195–223.

Mann, C. R. *When Women Kill.* Albany, NY: State University of New York Press, 1996.

Matthiessen, P. *Under the Mountain Wall: A Chronicle of Two Seasons in the Stone Age.* New York: Viking, 1962.

Meloy, J. R. "The Nature and Dynamics of Sexual Homicide: An Integrative Review." *Aggression and Violent Behavior,* vol. 5 (2000), pp. 1–22.

Mullen, P. E., M. Pathe, and R. Purcell. *Stalkers and Their Victims.* Cambridge: Cambridge University Press, 2000.

Muller, W. *Yap, Band 2, Halbband 1.* HRAF trans. Hamburg: Friederischesen, 1917.

Mulvihill, D. J., M. M. Tumin, and L. A. Curtis. *Crimes of Violence.* Vol. 11. Washington, D.C.: U.S. Government Printing Office, 1969.

Nisbett, R. E., and D. Cohen. *Culture of Honor: The Psychology of Violence in the South.* Boulder, Col.: Westview Press, 1996.

Packer, C., L. Herbst, A. E. Pusey, J. D. Bygott, J. P. Hanby, S. J. Cairns, and M. Borherhoff Mulder. "Reproductive Success in Lions." In T. H. Clutton-Brock, ed., *Reproductive Success: Studies in Individual Variation in Contrasting Breeding Systems* (Chicago: University of Chicago Press, 1988), pp. 363–83.

Pillsworth, E. G., M. G. Haselton, and D. M. Buss. "Ovulatory Shifts in Female
    Sexual Desire." *Journal of Sex Research,* vol. 41 (2004), pp. 55–65.

Pincus, J. H. *Base Instincts: What Makes Killers Kill.* New York: Norton, 2001.

Pinker, S. *How the Mind Works.* New York: Norton, 1997.

Pinker, S. *The Blank Slate: The Modern Denial of Human Nature.* New York:
    Viking, 2002.

Prentky, R. A., A. W. Burgess, F. Rolous, A. Lee, C. Hartman, R. Ressler, and
    J. Douglas. "The Presumptive Role of Fantasy in Serial Sexual Homicide."
    American Journal of Psychiatry, vol. 146 (1989), pp. 887–91.

Reinhardt, J. A. *The Murderous Trail of Charles Starkweather.* Springfield, Ill.:
    Charles C. Thomas, 1960.

Ressler, R. K., A. W. Burgess, and J. E. Douglas. *Sexual Homicide: Patterns and
    Motives.* New York: Free Press, 1992.

Rhodes, R. *Why They Kill.* New York: Knopf, 1999.

Richie, M. A. *Spirit of the Rainforest: A Yanomamö Shaman's Story.* Chicago:
    Island Lake Press, 1996.

Royle, T. *A Dictionary of Military Quotations.* New York: Simon & Schuster,
    1989.

Rule, A. *Small Sacrifices: A True Story of Passion and Murder.* New York: New
    American Library, 1988.

Russell, D.E.H. *Rape in Marriage.* Bloomington: University of Indiana Press, 1990.

Safilios-Rothschild, C. "'Honor' Crimes in Contemporary Greece." *British
    Journal of Sociology,* vol. 20 (1969), pp. 205–18.

Saran, A. B. *Murder and Suicide Among the Munda and the Oraon.* Delhi:
    National Publishing House, 1974.

Sargent, W. *People of the Valley.* New York: Random House, 1974.

Schmitt, D. P., and D. M. Buss. "Mate Attraction and Competitor Derogation:
    Context Effects on Perceived Effectiveness." *Journal of Personality and Social
    Psychology,* vol. 70 (1996), pp. 1185–1204.

Schmitt, D. P., and D. M. Buss. "Human Mate Poaching: Tactics and Temptations
    for Infiltrating Existing Mateships." *Journal of Personality and Social
    Psychology,* vol. 80 (2001), pp. 894–917.

Schmitt, D. P., et al. "Patterns and Universals of Mate Poaching Across 53 Nations:
    The Effects of Sex, Culture, and Personality on Romantically Attracting

Another Person's Partner." *Journal of Personality and Social Psychology,*
vol. 86 (2004), pp. 560–84.

Shackelford, T. K., D. M. Buss, and V. Weeks-Shackelford. "Wife-Killings
Committed in the Context of a 'Lovers Triangle.'" *Journal of Basic and
Applied Social Psychology,* vol. 25 (2003), pp. 137–43.

Shostak, M. *Nisa: The Life and Words of a !Kung Woman.* Cambridge, Mass.:
Harvard University Press, 1981.

Smith, W. R. *Kinship and Marriage in Early Arabia.* Cambridge: Cambridge
University Press, 1885.

Spencer, W. B., and F. J. Gillen. *The Arunta: A Study of a Stone Age People.*
London: Macmillan, 1927.

Sprecher, S., A. Aron, E. Hatfield, A. Cortese, E. Potapova, and A. Levitskaya.
"Love: American Style, Russian Style, and Japanese Style." *Personal
Relationships,* vol. 1 (1994), pp. 349–69.

Symons, D. "Beauty Is in the Adaptations of the Beholder: The Evolutionary
Psychology of Human Female Sexual Attractiveness." In P. R. Abramson and
S. D. Pinkerton, eds., *Sexual Nature, Sexual Culture* (Chicago: University of
Chicago Press, 1995), pp. 80–118.

Thornhill, R., and J. Alcock. *The Evolution of Insect Mating Systems.* Cambridge,
Mass.: Harvard University Press, 1983.

Thornhill, R., and S. W. Gangestad. "The Scent of Symmetry: A Human Sex
Pheromone That Signals Fitness?" *Evolution and Human Behavior,* vol. 20
(1999), pp. 175–201.

Tooby, J., and L. Cosmides. "The Evolution of War and Its Cognitive Foundations." *Institute for Evolutionary Studies, Technical Report #88-1,* 1998.

Townsend, J. M. *What Women Want, What Men Want.* New York: Oxford
University Press, 1998.

Trivers, R. L. "Parental Investment and Sexual Selection." In B. Campbell, ed.,
Sexual Selection and the Descent of Man: 1871–1971 (Chicago: Aldine, 1972),
pp. 136–79.

Turvey, B. *Criminal Profiling: An Introduction to Behavioral Evidence Analysis.*
2nd ed. New York: Academic Press, 2002.

[Vason, G.] *An Authentic Narrative of Four Years' Residence at Tongataboo, One
of the Friendly Islands, in the South Pacific, by George Vason Who Went*

Thither in the Duff, Under Captain Wilson, in 1796. London: Longman, Hurst, Rees, & Orme, 1810.

Wallace, A. *Homicide: The Social Reality.* Sydney: New South Wales Bureau of Crime Statistics and Research, 1986.

Williams, G. C. *Adaptation and Natural Selection.* Princeton, N.J.: Princeton University Press, 1966.

Wilson, E. O. *Sociobiology: The New Synthesis.* Cambridge, Mass.: Harvard University Press, 1975.

Wilson, M., and M. Daly. "Lethal and Nonlethal Violence Against Wives and the Evolutionary Psychology of Male Sexual Proprietariness." In R. E. Dobash and R. P. Dobash, eds., *Violence Against Women: International and Cross-Disciplinary Perspectives* (Thousand Oaks, Calif.: Sage, 1998), pp. 199–230.

Wilson, M., M. Daly, and S. Gordon. "The Evolved Psychological Apparatus of Human Decision Making Is One Source of Environmental Problems." In T. Caro, ed., *Behavioral Ecology and Conservation Biology* (New York: Oxford University Press, 1998), pp. 501–23.

Wilson, M., H. Johnson, and M. Daly. "Lethal and Nonlethal Violence Against Wives." *Canadian Journal of Criminology,* July 1995, pp. 331–61.

Wilson, M., M. Daly, and N. Pound. "An Evolutionary Psychological Perspective on the Modulation of Competitive Confrontation and Risk Taking." In D. Pfaff et al., eds., *Hormones, Brain and Behavior,* vol. 5 (San Diego: Academic Press, 2002), pp. 381–408.

Wrangham, R. "Evolution of Coalitionary Killing." *Yearbook of Physical Anthropology,* vol. 42 (1999), pp. 1–30.

Wrangham, R., and D. Peterson. *Demonic Males.* Boston: Houghton Mifflin, 1996.

Yate, W. *An Account of New Zealand.* London: Seeley & Bunside, 1835.

Zerjal, T., Yali Xue, Giorgio Bertorelle, R. Spencer Wells, Weidong Bao, Suling Zhu, Raheel Qamar, Qasim Ayub, Aisha Mohyuddin, Songbin Fu, Pu Li, Nadira Yuldasheva, Ruslan Ruzibakiev, Jiujin Xu, Qunfang Shu, Ruofu Du, Huanming Yang, Matthew E. Hurles, Elizabeth Robinson, Tudevdagva Gerelsaikhan, Bumbein Dashnyam, S. Qasim Mehdi, and Chris Tyler-Smith. "The Genetic Legacy of the Mongols." *American Journal of Human Genetics,* Jan. 17, 2003. Published electronically.

INDEX

FOR THE BEST IN PAPERBACKS, LOOK FOR THE 🐧

In every corner of the world, on every subject under the sun, Penguin represents quality and variety—the very best in publishing today.

For complete information about books available from Penguin—including Penguin Classics, Penguin Compass, and Puffins—and how to order them, write to us at the appropriate address below. Please note that for copyright reasons the selection of books varies from country to country.

In the United States: Please write to *Penguin Group (USA), P.O. Box 12289 Dept. B, Newark, New Jersey 07101-5289* or call 1-800-788-6262.

In the United Kingdom: Please write to *Dept. EP, Penguin Books Ltd, Bath Road, Harmondsworth, West Drayton, Middlesex UB7 0DA.*

In Canada: Please write to *Penguin Books Canada Ltd, 90 Eglinton Avenue East, Suite 700, Toronto, Ontario M4P 2Y3.*

In Australia: Please write to *Penguin Books Australia Ltd, P.O. Box 257, Ringwood, Victoria 3134.*

In New Zealand: Please write to *Penguin Books (NZ) Ltd, Private Bag 102902, North Shore Mail Centre, Auckland 10.*

In India: Please write to *Penguin Books India Pvt Ltd, 11 Panchsheel Shopping Centre, Panchsheel Park, New Delhi 110 017.*

In the Netherlands: Please write to *Penguin Books Netherlands bv, Postbus 3507, NL-1001 AH Amsterdam.*

In Germany: Please write to *Penguin Books Deutschland GmbH, Metzlerstrasse 26, 60594 Frankfurt am Main.*

In Spain: Please write to *Penguin Books S. A., Bravo Murillo 19, 1° B, 28015 Madrid.*

In Italy: Please write to *Penguin Italia s.r.l., Via Benedetto Croce 2, 20094 Corsico, Milano.*

In France: Please write to *Penguin France, Le Carré Wilson, 62 rue Benjamin Baillaud, 31500 Toulouse.*

In Japan: Please write to *Penguin Books Japan Ltd, Kaneko Building, 2-3-25 Koraku, Bunkyo-Ku, Tokyo 112.*

In South Africa: Please write to *Penguin Books South Africa (Pty) Ltd, Private Bag X14, Parkview, 2122 Johannesburg.*